Game Play

Game Play

Paratextuality in Contemporary Board Games

Paul Booth

Bloomsbury Academic
An imprint of Bloomsbury Publishing Inc

B L O O M S B U R Y
NEW YORK • LONDON • NEW DELHI • SYDNEY

Bloomsbury Academic
An imprint of Bloomsbury Publishing Inc

1385 Broadway	50 Bedford Square
New York	London
NY 10018	WC1B 3DP
USA	UK

www.bloomsbury.com

BLOOMSBURY and the Diana logo are trademarks of Bloomsbury Publishing Plc

First published 2015

© Paul Booth, 2015

Library of Congress Cataloging-in-Publication Data
A catalog record for this book is available from the Library of Congress.

ISBN: HB: 978-1-6289-2744-3
PB: 978-1-6289-2743-6
ePub: 978-1-6289-2742-9
ePDF: 978-1-6289-2741-2

Typeset by Deanta Global Publishing Services, Chennai, India
Printed and bound in the United States of America

I dedicate this book with love to my family, who have been playing games with me since I was young. Thank you for the fun times and great memories ... and for letting me win once in a while.

Contents

List of Illustrations

Acknowledgments

This book would not have been possible without the help and support of many. First, I thank all my friends and family who came over for the monthly board game days (and nights)—Anna Booth, Katie Booth, Amber Davisson, Alan Francisco, Ashlyn Keefe, Kate Lander, Brendan Riley, Natalie Wolfe, and Chris Wood—this book would not have happened without your patience, sense of fun, and stimulating conversations. Thank you for the times that you put up with some strenuous rule reading, and for being willing to try out pretty much any game. Brendan, especially, has been a wonderful gameplaying friend for over a decade and I am grateful for his continued friendship and the wonderful game nights with Jenny, Avery, and Finn.

The seeds for this book were first planted by Bethan Jones and Wickham Clayton, who edited a special issue of *Intensities: The Journal of Cult Media* about transmedia and board games. I contributed "Playing Dead: Transmedia Pathos and Plot in *The Walking Dead* Board Games," which has become Chapter 3 in this volume. I am particularly grateful to them for providing abstracts for the other articles so that I could properly shape additional chapters and research. Some of the research in this book also comes from "Crowdfunding: A Spimatic Application of Digital Fandom," which I wrote for Lucy Bennett, Bertha Chin, and Bethan Jones's special issue of *New Media and Society* on crowdfunding, and I am appreciative of their feedback on the content, as well as the feedback of the anonymous reviewers.

Both Matt Hills and Nicola Balkind were kind enough to send me pre-publication versions of some of their work, and I am grateful for their thoughtful conversations. Many thanks to Ian Peters, who commented on a version of Chapter 5, and who along with Lincoln Geraghty and Kyle Moody helped shape the direction of the book for the 2015 Society for Cinema and Media Studies conference. Thanks to Milan Rancic for permission to use his *Battlestar Galactica* fan card. Many thanks also to the thoughtful comments of Jonathan Gray in the early stages of writing; they helped immensely in the development of these ideas. I am also so thankful for, and appreciate, the keen eyes of Tom Vincent, editor extraordinaire, and the thoughtful editorial comments of Ashlyn Keefe. Now the student has become the master.

When one first expresses an idea to write a book about board games based on cult media, one tends to invite some sideways glances and cocked eyebrows. I am grateful to be working at an institution that not only didn't bat an eye, but also actively encouraged me to continue this line of research. Many thanks to DePaul University's University Research Council, whose grant allowed me to purchase many of the games studied in this book. I have been so lucky to find a group of editors at Bloomsbury who have also given their time and energy—Katie Gallof is a dream to work with and I am indebted to Mary Al-Sayed for all her design work and help.

As always, I am indebted to my family. Colin and Deb Booth are not only great parents, but also great people. I wish I had realized that when I was a teenager, but I am glad that I do now. My sister, Anna, is perhaps the most competitive game player I have met and makes every game much more fun. My thanks also to Tom Vincent and Wendy Vincent—your support means a lot. And thanks to Gary and Jane Booth, who very kindly held onto some games for me in the UK.

It is true that the best writing happens with a cat on your lap, and so I am so thankful that Gizmo spent a great deal of time there. If Black Kitty had been braver then perhaps my writing would have been better. And to my stalwart friends Slinky and Rosie, I can only praise you by giving you more treats, rubbing your belly, and throwing the ball a few times. It is not really repayment enough for the companionship. But without a doubt, none of this would have been possible without Katie, who not only read through the manuscript and offered valuable insights on every detail, but also encouraged me throughout the entire project. And although we both always want to be the green piece, I am so grateful that you let me have it once in a while.

Introduction

Board games in a digital culture

We are in the midst of a board game renaissance. Board games are commonly associated with family game nights, rainy days on vacations, or lazy Sunday afternoons, so there is something heartwarming about learning that hundreds of thousands of people still get together on weekends or in the evenings, in dining rooms and pubs, with friends and loved ones, simply to play games.[1] And it is a growing movement. Board game sales have increased more than 20 percent since 2009.[2] According to the Toy Association's annual sales data, annual board game sales increased by $60 million in 2013. In comparison, action-figure sales increased by just $20 million.[3] But beyond their popularity, board games have also increased in complexity—more strategic games like *Settlers of Catan* have joined perennial favorites like *Monopoly* and *Scrabble* at the table. These complex board games—usually involving more strategy than luck and deeper player investment in the game's play mechanics, narratives, and rules—were once associated with geek subcultures, but are now becoming more mainstream. It is not unusual to find some of these games in mainstream big-box stores like Target and Wal-Mart.[4] The board game's continued perseverance even in a flagging economy highlights its importance to contemporary notions of sociality and play in our complex media environment.[5]

As complex board games become more popular, a thriving culture of board game players has become more visible, thanks, in part, to the rise of geek chic culture and cult fandom. For example, ex—*Star Trek* actor and professional geek Wil Wheaton hosts the popular web series *Tabletop*, which regularly receives half a million views. Digital crowdfunding sites like Kickstarter, Indiegogo, or Gofundme harness the finances of thousands of game players to fund new types of board games. In 2013, the amount of money crowdfunded for board games exceeded the amount raised for video games by almost $10 million.[6] Perhaps a turn to board games represents a reaction to this very digital culture. As electronic games have become more complex, more graphically intense, and demanding of ever more expensive technologies to play them, the relative familiarity and simplicity of board games and the intimate socialization needed to play them form a new, yet somehow recognizable, game experience.[7] Board games remind us of our face-to-face past, and recall a type of pre-digital ludism where we all circle around the "campfire" of the game board.

Despite this seemingly Luddite turn to board gaming, digital media are also playing a stronger role in the acceptance and visibility of board gaming. For instance, as Stewart Woods points out, the growth of the Internet "has resulted in the emergence of virtual 'communities of interest' centered on particular topics and a shared enthusiasm for specific culture products and/or activities."[8] The website boardgamegeek, launched in 2000, is an example of one of these communities of interest, and its rising popularity indicates that board gaming as a hobby is on the increase: Stewart Woods lists it among the top 7,000 websites, and as of this writing (January 2015), it is listed among the top 3,000 worldwide and among the top 1,000 in the US.[9] Although the Internet has not created a board game culture, it has certainly fostered and nurtured one.

Today, our "media life" is becoming more and more inundated with multiple media outlets, and board games are reflecting this multimedia experience.[10] One important facet of board game culture is a rise in the number of licensed board games, or those based on extant media products. Although not a new phenomenon in and of itself (e.g., boardgamegeek features an 1882 game based on Lewis Carroll's *Alice in Wonderland* created by Sir John Tenniel),[11] the licensing of board games today reveals a heightened complexity just as the media environment itself has become more complex. Through transmediation (the expansion of a narrative across multiple media products), adaptation (the process of recasting a text into a new format), and franchising (the addition of multiple media products under one brand), the idea that any one media text exists in a vacuum has been complicated.[12] For example, 2012's highest grossing film, Marvel's *The Avengers*, is transmediated, adapted, and franchised—that is, the narrative of the film advances plot threads developed across multiple other films, it is adapted from a series of popular comics, and the film has spawned not only a number of sequels, but also a television show, video games, toys, costumes, and other ancillary products, all franchised under the *Avenger's* brand. The complexity of the media environment is reflected in the rising complexity between its associated ancillary products.

As part of, and also apart from, the media environment, board games are situated in a nebulous region of media studies—they are often relegated to the "closet" of the academy. They are rarely narratively consequential for the franchise, but thrive on the narrative development of their requisite media products. Board games that are based on media products reflect a heightened level of complexity at the heart of contemporary media culture. They ask players to perform a version of a media text, one that differs from the original. In turn, the game itself is a type of performance, relying on players to make sense of the multiple sites of interaction between these "paratextual" board games and their primary media text. The term paratext describes a text that is separated from a related text but informs our understanding of that text—a film trailer is a paratext for the film, made up of elements from the film but separated from it. Each paratextual board game analyzed within *Game Play* performs a version of its text; each performance highlights a different player intersection with the primary text.[13] Using board games to analyze media illustrates the performative aspects of media interpretation and reveals the multiple ways all viewers play with their media.

This performativity at the heart of media studies necessarily involves an interdisciplinary conversation between topics in media (e.g., paratextuality, transmediation, adaptation) and topics in game studies (e.g., game mechanics, concepts of play, win conditions, cooperative play). *Game Play* will reveal that paratextuality is never an "also and" part of the media text; paratexts are textual in and of themselves, and paratextual board games reflect cultural concerns that map onto the media landscape in unique and informative ways. Even while being a ludic experience, a game constructs messages with particular meanings for specific audiences. Game designer Raph Koster argues that games are about patterns, and like a media text, a good board game can use these patterns—aesthetics, character, story, and theme—to create meaning, both obvious and hidden. Games reflect culture.[14] As Mary Flanagan asserts, games are "legitimate forms of media," and the way games "reflect the norms and beliefs of their surrounding cultures is essential to understanding both games themselves and the insights they may provide into human experience."[15]

Game Play explores the relationship between cult narratives, cult board games, and game players through an investigation of paratextual games as they adapt, reflect, problematize, and exemplify characteristics of contemporary media culture. I am defining "cult narrative" and "cult board game" as those based on media franchises that have garnered overt fan cultures and have "geek" followings, what Matt Hills has defined as "passionate, enduring, and socially organized fan audiences."[16] In *The Cult TV Book*, Hills later defines cult media as "something 'special,' something at least a little bit 'underground' or even transgressive."[17] Similarly, many complex board games are, as defined by Woods, specifically designed for cult audiences who lie "outside the mainstream [and] whose interests lay largely outside of both classical abstract games and those that dominate the mass-market."[18] *Game Play* challenges these definitions by illustrating the performances of "cult media" and "player" in these games. Many of the paratextual games examined in this book are both commercial and critical successes and have immense replay value—my board game group, for instance, clamored to play *Battlestar Galactica: The Board Game* again, and no one could stop my wife from playing *Game of Thrones: The Card Game* for hours on end. *Game Play* describes the ways in which we make sense of texts, not just as things we passively sit back and consume, nor just as products that we actively make meanings of, but as performed, lived, and experienced games that we play.

Board games as paratexts

Rather than the more commercial moniker "licensed board games," which brings to mind generic instances of already extant board games overlaid with television and film themes, I use the term "paratextual board game" throughout the book to highlight the multiple ways that these games can be seen to interact with media franchises. Games are not "opposite" media texts, nor are they precisely the same—they form a unique textual enterprise that troubles the stolid conceptions of textuality and gaming. Rather than "either/or," paratextual board games allow a free and open interpretation, where "meaning"—like the text itself—is performed at specific sites of audience play.

I prefer "paratext" because it foregrounds this unique textuality of board games. The *Walking Dead* board games may be ancillary to the comic and the television show—but this does not mean that they are therefore less valid as media texts. The analysis of board games within *Game Play* is not just about the games themselves; it is about the way these games problematize the very notion of a clear-cut "textuality" in a new media environment. For example, *Star Trek: Expeditions* places the player at the heart of the Kirk/Spock/McCoy/Uhura team from the 2009 *Star Trek* reboot film. Using an original narrative, the game exists in tandem with the movie. One does not have to watch the film to play the game, nor does one have to play the game to understand the film. But the affective relationship between the game and the player alters the understanding of the film's meaning through the emotional dedication of the players/fans. Similarly, knowing the film reveals the paratextual significance within the game. Some players may approach the game as a paratext, a subsidiary of the "main" text. Others may play the game before (or even instead of) viewing the "original" text. Even if I have never read *The Lord of the Rings*, I can still enjoy the *Lord of the Rings* board game; the two are not as much separate texts as they are conjoined textual moments.

The term paratext developed from the narratological writings of Gerard Genette, for whom the paratext exists at the "threshold" of literature, between the "inside and the outside of a text." For example, the cover of a book is a paratext, as it is both part of the book product, and yet substantially different from the content of the book. Despite the maxim, we do tend to judge a book by its cover, as the cover image influences our understanding of what is inside. However, the paratext is not just a thing but also one that is "empirically made up of a heterogeneous group of practices and discourses of all kinds."[19] That is, a paratextual discourse is not just part of a book but also part of the unique practices that encourage interaction with a book. Jonathan Gray argues persuasively in *Show Sold Separately* that paratexts exist in the space between text, audience, and the industry, "conditioning passages and trajectories that criss-cross the mediascape, and variously negotiating or determining interactions among the three."[20] In other words, paratexts help us understand the larger connections between elements of the contemporary media environment.

In game studies, the term "paratext" has mainly been used to describe video games and their ancillary products. Gray describes licensed video games—promotional games based on films or television series—as allowing players to enter cult worlds and "explore them in ways that a film or television show often precludes, and/or that amplify the show's meanings and style."[21] Mia Consalvo has applied the term to describe commercial and noncommercial artifacts that shape "our experiences of gameplay."[22] The paratexts she describes, including video game walk-through guides, cheats, and strategy books, have become essential elements themselves, and a diverse array of paratextual content, from player-created websites to branches of video game publishing, has developed more formalized structures for understanding the context of video game play. Ian Peters writes about video game "feelies"—material artifacts that are packaged with video games—as paratexts that offer further insight into "the accumulation of material culture in the digital age," and ask us to "reevaluate our notions of the material and the immaterial."[23] Importantly, he notes how paratexts can become as important as—or even more important than—the original text, especially given the commercial value of ancillary products surrounding media texts such as video games.

While studies of paratextuality in video games reveal the interaction between the paratext and the primary text, rarely have board games been analyzed as paratexts, and even rarer still have they been discussed as key moments of original textual meaning. One exception is Bethan Jones, who writes of the *Discworld* board games that beyond a paratextual connection, they "provide players with new ways of understanding both the geographical spaces … and the characters inhabiting the universe."[24] Yet, as board games develop as paratexts, they can become as important to the player as the original text through their unique interaction and subcultural value among game players. Paratextual board games allow players to enter a cult world, but use a more tangible and material presence than video games to harness player affect. Other material paratexts, like action figures, can become integral to the way individuals interpret and work through the sociopolitical meanings of a cult franchise, as Lincoln Geraghty has described.[25] Yet, in comparison with action-figure play, board gaming is more directly structured around the cult diegesis directly and provides more opportunities for creator-designed meaning.

Thus, board games as paratexts have been little explored in media research, yet they represent a major facet of our paratextual media environment.[26] *Game Play* fills this gap in the literature through in-depth analyses of paratextual board games as both reflexive of and contributing to our contemporary digital media environment. The idea that paratextual board games are media products is not necessarily a popular one. They are often released simultaneously with the media text upon which they are based, and critics tend to perceive this synergy as an attempt to capitalize on the popularity of a blockbuster film or popular television show. David Parlett, author of *The Oxford History of Board Games*, describes them quite pejoratively: "essentially trivial, ephemeral, mind-numbing, and ultimately [of a] soul-destroying degree of worthlessness."[27] In a later chapter, he notes his "disgust" when a game is branded "in reference to a … popular TV domestic sitcom."[28] Jack Botermans, Tony Burrett, Pieter van Delft, and Carla van Splunteren, in their encyclopedic *The World of Games*, disregard the entire genre, skipping any analysis and writing merely that they are "readily available commercially and rules of play are always included in the game."[29] John Sharp calls the idea that games could be media a "flawed assumption," comparing licensed games to "a sugary snack … that is eaten and quickly forgotten."[30] For Woods, licensed board games are simply gussied up with interchangeable themes: take some game mechanics, paste a *Star Trek* theme over them, and you have a licensed board game. For Greg Costikyan, "the very theme-ness of 'theme games,' with their reliance on thematic color," is interpreted negatively by "serious game players." But he later tempers this analysis when discussing what he calls "Ameritrash" games (modern American complex board games), which focus on a "tight connection between theme and mechanics"; he singles out the production company Fantasy Flight Games as producing "excellent Ameritrash games today, with titles like *Arkham Horror* [see Chapter 1] and *A Game of Thrones* [see Chapter 7]."[31]

Indeed, a focus on this tight connection can be interpreted in many ways. Derek Johnson argues that while this type of media franchising, an industrial process by which a media text may be replicated across multiple cultural contexts, may be sneered at, it is also the result of longstanding economic concerns: the existence of a popular media text means it is ready-made for franchising through ancillary products.[32] As game designer Nick Bentley argues, two of the major factors behind the popularity of any game are strong brands and investment in those brands.[33] In a paratextual media environment, where interrelated media products are standard, it is crucial to look beyond the text to see how the text's ancillary products influence our interpretation of textuality itself. If the perception is that these board games attempt to emulate the original media text by mirroring mainstream texts rather than focusing on more original experiences, then such assumptions serve to delimit and define any interpretations of the games, ascribing to them characteristics they may not necessarily have.

Johnson's analysis of media franchising investigates industrial and economic shifts. In contrast, I hope to explicate some aesthetic, ludic, and textual concerns of cult franchises and further develop the "philosophy of playfulness" that I first discussed in *Digital Fandom* in relation to fan activities.[34] The cultural and technological transition from analog to digital technology has brought new ways of conceptualizing the media. *Game Play* examines the influence of new media technology in the context of ludic environments. I want to look at the way media like board games reflect, problematize, and exemplify the characteristics of today's media landscape. Board games have always reflected the culture in which they developed. Contemporary board games are no different in today's highly mediated and digital society.

The rise of the board game

As I noted, few academic studies have critically examined board games. One exception, Kurt Lancaster's *Interacting with Babylon 5*, analyzes the multiple ways that fans of *Babylon 5* interpret and perform their fandom of the show. Lancaster describes the paratextual games that fans play to immerse themselves in the vast world of *Babylon 5*, including *Babylon 5 Wars,* a simulation board game in which players/fans perform the role of captain. For Lancaster, *Babylon 5 Wars* is most specifically a way for fans "to 'visit' and perform simulated battles from episodes of *Babylon 5* … [and] immerse themselves in this universe."[35] The board game becomes a way for fans to develop their own interactive narrative via players' own imaginative play. In his analysis, Lancaster utilizes the board game's two key characteristics—its ability to generate narrative and its sense of play—to articulate how fans perform and ultimately interact with the game system as generative of story.

Stewart Woods, another scholar to write in depth about complex board games, uses a genre approach to separate board games into three broad categories: classical games, mass-market games, and hobby games. Woods's analysis offers a multi-game study of the Eurogame, a modern complex board game that "typically facilitate[s] indirect rather than direct conflict, deemphasize[s] the role of chance, offer[s] predictable playing times, and [is] of a high standard in terms of component quality and presentation." Importantly, even in his far-reaching study, Woods relegates licensed board games to a minor subset of mass-market games, arguing that "the mechanics … are typically derivative and uninspired." At the same time, he also argues that "the increased complexity and variety of modern commercial games often sees them weaving several mechanics together in ways that defy such simple categorization."[36]

Yet, I will demonstrate that the paratextual board game makes use of Eurogame characteristics in a variety of ways, while introducing more complexity within its relationship to its requisite text and to the media environment. For instance, Woods's three categories offer insight into the way authorship in particular comes to define traditional board game classification, while paratextual board games complicate authorship. Classical games are identifiable as those with no readily attributable authorship, and which no company can claim as its own—Chess and Backgammon could be considered classical in this sense. As he describes, classical games "hold … the attention of the game player rather than the thematic elements that are so central to both mass-market game and many hobby game forms." Mass-market games are commercial titles that are produced and sold in large numbers year after year, and which constitute the common perception of commercial board games. These are games that tend not to have specific authors attached to them, but are rather known through their corporate ownership—Parker Brothers, Milton Bradley, etc. Mass-market games include traditional board games like *Monopoly* and *Scrabble*, party games like *Catchphrase*, and trivia games like *Trivial Pursuit*. For Woods, licensed games, as a type of mass-market game, were influenced by "the arrival of television … since each new television show brought with it another opportunity to repackage familiar mechanics with a new theme."[37] In contrast, hobby games have clear authors, and some game designers (Reiner Knizia, for instance) have become quite famous in the gaming world. The names of these game auteurs are often prominently displayed on the boxes of hobby games. Like the paratextual board games I describe in *Game Play*, hobby games have clear game mechanics, tend to be playable in just a few hours, and include less player elimination. Game play may rely more on strategy than on luck.

Paratextual board games, as I describe in this book, are clearly akin to hobby games. At the same time, paratextual board games complicate this notion of authorship, for they not only have clear game authors but they also have to rely on the auteurs and authors of the cult world upon which they are based. It is not just *A Game of Thrones: The Board Game*, it is George R. R. Martin's *Game of Thrones: The Board Game* (designed by Christian T. Petersen). And, as I point out, players themselves interject their own moments of authorship into each game play session. No paratextual board game is complete without a player. There are thus multiple "authors" for each paratextual board game—game designer, media producer, game player.

I should clarify at this point, then, that there are also multiple types of paratextual board games, and I have concentrated on just one type in this book. On the more superficial end of the spectrum, there are literally hundreds of examples of themed *mass-market* board games built around the topic of a media text, but which do not actually use the characteristics of that text in the gameplay (this is the type of mass-market game described by Woods). For this type of licensed game, the base game predetermines and delimits the type of play engendered by the paratextual relationship. For example, many various themed Monopolies have been developed, including *Star Wars Monopoly*, *The Godfather Monopoly*, *Disney Pixar Monopoly*, *Wizard of Oz Monopoly*, etc. These games use only the most cursory characteristics of the media text—place names around the board, character statues as playing pieces, and changed versions of community chest and chance cards—but retain the basic play mechanics familiar to fans and players of *Monopoly*. These games are based more on *Monopoly* than on the original text. Even if there are minor variations between editions of *Monopoly*, what George Elias, Richard Garfield, and K. Robert Gutschera call "conceits," I consider these iterations as versions of the same game, and do not consider them in detail in this book.[38] Similarly, I do not discuss in detail themed versions of other classic games (*Doctor Who Yahtzee*, *Pirates of the Caribbean Scrabble*, *Simpsons Operation*). Although some of these versions do feature slightly adjusted rules (extra points for a *Pirate* word in *Scrabble*, for example), I am instead interested in originally created paratextual board games, those based on media products but using new game mechanics to complement the original text. These licensed games are *paratexts* in a commercial sense, and therefore inhabit the media environment in a way that Geraghty might call games of "capital consumption"; they are not adaptations of other games, with the play mechanics of the other games taking precedence over the paratextual gameplay.[39] Each of the paratextual games I examine in this book has sufficiently different enough ingredients to make distinct games. And so while *Doctor Who Monopoly* might have one or two elements that set it apart from traditional *Monopoly*, for the most part the ingredients are similar enough to make them virtually identical. In contrast, the ingredients of *Doctor Who: The Interactive Electronic Board Game* create a game with unique mechanics that separate it from any other game brand.

Nor do I look at trivia games based on media products—most popular cult franchises have a requisite *Trivial Pursuit* edition released, and many have a *Scene It?*; and while some franchises have designed unique trivia games (e.g., *Star Trek: The Game*, *Doctor Who DVD Board Game*), I consider them trivia games as well. Trivia games position the game texts in a nondiegetic way: the franchised text becomes external to the game in order that questions be asked about them. The paratextual games I examine in this book seemingly exist within the cult media texts' diegesis, extending and developing it in varied ways.

To narrow the focus even further, and to help navigate the complexities of the contemporary media environment, I focus my discussion in each chapter on a ludic comparison between two adaptations of the same franchise. With two exceptions, each chapter focuses on a cult franchise text (e.g., *The Walking Dead*, *The Lord of the Rings*, *Star Trek*, *The Hunger Games*, etc.) with more than one media text associated with it (e.g., *The Walking Dead* has both a television series and a graphic novel with separate, but linked, narratives; *The Hunger Games* is both a film series and a book series, as is *The Lord of the Rings*.) Each different text has spawned a different board game, and through cross-game comparisons, I reveal the cross-media relationships of these cult franchises. As game designer Kevin Wilson describes, in order to create a board game designed for different media, he "acknowledges the strengths and weaknesses of the medium [he is] working in."[40] Two of the chapters do not use this cross-franchise analysis because of the unique characteristics of their media texts. In the first chapter, I focus on *Arkham Horror,* a game based on the work of H. P. Lovecraft. It is a popular game with many expansions. However, there is no specific adaptation of the Lovecraft universe on which it is based. While specific films and television shows have borrowed heavily from Lovecraft's mythos, there have been few direct adaptations of his work. Additionally, in the conclusion, I discuss electronic interactivity in two *Doctor Who* board games. Each game references a different Doctor and a different version of the show.

Two consequences of this focus become quickly apparent: first, there are relatively few media products that have both adaptations *and* board games based on those adaptations. The most common franchises to have spawned multiple board games also tend to be made for particular fan audiences. While this makes narrowing down the type of game easier, it also restricts the focus. While there are many hundreds of board games based on children's programming (e.g., cartoons, Disney movies) or programming based on other genres (e.g., soap operas), few complex paratextual board games are based on *multiple* texts within a franchise. This is a notable limitation that presents further opportunities for additional study. Second, although these specific genres/texts might appear to lend themselves to particular forms of board game play (e.g., wargaming, fighting games), in actuality there is a diverse array of game mechanics and play types for the games based on these cult media products.[41] For instance, many of the complex games discussed in this book involve cooperative play, increased character development, and narrative play. As board gaming becomes more mainstream, new styles of play will appeal to new audiences and players.

I will be examining paratextual board games using what Elias, Garfield, and Gutschera call a "systemic analysis," in which the unique characteristics of the game system help make the game what it is.[42] These ingredients, things like *rules, standards, outcomes, mechanics, constituent elements,* and *ending conditions,* are what make each game unique. Although I concentrate each chapter's analysis on the games within a particular franchise, the conclusions I draw are applicable to other paratextual games as well; they are not unique to the exemplar text. In order to develop this systemic analysis, I have undertaken a mixture of textual analysis and autoethnographic methods.

For the majority of the cases discussed in this book, I use a textual analysis to uncover the workings of the game. In this, I refer to the classic definition of textual analysis as articulated by Alan McKee: "when we perform textual analysis on a text, we make an educated guess at some of the most likely interpretations that might be made of that text."[43] This form of cultural/textual analysis examines texts as *meaning-containing*. Games are particularly difficult texts to examine using textual analysis. There are some elements that are easily dissected and discussed. For example, the rules form a type of text that we can read as both instructional and algorithmic in its interpretation. The game pieces, as well, can be a form of rhetorical text, in that they encourage players to perceive the game in a particular way through their artwork and aesthetics.

But there are other elements of games that make them particularly *unsuited* for textual analysis, and in those cases, based on the informed textual analysis of the game elements, I will generally use what Matt Hills has termed an autoethnography. This autoethnographic exploration will view the game's particular ludic functionality through the lens of actual gameplay. This method asks the researcher to examine his or her own place within the media environment. During the research for this book, a group of friends and I met once a month to play and become familiar with all the games analyzed. Sometimes we played more than one game per session; at other sessions (*Arkham Horror*), we couldn't even complete one full game without some members having to go home. For Hills, an autoethnographic methodology not only examines the tastes, values, attachments, and investments of the community under study but also asks the person undertaking it to "question their self-account constantly, opening 'the subjective' and the intimately personal up to the cultural contexts in which it is formed and experienced." Hills' autoethnography places the researcher squarely in the center of the analysis in order to reveal "the narcissistic limits of 'intellectual rigour' as well as the narcissistic limits of 'common sense.'"[44] Autoethnography requires constant questioning of the self.

For the purposes of this study, the autoethnographic methodology espoused by Hills is turned slightly as I examine not just my own experiences as a game player and media fan, but also those of the group members who came over once a month to play these games. By interrogating not just the game but also the interaction of the game with the players, I hope to gain insights into how paratextual board games function across multiple play sessions. The game group that I played with reflects important autoethnographic details. We are all early career professionals or scholars, well educated, male and female, middle class, and white. Further, although not everyone was familiar with every media text, enough of us playing had background knowledge—and often highly tuned fan knowledge—of both the games and the franchises. Our demographics illustrate additional limitations to this type of analysis—any particular autoethnographic analysis is caught up in a particular time and place, as well as the particular subjective experiences of the researcher and his or her team. In my case, it is clear that my own tastes have influenced how the game night progressed (would they be different if I hadn't purchased pizza for everyone?), and that the group's background reflected how we interpreted the different games. The specific contexts of each gameplay session revealed multiple discourses that foregrounded the different games.

Summary of chapters

Studying games as cultural artifacts allows us to focus on new ways of interacting with the world around us. To analyze this, *Game Play* engages in new forms of audience-generated play with and about the media, something I have previously called a philosophy of playfulness:

> The contemporary media scene is complex, and rapidly becoming dependent on a culture of ludism: today's media field is fun, playful, and exuberant. More so than at any other time, the media we use in our everyday lives has been personalized, individualized, and made pleasurable to use.[45]

Game Play takes this philosophy of playfulness as its central theme, merging the implicit ludism of the media environment with the explicit ludism of gaming. Although today's media can illustrate a philosophy of playfulness more obviously, human beings have always enjoyed playing and games. Early play researcher Johan Huizinga hypothesized that it is the notion of structured play that makes us human, calling us Homo Ludens (playful man) to differentiate our form of play from what he considered less structured play within the animal kingdom.[46] Throughout human history, playing and games have structured our leisure time and developed our informal learning strategies. From early games like Chess and Go to modern-day video games and location-based digital gaming, it is hard to imagine a more universal or successful form of play than the game.

At the same time, contemporary games are more narratively driven than ever before, especially those based on media products. Our philosophy of playfulness energizes our interactions with media today.

The first part of the book explores what Katie Salen and Eric Zimmerman define as the three main concepts undergirding games—all games have a rules-based structure, invoke meaningful play, and exist contextually within a particularly diverse culture.[47] In the first chapter, I discuss the idea of rules by critically engaging with media theorist Lev Manovich's discussion of new media and algorithms.[48] As I demonstrate using the horror-themed game *Arkham Horror*, digital algorithmic structure is exemplified by paratextual board games. *Arkham Horror* is based on the works of H. P. Lovecraft and his mythos of the Ancient Ones. This mythos establishes a nonlinear, multimodal interpretation of dimensionality, which is a concept I term *unstructure* and a characteristic the game attempts to emulate. However, through a mechanical investigation of the game, I show how rules-based elements within board games reflect new media characteristics, and contemporary players must negotiate these characteristics as they play through paratextual media games.

In the second chapter, I synthesize Henry Jenkins's concept of convergence culture with meaningful paratextual play.[49] According to Jenkins, convergence is the melding of top-down and bottom-up cultural processes of production and consumption. Games based on two franchises of *The Lord of the Rings* demonstrate this type of convergence. To develop a more meaningful understanding of convergence across media outlets, I examine *cooperation* as a key game mechanic, which exists in contrast to *competition* throughout complex gaming. Through a detailed examination of these characteristics as they manifest in games based on books and games based on films, I augment contemporary research into media convergence through analyses of hierarchy in both media and game play.

The final chapter of the first section looks at a cultural aspect of new media: transmediation within narrative and games. Through analyses and comparisons of the *Walking Dead* board games, I argue that to effectively integrate board games into a narrative franchise requires a more inclusive view of the concept of transmedia storytelling. Previous analyses of transmediation, most taking their cue from Henry Jenkins's definition, articulate the term as a plot-based aspect of narrative.[50] However, integrating games into a narrative franchise means expanding the term to include *affect* and *pathos* as additional components of narrativity. I conclude that the affect of individual audience members generated via character pathos is a relevant aspect of game/story transmediation. Using the *Walking Dead* board games as case studies,

I extend research into transmediation as it portends a more affective media environment.

The second part of the book explores different aspects of gaming and new media theory as they intersect. In the fourth chapter, I examine two games based on two *Battlestar Galactica* television series. I analyze the ways individual players become enveloped in both the cult text and the paratextual board game simultaneously. I focus on two related concepts that the *Battlestar Galactica* paratextual board games reflect: first, how board games based on media products mirror both a *spatial understanding* and a *temporal construction* of the game world; and second, how the hidden enemy trope of the contemporary *BSG* game reflects the integration of everyday technology into contemporary environments. We *all* become Cylons through the role-play in the *Battlestar Galactica* game.

In the fifth chapter, I advance a discussion of game mutability by approaching Axel Bruns' notion of produsage from the standpoint of game play in two *Star Trek*—based board games.[51] Produsage is defined as the intersection of production and usage within a digital environment, and looks not just at the way individual texts become converged online, but also at how nothing is ever *finished*—everything is always *in process*. Produsage is a useful tool for examining the interactive nature of online communication, but it can apply to board games as well. Specifically, *Star Trek* is a text that is continually in process. Fans reinterpret and reexamine the classic series as well as the sequel series like *The Next Generation* and *Deep Space Nine* and the Alternate timeline of the new reboot series. At the same time, ludic extensions to the *Star Trek* franchise develop deeper, more rich integrations of the complexities of the narrative world for fans to investigate.

In the sixth chapter I investigate the notion of fan participation in paratextual board games using games based on the *Hunger Games* film and book series. In the game based on the film series, everyone plays as protagonist Katniss Everdeen. The game relies on players being able to manage resources and develop mechanisms for survival. In contrast, the game based on the book series focuses on strategic alliances between characters. Players compete in challenges based on the characteristics of whichever District's participant they have chosen. While the game based on the novel opens up spaces for fans to creatively imagine their own narratives, the game based on the film closes up the gaps within the narrative, which also serves to close out fans from participating in their own narrative construction.

In the seventh chapter, I expand on the discussion of fandom by analyzing games based on the two *Game of Thrones* franchises. This analysis compares the serialization of the television series and the novels with the complex database of information contained in both of the franchises. The game based on the television show reflects a serialized play of individual character cards, while the game based on the book series relies more on a complex database of information to win. Such play differences speak to the larger paradigm of networking as a facet of contemporary digital culture, which relies on individuality *and* social interactivity to develop. Through detailed interpretations of both games, I contrast game narratives with information databases.

In the eighth chapter, I conclude my analyses by examining what I term "ludic interaction" within paratextual board games. I use adaptation theories to augment our understanding of paratextual board games, specifically looking at two board games based on *Doctor Who*. These two *Doctor Who* games reveal a sense of *ludic interaction*, or how paratextual board games reflect not the content but the *feeling* of the original text. Board games based on media are not necessarily novel, but their complexity and popularity develop new audiences and discourses surrounding them.

The principles of paratextual board games

Throughout this book I identify key "takeaway" points about paratextual board games that establish some of their textual or structural similarities. By noting ways to better understand, identify, and analyze paratextual board games, each chapter points toward these principles, and my hope is that scholars, teachers, game designers, and players will be able to use them to teach and to better understand paratextual board games as part of the converged media environment. Although each chapter concentrates on the games in a particular franchise, these principles apply outside that franchise as well.

- Principle 1: Paratextual board games rely on two sets of guiding rules: the rules of the game and the rules of the world upon which the game is based. These rules do not have to match, and can work well even when in conflict with one another.
- Principle 2: The rules governing paratextual board games work algorithmically, and, in conjunction with uncertainty like randomness and player action, create *unstructure*.
- Principle 3: Paratextual board games create meaning from the tension between an authorial presence and audience play; this meaning is created between player, designer, and original text.

- Principle 4: Paratextual board games use *play* as a specific mechanism by which players inhabit and make media their own.
- Principle 5: Through player/text interaction, paratextual board games can transmediate pathos and affect better than they can transmediate narrative.
- Principle 6: Paratextual board games rely on mixing familiar characters and unfamiliar characteristics to facilitate player investment.
- Principle 7: Just as a media text takes place within a specific spatial-temporal environment, paratextual board games mirror this space/time amalgam via the board and the pacing of the game play.
- Principle 8: Paratextual board games can offer players the opportunity to mirror characteristics of particular characters within the specific spatial-temporal environment of the media text.
- Principle 9: The materiality of the game pieces in paratextual board games facilitates fan interaction with the game as a system while also externalizing the game as an additional episode within the media franchise.
- Principle 10: Mutable elements randomize game play while also reinforcing the paratextual game structure.
- Principle 11: Paratextual board games harness the affective power of fandom to help generate player interaction within the game.
- Principle 12: Paratextual board games can either allow players to create their own stories or discourage players from doing so within the larger narrative framework of the text, depending on the structure of the game's narrative elements.
- Principle 13: Paratextual board games expose the database and the serial at the heart of licensed gaming, revealing connections between players, texts, and actions through the mechanisms of play, algorithmic procedure, narrative, and player interaction.
- Principle 14: Paratextuality can be achieved in multiple ways through differing emphases on simulating thematic content.
- Principle 15: When seen as strict adaptations, paratextual board games close off interpretation of the media text; when seen as ludic interaction, they open up player dialogue with the media text.

Part One

Understanding Games

Ludifying Lovecraft in *Arkham Horror*

The most merciful thing in the world, I think, is the inability of the human mind to correlate all its contents.

H. P. Lovecraft, "The Call of Cthulhu"

Darrell Simmons was on the move. A local photographer for the Arkham paper, Darrell had seen something that chilled his blood, but was indescribable. Armed only with a camera and his wits, Darrell left his office intent on proving that things were not normal in Arkham. Or maybe just to prove to himself that his fears—those overriding fears that permeated his grasp on reality—were valid. Darrell entered the Twilight Lodge and saw Carl Sanford in front of him. A cold shiver ran down Darrell's spine as Carl led him into a study, intoning quietly but insistently to himself. Darrell's ability to withstand fear became compromised— normally able to block out even the most uncomfortable of feelings, he had recently needed some luck, so he had adjusted his abilities. The hypnotic tones of Carl lulled Darrell into a trance, and soon Darrell lost all sense of time and place, his consciousness taken out of the world and into that fearful, otherworldly nonplace, R'lyeh. His clues gone, his sanity near zero, Darrell contemplated how it all started....

With over 700 pieces, a table-sized game board, and a 24-page rule book, the game *Arkham Horror* is notoriously complex, a characteristic that game designer Ira Fay argues "creates excitement in the players."[1] Memorizing the rules is difficult; when my game group first sat down to play, they had already watched a couple of online videos illustrating how to play (one was ninety minutes long), and had read an abbreviated (10-page) set of rules. I started setting up the board and learning the rules myself two hours before the first guest was scheduled to arrive; by the time they all did, I still had five pages to go.

Rules are an integral part of games. In fact, some would call games entirely dependent on the rules—Salen and Zimmerman argue that "to play a game is to follow its rules."[2] We can tell the difference between different games, however common the aesthetic and surface details, by the differences in their rules (although Elias, Garfield, and Gutschera argue that game rules are less important than scholarly literature has implied.)[3] Rules, as Rachel Wagner notes, "shape games by setting the standards for behavior and the tolerance for play in relationship to those standards."[4] Without rules, there would be no structure in the games we play. Rules also undergird and support our cultural understanding of how games function in society. Johan Huizinga describes games as organized around the "proper boundaries of time and space according to fixed rules."[5] Roger Caillois famously uses "rules" as one of the six defining characteristics of play, writing that play happens "governed by rules; under conditions that suspend ordinary laws, and for the moment establish new legislation, which alone counts." These rules, he describes, are sacrosanct to the game world:

> The confused and intricate laws of ordinary life are replaced, in this fixed space and for this given time, by precise, arbitrary, unexceptionable rules that must be accepted as such and that govern the correct playing of the game.... The game is ruined by the nihilist who denounces the rule as absurd and conventional, who refuses to play because the game is meaningless.... That is why its rules are imperative and absolute, beyond discussion.[6]

Rules thus govern the game, and help to define the game for what it is and also what it is not.

At the same time, for paratextual board games, the rules of the game are developed in conjunction with another set of rules: the rules surrounding the cult world upon which the game is based. Every fictional cult world has its own rules that determine such factors as the inhabitants, character relationships, fictional cultures, natural laws, and history of the world.[7] For example, in the cult world of J. R. R. Tolkien's Middle-earth (see Chapter 2), Elves and Dwarves exist alongside human beings, and magic governs the realm. In the cult world of *Star Trek* (see Chapter 5), the rules governing the meeting of cultures (at least for the United Federation of Planets) are inscribed as the Prime Directive, demanding noninterference. In the cult worlds of H. P. Lovecraft, as I show in this chapter, ancient entities have shaped humankind's development through the seemingly magical manipulation of anxiety and fear. There are thus two sets of rules at work at once within the paratextual board game: the rules of the game, that set it apart from the "real world" and place it into a "magic circle" (Huizinga's term for the playspace of the game world) and the rules of the cult franchise that govern the player's understanding of the larger world of the game. This understanding is reflected in the first principle of paratextual board games:

Principle 1: Paratextual board games rely on two sets of guiding rules: the rules of the game and the rules of the world upon which the game is based. These rules do not have to match, and can work well even when in conflict with one another.

In the same way that rules control both the way games are played and the way cult texts are perceived, so too do rules underlie the way that media technologies are used and understood. Rules are a determining part of the new media environment, and thus understanding games—even so-called "old fashioned" board games—becomes a metaphor for understanding how we take part in the new media environment. A third set of rules applies to this discussion: the algorithmic rules that govern new media. Using the work of Lev Manovich, I discuss how the complexity of rules in both paratextual board games and in their requisite cult franchises reflects the larger cultural ramifications of an algorithmic understanding of contemporary media. This leads to the second principle:

Principle 2: The rules governing paratextual board games work algorithmically, and, in conjunction with uncertainty like randomness and player action, create unstructure.

Here, I am defining *unstructure* not as the absence of structure, but as the inability to define or recognize the underlying basis for a structure within a system. Unstructure exists when elements appear random, but we simply don't know enough about a system to see the organizational patterns. As author Arthur C. Clarke famously writes: "Any sufficiently advanced technology is indistinguishable from magic."[8] When we do not understand something, it can appear to be random. Unstructure is the deliberate application of this structured randomness for an effect.

In general, we base our understanding of structure on the norms of linearity. Understanding unstructure can be elemental in the conceptualization of paratextual game rules as an alternative to this norm. Unstructure reflects in the work of H. P. Lovecraft, whose Cthulhu mythos and otherworldly descriptions of ethereal horror manifest in a universe where the "rules" we live by are undermined by beings beyond our control, creating discomfort at the unexplained randomness.

Lovecraft's unstructure, the horror of the non-rule, contrasts with the very games based upon his universe. There are multiple board games built around

Lovecraft's universe. In this chapter, I will be focusing on *Arkham Horror*, because of its popularity and its complexity. *Arkham Horror*'s connection to Lovecraft is overt, and is one of the most popular complex board games on the market. Its original edition, designed by Richard Launius and published by Chaosium, sold out in 1987. A newer edition, designed by Kevin Wilson and published by Fantasy Flight Games, also sold out in its initial run, with over 140,000 units purchased.[9] Other board games, like *Eldritch Horror* and *Elder Sign*, also connect to Lovecraft's work, especially in the genre thematic and the monsters that populate the games. I focus on *Arkham Horror* because it precedes the others: *Eldritch Horror* is itself based on *Arkham Horror* (the box advertising, "Inspired by *Arkham Horror*") and *Elder Sign* makes use of the same characters and Ancient Ones as does *Arkham Horror*. Importantly, both *Elder Sign* and *Eldritch Horror*, like *Arkham Horror*, are complex games with long rule books and multiple rule guides: they use their rules to create unstructure within the game. *Arkham Horror* is billed on its box cover as being "the classic game of Lovecraftian horror," and, indeed, many of the places, characters, and enemies in the game draw their names and characteristics from the writing of Lovecraft. Game designer Kevin Wilson notes that he used the Lovecraftian role-playing game *Call of Cthulhu* as a basis for some of his revisions to the game, and the game box itself calls *Arkham Horror* "A Call of Cthulhu Boardgame."[10]

One of the consequences of rule-heavy games is a reliance on story and structure. For instance, in Reiner Knizia's *Lord of the Rings* game, which I explore in the next chapter, certain events must happen at certain times within the game. Players can make choices about how to prepare for these events, but this structure must exist. When players have the opportunity to make more independent decisions, the game becomes less story oriented and more ludic. At the same time, paratextual board games exist in a system of already established rules: the cult universe in which they reside has its own system for how the world works. The rules of *Arkham Horror* sometimes mirror Lovecraft's world, but also differ in crucial ways. What happens when a cult universe reveals an absence of rules? For Lovecraft, horror arrives from the unknowable—not the foreign made manifest necessarily, but the presence of things outside the realm of our own human understanding. This mythos establishes a nonlinear interpretation of narrative, a characteristic *Arkham Horror* attempts to emulate.

At first glance, the Lovecraftian mythos would seem antithetical to rules-based games as its peculiar aspect lies in its indefinability: like Cthulhu itself (which has a form but can change it, and which is amoral but influences humanity in immoral ways), the series of short stories from which the mythos develops has created a sprawling yet indefinable narrative. The unstructure of Lovecraft's worlds can be found in the way that his stories themselves only sort of cohere. According to Lovecraft expert Robert M. Price, Lovecraft's works do not fit together neatly—"the fit [between all the titles] is not exact, nor need it be."[11] Although general themes of Lovecraft can be teased out, at any one specific instance no individual text can be said to fulfill all the "rules" of the Lovecraftian universe.[12] And it's not just one "universe"—unlike an auteur such as George Lucas, for instance, whose Lucasfilm has maintained the authority to artificially determine what is or is not part of the *Star Wars* canon, Lovecraft's stories have been assigned into various cycles, myths, or universes, at various times, by various authors and scholars.[13] Lovecraft "left it to subsequent systematicians to lend artificial order" to his catalog.[14]

In order to detail how unstructure functions in paratextual board games, I first analyze the way rules work in *Arkham Horror*, then apply these rules to an analysis of the game play in *Arkham Horror*, and finally discuss the way that the rules determine the story of the game. Lovecraft's unstructure manifests in *Arkham Horror* when the numerous rules of the game as laid out in the 24-page rule book ideologically contradict the more fluid and open rules of the Lovecraftian universe detailed in his overarching Cthulhu mythos. Ludic necessities override paratextual connectivity. *Arkham Horror* uses rules as a way of maintaining variability within game mechanisms to shift the prominent traits of the main characters, offering multiple routes through narrative by changing the stories within its many play options.

Algorithms, games, and Lovecraft

For Salen and Zimmerman, any set of game "rules" can be broken into discrete, formal structures. There are the operational rules, or the "guidelines players require in order to play"—for example, the rules written in a rulebook. In addition, there are the implicit rules of the game, which are largely the social and cultural contracts that we subscribe to when we agree to play with each other. Some implicit rules of games may include letting someone have a "do-over" if they are inexperienced at the game, making the loser buy a round, or refraining from punching the winners if they beat you. Mediating between the operational and the implicit rules of the game are the constitutive rules of the game, the "underlying formal structures that exist 'below the surface' of the rules."[15] Constitutive rules are the mathematical logics that guide the allowable permutations of a game. Rules have a "mechanical rigor" and an "algorithmic specificity" that help determine the play experience.[16] Matthew Berland goes so far as to argue that "playing strategic tabletop games requires that individuals think like a computer."[17] The constitutive rules are what lead games researcher Greg Costikyan to argue that, for instance, Tic-Tac-Toe is "a trivial" game because "you know that the outcome of the game is utterly certain." The game is only enjoyable when "the naïve player has not yet learned, or figured out, that the game has an optimal strategy."[18] Once the underlying logic of the game has been uncovered, the uncertainty in outcome is resolved.

As Berland intimates, today's complex paratextual board games reflect an algorithmic approach to contemporary media. For new media theorist Lev Manovich, the rules governing digital technology represent one of the core tenets of a profound shift toward algorithmic functionality in our everyday lives. Yet, as Mark Deuze notes, new media characteristics "are not brand new phenomena that jumped into being the moment the first computer went online."[19] Paratextual board games—as with all board games—already reflect the algorithmic characteristics of new media technologies, and as such, form a type of symbolic partnership with new media that refocuses attention on how we interpret ludic elements within our contemporary media environment.

Through manipulation, says Manovich, all new media objects are subject to algorithmic change, and become programmable. This programmability happens because new media objects are numerical (based in binary code), modular (constructed of interchangeable parts), automated (can work without human intervention), and variable (can be adjusted to suit the context). These four characteristics reveal a fifth—that "the logic of a computer can be expected to significantly influence the traditional cultural logic of media." In other words, the metaphor of the computer guides the way we see the world around us— the way we interpret information (we "input" it), understand the relationship between people and objects (we are "networked" to others), even describe the functionality of the human body (the brain is a giant "hard drive")—and has been "transcoded" into all levels of human culture.[20] Importantly, the transcoding nature of new media reveals the algorithms of contemporary culture—the scripts that automate and structure our everyday lives.

Aspects of paratextual board games reveal their algorithmic bases. Any particular session of game play can contain elements that are manipulable through rules-based play. In *Arkham Horror,* many choices are mathematical. For example, when fighting a monster, a player must compare a numerical assessment of the monster's "combat rating" to the character's "fight" score, and then add the role of a die. The die offers a sense of uncertainty, a random element that may affect whether the player wins or loses the fight, but the algorithmic structure by which the fight progresses is mathematical and systematic. Yet, the base skill set is highly changeable, manipulable by the players. Paratextual board games mirror our experiences within the cult world upon which they are based. All paratextual board games ask us to play for a time within an alternate world. This world is necessarily incomplete; it relies on us to fill in the contextual details. These details, as Marie-Laure Ryan describes, emerge from our own interpretation of the world around us.[21] Like the fiction upon which it is based, *Arkham Horror* asks us to re-envision the world. We are not in Lovecraft's universe, except insofar as we allow ourselves to develop an understanding of the universe influenced by the same elements that influenced Lovecraft. Interpretation is key—we see chaos and horror in our lives and justify it, balance it with what we "know" to be true. Lovecraftian horror, the type of horror that excels at being unknowable, influences our knowledge of the diegesis of the game.[22] It is not enough to see Middle-earth in *The Lord of the Rings* board games, but we also have to input our own interpretation of what Middle-earth means, and how it developed out of an understanding of our culture, to make the game have meaning for us. Working in concert with each other, randomness and strategy in *Arkham Horror* balance the structural effect of both the game and the fiction rules.[23]

The modularity of *Arkham Horror* reveals additional elements of algorithmic culture. The game focuses on the town of Arkham as the site of an otherworldly occupation; Ancient Ones, who have secretly controlled humanity for thousands of years, have emerged to take over the Earth. With them are various monsters— zombies, cult leaders, vampires, etc.—who lurk in various buildings and streets in Arkham. Playing as a band of intrepid heroes, the players move throughout the town defeating monsters, exploring environments, having encounters with the people of Arkham, opening (and closing) gates to the Other World, and (hopefully) earning Elder Signs, which can be used to seal those gates. These Other World gates send players out of Arkham, where they are instructed to move differently or have different encounters. The different dimensions call for new sets of rules, which help determine the play of the Other World. One could change the rules for the Other World without affecting the overall universe of *Arkham Horror* or the larger diegetic game play.

Exterior to the game's diegesis, however, paratextual board games also reflect algorithmic modularity, in that their peculiar relationship with the original media text means some aspects of the game reside uniquely within the game diegesis while other aspects are a "crossover" from the original text. Most paratextual board games will use characters from their original text, as do the *Lord of the Rings* games I discuss in the next chapter, the *Walking Dead* games in Chapter 3, or *Star Trek: Expeditions* in Chapter 5. But for *Arkham Horror,* the creation of unique characters leads to interchangeability within the game. Like the *Battlestar Galactica* game I discuss in Chapter 4 or the *Game of Thrones: The Card Game* of Chapter 7, the *Arkham Horror* franchise includes room for expansion packs that augment the play of the game via the addition of modular elements. For example, beyond the base set, which comes with over 700 pieces and cards, I can also purchase at least eight different expansion packs of more cards, pieces, and narrative elements, including the *Dunwich Horror,* the *Innsmouth Horror,* and the ominously titled the *Lurker at the Threshold.* Such expansion packs are common for complex paratextual board games, adding texture and meaning to a cult world—as well as increasing revenue for franchises and game companies, as the expansion packs can range from \$24.99 to \$54.99 each. Being able to touch and feel these multiple components also helps create affect in players, as the tactile nature of multiple sets of games, tokens, and figures helps produce an emotional connection to the game, and a sense of completion (or desire) for those that collect miniatures.[24]

The algorithmic nature of paratextual board games extends to a sense of automation as well. Unlike digital games, where the calculations and algorithms are all hidden from the player, paratextual board games rely on players knowing and understanding every rule.[25] It is not uncommon for players to spend time looking up rules in the book when they do not know them off the top of their heads—and during our gameplay session, there were breaks of fifteen minutes or so when we would argue over the semantics of the wording to figure out what the game meant. For instance, *delaying* a character is different from *devouring* a character, which is different again from *arresting* a character or making a character go *insane* or *unconscious.* We often had to go online to see videos and other resources to aid our understanding of the rules, revealing the importance of knowing them for continued play.[26]

The very paratextuality of media-based board games also reflects an automation, such that the more a player knows about the cult world upon which the game is based, the more his or her interpretation of the game becomes based in that world's contextual information. Relying on the automated understanding of the cult world reveals an underlying tension in paratextual board games between an element of narrative surprise and a reliance on familiar tropes. Because players know that *Arkham Horror* is based on Lovecraft, they can assume that other worldly demons and monsters will appear. If monsters did not appear, the game would appear out of step with the original text. Other paratextual games reveal additional moments of automation between cult text and game: *District 12*, based on the *Hunger Games* film, does not introduce the characters of Gale, Prim, and Peeta (see Chapter 6). Rather, the players are expected to know who these characters are (and why they are in certain locations, like the bakery or the woods) before the game begins. *Battlestar Galactica* expects its players to automatically know that Cylons are bad and humans are good. Paratextual games rely on audience foreknowledge (although audiences do not always need that knowledge to enjoy the game).

The combination of the complexity of a paratextual board game's rules, the characteristics of its play, and the input of different players creates a variable algorithm that makes each session unique but recognizable as the same game. We say we are playing *Arkham Horror* even though we may use different characters, cards, monsters, locations, and even a final enemy. All game sessions of *Arkham Horror* look similar, but minute variations at the start make each play of the game vastly different from the others. For instance, at the beginning of the game, each player randomly draws one of sixteen characters. Each character has different attributes that change the way the game progresses, including special abilities and different skill levels in speed, sneaking, fighting, will power, lore knowledge, and luck. Each character starts in a different area of Arkham. At the start of each turn, players can construct their own custom skill levels, and although only eight players can play at one time, the large pool of sixteen choices opens up different ways to play. Different characters may have different backstories, so from a narrative point of view, the game may subtly shift depending on whether one is playing as adventurer and archeologist Monterey Jack (who continually uncovers magical artifacts), as gangster Michael McGlen (whose stamina is extraordinarily high), or as dilettante Jenny Barnes (who earns money at every turn). And ultimately, the characteristics that define each character—the amount of stamina and sanity, the special powers they possess—will influence the game play.

Additionally, the first player starts the game by randomly drawing one of eight Ancient Ones who will slowly awaken as the game progresses (Figure 1.1).

Figure 1.1 "Azathoth" and "Nyarlathotep," two Ancient Ones from *Arkham Horror: The Board Game* © 2005 Fantasy Flight Publishing, Inc. Photo by the author.

Each Ancient One has different effects that change the game play—the biggest and baddest of them all, Azathoth, has an ability to attack infinitely, and thus the game is over if Azathoth awakens. In one of Lovecraft's descriptions of this Ancient One, he describes this terrible power as an

> amorphous blight of nethermost confusion which blasphemes and bubbles at the center of all infinity—the boundless daemon sultan Azathoth, whose name no lips dare speak aloud, and who gnaws hungrily in inconceivable, unlighted chambers beyond time and space amidst the muffled, maddening beating of vile drums and the thin monotonous whine of accursed flutes.[27]

In contrast, the Ancient One Nyarlathotep controls different monsters, which means more monsters can be engaged in the game, but has a relatively low combat score itself (4), meaning it is not too difficult to defeat Nyarlathotep once it awakens. This also matches Lovecraft's description of the demon:

> swarthy, slender, and sinister, always buying strange instruments of glass and metal and combining them into instruments yet stranger. He spoke much of the sciences—of electricity and psychology—and gave exhibitions of power which sent his spectators away speechless, yet which swelled his fame to exceeding magnitude. Men advised one another to see Nyarlathotep, and shuddered. And where Nyarlathotep went, rest vanished; for the small hours were rent with the screams of a nightmare.[28]

Nyarlathotep tends to be more closely aligned with the knowable, human world and is thus less abject than the Ancient Ones that exist outside humanity's understanding entirely. The rules of the game present variations that significantly affect both the narrative of and the play within the game; yet, because those rules are *part* of the game, the variations become the element that defines the game.

The horror of structure and unstructure

If, as I have shown, algorithms guide the most basic understanding of paratextual board games, then it seems contradictory to base a complex game on the work of H. P. Lovecraft. The detailed mythos built up in Lovecraft's work describes a world existing *outside* of rules, a world based on the cosmic horror of the unknown and the unknowable. Yet, as I will show in this section, *Arkham Horror* uses that sense of algorithmic structure as a way of mirroring the very non rules—based mythos of Lovecraft. By relying on multiple sets of rules at once, the game creates what I have termed *unstructure*—a feeling of randomness generated by an unknowable structure.

Lovecraft's plots revolve around the fact that the existence of ancient supernatural entities outside of traditional Euclidean and Cartesian realities affects the emotional responses (especially fear, dread, horror, and terror) of individuals. Despite trying to fight back, humans find that victories are usually temporary and costly. But according to Lovecraft expert Donald R. Burleson, Lovecraft's themes go deeper than this, and reflect his belief that human beings are insignificant in the universe, and our very awareness of this fact leads to madness.[29] Yet, as I noted, there is no one "order" to Lovecraft's work—it is not a series like Lewis's Narnia books or a complete world like Tolkien's Middle-earth. Rather, Lovecraft's oeuvre is best understood as fitting together thematically. It is not that the volumes are random and out of order, but that readers (as well as Lovecraft himself) have no overarching organization to guide them. This is *unstructure*, where randomness implies a lack of structure. There may be a basic arrangement of elements, and although we may not understand the organization, we know that there must be something underlying it. In this sense, the Lovecraftian universe is fraught with unstructure.

Defining any one aspect of Lovecraft's "rules" works against the very nature of Lovecraft's universe. In this sense, Lovecraft's stories are fluid and dynamic, where, as Price describes, "the realms of magic turn out to be unsuspected dimensions of non-Euclidean geometry." We cannot understand the structure of the universe, although we recognize that there is a structure there. In a way, the symbolic nature of the Lovecraft universe, a storyworld "so massive and complex ... that no writers can ever utilize enough of it for the reader to surmise the writer's principle of selection," mirrors that of Lovecraft's Ancient Ones themselves. So immense as to be virtually sizeless, the Ancient Ones are a corpus unto themselves. But they are never consistently the same. For example, in one story about the Ancient One Azathoth, "we would have encountered a nightmare 'daemon-sultan' bearing little resemblance either to the 'monstrous nuclear chaos' of Lovecraft's science fiction ... or the mindless demiurge of the Cthulhu Mythos tales." Lovecraft's Azathoth is not consistent, and nor should it be: the sheer unknowability (and unstructurable presence) of ancient aliens/gods/creatures means that conceptualizing Azathoth *as* something defeats its very purpose. The same can be said for Lovecraft's creation Nyarlathotep, a creature with many guises and many forms, which Lovecraft also uses throughout his oeuvre in multiple ways: "he inserts the name Nyarlathotep into the denouement of the 'The Rats in the Walls,' where it has neither weight nor much significance. ... Here is the Cthulhu Mythos in a nutshell," argues Price.[30]

Yet, *Arkham Horror*'s structural reliance on enemy characteristics belies this mutability. In the game, any Ancient Ones must remain fixed, denying the uncertainty of Lovecraft's universe. In what Lovecraft himself described as his own favorite among his stories, "The Colour Out of Space," the text "symbolically raises questions ... about categoricality and systematization." In this way, Lovecraft's stories eradicate "the basic notion of any stable system that purports, in a settled and comprehensive way, to account for the world as perceived by humankind."[31] *Arkham Horror*, in turn, almost completely negates Lovecraft's world by relying on its underlying algorithms, which players *must* comprehend.

Reading Lovecraft as a whole means artificially creating a structure that the author may never have intended: understanding earlier stories in light of later ones opens up what Jacques Derrida calls "the dangerous supplement," or a sense that the sequel in some way determines aspects of the original.[32] The placement of a text within Lovecraft's mythos is a complex process. Some Lovecraft scholars take great pains to point out which texts do, and which ones do not, fit into the larger scheme. Lin Carter places artificial boundaries between the works, creating a structuralist methodology for examining the mythos: to maintain a discrete border for the mythos, each story must "present us with a significant item of information about the background lore of the Mythos, thus contributing important information to a common body of lore."[33] Yet, Price asks, "Is this manner of reading fair to the texts? Is it realistic? Here is how I resolve the matter. It is entirely a question of which of the [Mythos] stories you consider any individual story to be a part of."[34]

Such work in concretizing the unconcretizable must be present when translating a cult narrative to a board game. *A Game of Thrones: The Board Game* must make tangible the multiple relationships between characters; *Star Trek: Fleet Captains* must represent the damage ships take during battle. For *Arkham Horror,* the game uses a procedural rhetoric to formalize the roles of the Ancient Ones, the characters, and the entire Lovecraftian mythos in a way that never formally took place in Lovecraft's works. Ian Bogost has defined the phrase "procedural rhetoric" in game studies to refer to the "practice of using [game] processes persuasively."[35] Games become a way of informally educating from a particular point of view, using play as a pedagogical mechanic.[36] Wagner expands on Bogost's definition, arguing that "to examine procedural rhetoric, then, is to look at how arguments are addressed to users via the things they are doing in interaction with the game."[37] Bogost holds that such procedural translation lies at the heart of paratextual video games, arguing that by "taking themes and figures from [literature] and applying them to games," we can see how games do not so much remake as they reapply traditional modes of understanding.[38] This is how Wilson redesigned the complex set of rules, mythologies, and underlying stories at the heart of *Arkham Horror*, writing that he had to "respect … a medium's strengths and weaknesses, but at the same time [look] to see what storytelling techniques other media have to offer."[39] *Arkham Horror* uses procedural rhetoric to attempt to mirror the unstructure of Lovecraft's work, through (1) the cooperation mechanics of players within the game and (2) a focus on individual components working within the game to focus on hybridizing story and play. In this case, "procedural rhetoric" refers to the rules of the game as they attempt to mirror the unstructure of the underlying mythos. As Flanagan notes, even play itself is a type of unstructural "subversion," as it can be a "transgressive and subversive" action.[40] Ultimately, these attempts to concretize the unstructure of Lovecraft represent a method of rhetorically hybridizing rules and a story that highlights the unique positioning of paratextual board games within the media environment.

Cooperation

One of the ways *Arkham Horror* uses its algorithmic structure to realize the unstructure of Lovecraft's universe is through the board game mechanism of cooperation. Cooperation within *Arkham Horror* allows for a greater fluidity of human motivation to become part of the game. Much of the nitty-gritty mechanics of *Arkham Horror* can be electronically automated through digital apps that automate dice rolling, card shuffling, and other mathematical elements. Indeed, other Lovecraft games can be automated as well: a mobile game based on *Elder Sign* allows for the computer to do much of the mathematical work. Jonas Linderoth calls *Arkham Horror*'s cooperation "pure," since "all players work together towards a mutual goal."[41] This lies in opposition to what he defines as "tragedy of the commons" style of cooperation, where the system falls apart if players are too individualistic (which I will describe in the next chapter regarding the *Lord of the Rings* games), and cooperative games with a traitor mechanic (which I describe in Chapter 4 in reference to *Battlestar Galactica: The Board Game*). Cooperation in this "pure" mode means that no individual will "win" the game by himself or herself. All players, instead, win or lose as a group.

That cooperation is mandated in the game makes the underlying structure of the game more malleable. Each player controls one character, and all characters are bound by individual rules. But when different characters cooperate, the different rules can be enacted in multiple ways. For instance, Jenny Barnes, the dilettante, receives one dollar at the start of every turn. Dollars can be used to purchase items like equipment or to heal a character's stamina or sanity. Keeping Jenny busy buying items might help the group as items and money can be transferred between players as needed. Further, the professor Harvey Walters has the "strong mind" ability, which allows him to reduce all sanity losses by 1 point. He also starts the game with what is an enormous number of sanity points, 7 in total. If players are cooperating, they can use Harvey to seal gates or cast spells to combat monsters—his sanity allows him these abilities. Similarly, Michael McGlen, the gangster, has a high stamina (of 7) and his special rule ability is "strong body," which allows him to take less damage. Higher stamina allows a character to combat monsters more effectively. Dispersal of character allows the game players to cooperate and work together to use their abilities to defeat the monsters. Here, the individual characters themselves become subsumed within the game world as components within a larger universe. Cooperation changes game play. The many rules that guide these characters not only help to differentiate them from one another, but more importantly, also bring the different skills that the individual *team* will need to defeat the Ancient One.

This "coming together to defeat an evil" motif is a structural element of the game that the Lovecraft mythos does not necessarily invite; however, the structural elements of character individuality actually end up providing the same sense of unstructure as in Lovecraft. For example, even with a full game complement of 8 players, not every character in the game will be able to be played—there may be a noticeable absence of some characteristics. This randomness increases the level of unstructure in the game. Further, the cooperation mechanic forces players to communicate to defeat the Ancient One, but the more players that are in the game, the harder the game becomes: less cooperation is possible, more monsters are allowed on the board, the Ancient One can awaken earlier, and fewer monsters can be banished to the "outskirts" of the city. More cooperation means a more difficult game—and more unstructure within the organizational parameters of the game.

Individual components

Another method which *Arkham Horror* uses to realize the unstructure of Lovecraft's universe is through individual components in the game. For example, throughout the game various clues are scattered around the game board representing the town of Arkham. Clues are both a means of tracking progress in the game (the number of clues corresponding to how well the team is playing), and tools that all the investigators can use to defeat the Ancient One. The rule book states, "Clue tokens represent information about the mythos threat that an investigator may acquire. A player may spend Clue tokens, one at a time, after any skill check ... to roll one additional die."[42] In addition, as the town of Arkham is slowly being overrun with gates to the "Other World" (one gate appears at the end of every turn), the investigators have to close each one. If too many gates are open at once, the Ancient One immediately awakens and begins his destruction of the town. Clues can be used to seal these gates. A player can spend five Clue tokens to seal the gate forever. This is a powerful move in the game, as sealing six gates wins the game.

Yet, the "Clues" themselves are pieces of non-information—images of magnifying glasses instead of text. There is no actual, textual clue as to the meaning of the Ancient Ones; rather, the Clue tokens are simulacra of information.

Players can never "find out" the answer, the underlying structure: the Clue token simply provides a mechanism by which answers are known to be known. There are no answers at the end of the game; players simply stop (or do not stop) the monster. The structure of the game—the larger set of underlying thematics that rule this world—is able to mirror the "unknowability" of Lovecraft's mythos through the mechanism of literal undiegesis. As players, we have to know that knowledge exists without comprehending what that knowledge is. This unknowable unknown simulates the type of knowledge comprehension that characters create in Lovecraft's worlds as well, as characters must interact with the Ancient Ones all the while knowing that there are aspects that they don't know.

Further, the character attributes help to perpetuate a sense of unstructure in the game. At the start of every turn, players can adjust three different settings on their character's card—"speed/sneak"; "fight/will"; and "lore/luck" (see Figure 1.2). As characters increase *speed*, they must conversely decrease *sneak*. The same applies to *fight/will* (e.g., as their ability to fight increases, their desire to do so decreases) and to *lore/luck*. Ideologically, this last pairing is an interesting linkage, suggesting that as your knowledge of your enemies increases, your luck decreases (perhaps education reduces one's ability to rely on intangible results). The amount of change in these three pairs depends on the character's "focus"—Jenny Barnes has a focus of just one, meaning she can make

Figure 1.2 Character cards for "Jenny Barnes" and "Amanda Sharpe" from *Arkham Horror. The Board Game* © 2005 Fantasy Flight Publishing, Inc. Photo by the author.

only one adjustment per turn (perhaps her days as a Dilettante have left her a bit dazed?). In contrast, the student Amanda Sharpe has a focus of three, allowing her to change her various abilities more often. These seemingly minor individual character differences in the game actually have quite significant consequences: increasing Amanda's fight from two to four would decrease her will from three to one. This would then radically alter her ability to complete a "horror check." The horror check is a special kind of check enacted when encountering a monster. If Amanda fails her will check (and with a one, she is likely to), she would lose sanity and possibly be sent to the insane asylum.

The key Lovecraftian element of unstructure at the heart of this game mechanism is that it is unlikely that a player will know precisely which elements will need to be increased or decreased during a turn, as the events that befall one player may affect others. Amanda, increasing her speed because she thinks she will not have to sneak around a monster, may, in fact, be the complete opposite of what she "should" do given other players' involvement. The unknowability of future events is precisely the type of "aporia" that Price describes at the heart of Lovecraft's work—the philosophical state of puzzlement of the mythos.[43] It is, at once, both a sense of structure to the character and a sense of unstructure to the game story.

Ultimately, both the Clue tokens and the character adjustments serve as microcosms of the larger unstructure of the game, which, in turn, reveals the underlying unstructure of Lovecraft's original cult texts. And in a larger sense, it reveals the unstructure at the heart of contemporary digital culture—the "transcoding" of the game demonstrates the unknowability of today's technology. We use our technology without quite understanding what it does, or where the information goes. Despite the ubiquity of new media today, many people remain ignorant of its basic functionality. New media are sufficiently advanced technologies that appear magic. And although based on hundred-year-old stories, *Arkham Horror* reflects the unstructure of today's media environment.

Rules and story

So far, I have been noting some surface elements of the game: characters, clues, tokens, attributes. But looking more deeply at the rules and how they contribute to our understanding of Lovecraft's particular milieu allows us to develop a more robust analysis of how *Arkham Horror* uses structure to realize the unstructure of Lovecraft's universe. Specifically, I want to look at how the rules governing turn-taking and the functionality of each phase of the turn help to define the unstructure of Lovecraft. Like many paratextual board games, including *Game of Thrones: The Card Game*, as I discuss in Chapter 7, *Arkham Horror*'s game play is dominated by a series of turns and phases. Each turn is divided into five phases, and each phase sees each player performing various actions. As the rule book states, "during each phase, every player, starting with the first player and continuing clockwise, performs the actions that take place during that phase."[44] The next phase continues in the same manner, and so on. Thus, for players of *Arkham Horror*, a "turn" is quite different from what one might expect in a less complex game like *Monopoly*. A single turn may take upward of an hour to complete. Many of the other paratextual games I discuss throughout the book have similar structures, although most are not as laborious as this. Throughout the turn, the unpredictability and random nature of elements within each of the phases present carefully crafted moments of mythos and story. Below, I outline the phases (and the actions that occur in each one) in order to demonstrate how the complexity of the structured process of play deepens the underlying unstructure of the game. By increasing the chaotic randomness of the play in a measured way, each turn acts like a computerized algorithm. In fact, many of the actions can be phrased as if/then logical statements (I have added the *if*s and *then*s to the following outline, and the parenthetical statements reflect assumed instructions).

I.   Phase I: Upkeep
   a.   (*If* Cards exhausted, *then*) Refresh Exhausted Cards
   b.   (*If* character has Upkeep Action, *then*) Perform Upkeep Actions
   c.   (*If* player wishes, *then*) Adjust Skills

II. Phase II: Movement
   a.   (*If* character is in Arkham, *then*) Arkham Movement
      i.   (*If* leaving area with Monster, *then*) Evade (or Fight) Monsters
      ii. (*If* character ends movement on Clue, *then*) Pick Up Clues
   b.   (*If* character is in Other World, *then*) Other World Movement
   c.   (*If* character is Delayed, *then*) Delay Investigator

III. (*If* character is in Arkham, *then*) Phase III: Arkham Encounters
   a.   (*If* character is not on Gate, *then*) No Gate Encounters and player picks Encounter Card

        i. (*If* Encounter Card calls for Monster, *then*) Evade (or Fight) Monsters

   b. (*If* location has Gate, *then*) Move to the Other World through Gate

IV. (*If* character is in Other World, *then*) Phase IV: Other World Encounters

   a. (*If* character is on first spot, *then*) Draw Encounter Card

        i. (*If* Encounter Card calls for Monster, *then*) Evade (or Fight) Monsters

   b. (*If* character is on second spot, *then*) Draw Encounter Card

        i. (*If* Encounter Card calls for Monster, *then*) Evade (or Fight) Monsters

V. Phase V: Mythos

   a. Open Gate and Spawn Monster

        i. (*If* Location has Elder Sign, *then*) Do Nothing

        ii. (*If* Location has Open Gate, *then*) Monster appears at every Open Gate on board

        iii. (*If* Location has neither Elder Sign nor Open Gate, *then*)

           1. The Doom Track Marker Advances

           2. A Gate Opens, and

           3. A Monster Spawns

        iv. (*If* Gate Opens on Character, *then*) Character is moved to Other World

   b. Place Clue Token

        i. (*If* Location has Gate, *then*) Do Not Place Clue Token

   c. Move Monster

        i. (*If* Monster has Black borders, *then*) Move Monster Normally

        ii. (*If* Monster has Yellow borders, *then*) Do Not Move Monster

        iii. (*If* Monster has Red borders, *then*) Move Monster Twice

        iv. (*If* Monster has Green borders, *then*) Follow Instructions on Monster Card

        v. (*If* Monster has Blue borders, *then*) Move Monster to Street Area

   d. Mythos Ability—Draw Mythos Card

As this outline indicates, almost every action within each phase of each turn in *Arkham Horror* comes with an associated uncertainty. One does not even need to know *what* the action actually is. Much ambiguity within the game stems from elements that generate feelings of randomness: for example, the roll of dice as to whether one defeats the monster, the draw of a card revealing what encounters one might have. The multitude of rules creates a feeling of randomness within the game.

Phases III and IV demonstrate the importance of encounters within *Arkham Horror* not only by revealing uncertain (or unstructured) elements within the game, but also by continuing the storylines. *Arkham Horror* has twenty-seven different locations, split three each among the nine streets that line the town (Figure 1.3). At each location, a player draws an Encounter Card that reveals a particular narrative, motive, or event that can alter the progression of the game. As Kevin Wilson describes, "by carefully crafting these encounters for each location, it is possible to give each place a certain feel, with recurring characters and themes."[45] For example, while in the Rivertown street section of Arkham, a player might find herself in the Graveyard (not truly the wisest place to hide

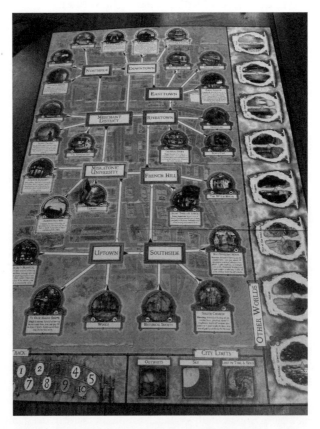

Figure 1.3 The town of Arkham, Game board from *Arkham Horror: The Board Game* © 2005 Fantasy Flight Publishing, Inc. Photo by the author.

from Lovecraftian monsters, to be sure). During Phase III, she may draw one of seven cards geared toward Rivertown, each with a different event. Wilson writes mini-narratives into the Encounter Cards drawn at each location. For example, one card reveals that at the Graveyard, "You find a man painting a picture of one of the horrible gargoyles lining the walls of the graveyard. Seeing you, he introduces himself as **Richard Upton Pickman**, a painter visiting from Boston." That player then has a choice (another if/then algorithm): "If you spend monster trophies [monsters that you have defeated] that have a total of 5 toughness, [then] Pickman takes a liking to you. Take his Ally card [he becomes an ally of yours]. If it is not available, [then] he teaches you an incantation instead. Draw 1 spell." One must have an immense amount of information in order to determine the effect of this card, and any future events will depend on that uncertainty throughout the game. Another card for the Graveyard reads: "Entering a stone crypt, you are surprised to find a beautiful fresco and some inspirational words upon the wall. There is an almost magical peace within the chamber" and you gain two sanity points for entering. Another card reads "A monster appears!" and you must then evade or fight. The point here is not that the Graveyard or any other location allows you to participate in the game in these various ways, but rather that building these types of different mini-narratives into the game allows for more unstructure to enter the game. Understanding the "narrative" of any one location requires a nonlinear reading of the cards, a nonlinear play of the game. Regarding one location in the game where a character named Harney Jones might or might not help out the player, Wilson reveals that "Due to the random nature of the location decks, it's possible for [Harney] … to die immediately the first time a player enters that location. However, with repeated plays, the players learn and remember the story as [Wilson] intended it."[46] Only with repeated play *and* engaged memory can the player understand this embedded narrative. The story told within each of these locations allows the *play* to happen while the *plot* engages in a nonlinear structure. Lovecraft's themes of timeless uncertainty and expansion here find root in the nonlinear expansion of a micronarrative within the larger game structure.[47] Drawing cards at random increases the unstructure of the game play.

As Costikyan reminds us, stories are linear while games are nonlinear.[48] *Arkham Horror*, though, reveals not only that linearity is *not* the key to understanding Lovecraft's universe but also that the whole idea of linearity as a structure is antithetical to the underlying story. The encounters may reveal part of a story or may reveal no story at all. But because that game is structured so as to allow nonlinear narrative expansion, the game reveals unstructure. We play through the many if/then algorithms of the game, only to find in the end that our decisions had no effect: three bad cards in a row or two poor dice rolls can change the flow of a game despite the player's best efforts.

"The inability of the human mind…"

As Costikyan argues, "if we want to get closer to games that also produce compelling stories, we're going to have to experiment with different approaches." Some examples include embedded narratives (like the Encounter Cards) and "imposing a defined narrative arc on the game, but allowing for a high degree of player freedom between those fixed points." But more importantly, we need to see a hybridization of form and content, something that paratextual board games bring with them inherently through their connection to cult narratives. Cult narratives already have a built-in structure—the storyworld exists and the game must be made to fit within its boundaries, however loose they may be. At the same time, a game must also demonstrate its own fluency with uncertainty:

> In other words, there's a direct, immediate conflict between the demands of the story and the demands of a game. Divergence from a story's path is likely to make for a less satisfying story; restricting a player's freedom of action is likely to make for a less satisfying game.[49]

The fact that the game *Arkham Horror* explicates so many rules might be the ultimate irony of the game: according to Barton St. Armand, Lovecraft's visions of an unknowable universe rest on the unstable world of unreal dreams, "outside of space, outside of time."[50] Rules, making the game *a game*, must necessarily exist within a specific time and a specific place. To ludify Lovecraft requires not just rewriting the underlying mythos, but undermining it as well. As Price argues, the Cthulhu mythos is itself largely amorphous: "it is not that *all* of [the stories] *did* happen, but that *any* of them *might* have."[51] The mythos is not about creating coherence but about nullifying the importance of coherence altogether. *Arkham Horror* thus reveals what may be the ultimate Lovecraftian element of the game: by using structure to create unstructure, it undoes the most Lovecraftian of elements to make the game even more Lovecraftian. In a chapter about the role-playing game *Call of Cthulhu*, Kenneth Hite discusses how the Cthulhu mythos serves as a background for a series of games with a "high degree of standardization." Indeed, because all the *Call of Cthulhu* role-play games and expansions feature the same type of play—"a dramatically constricted series of horrific discoveries in a mystery story plot"—the game itself is knowable and consistently structured. Although Hite concedes that many Lovecraft stories do not fit into this mold, he does argue that each follows a certain set of rules that determine the ending—good or bad, sane or mad. These rules, the "anti-mythology," roughly coincide with the "thematic and mythic" elements residing in his stories.[52]

For Price:

> There is no denying that Lovecraft was fashioning a common background for his narrative universe, but equally one cannot deny it is rife with contradictions, there is a limit to which one can read any one story as a chapter of some other. When we try to harmonize all the details, we are reading the story against the grain: we are taking what was intended to be background and yanking it into the foreground.[53]

Attempting to concretize the unstructure of the Lovecraftian universe(s) through a game becomes a way of hybridizing rules and story, and is something that paratextual board games are uniquely positioned for. Such reliance on hybridization and concretization mirrors the Manovichian sense of automation and variability within algorithmic culture. New media rely on rules to govern their behavior, but from those rules flow multiple and various ways of interacting with technology, media, and content. Paratextual board games reveal such interactions within analog media as well, not as separate paratextual connections, but rather as integral elements of the paratextual media environment in total.[54] Players of *Arkham Horror* enter the Lovecraftian universe during the game play, not because of the specific connections to Lovecraft's stories but because of the underlying algorithmic *unstructure* that governs the (unknowable) universe.

2

The Lord of the Rings as Convergent Game Play

All we have to decide is what to do with the time that is given to us.

Gandalf, *The Fellowship of the Ring*

Frodo Baggins was trapped. His friends Merry, Pippin, and Sam had already trudged toward the Doors of Durin, eager to meet up with Gandalf, Legolas, and Aragorn. But poor Frodo was stuck. In front of him, Buckleberry Ferry heralded escape and, possibly, a chance to rejoin his friends. But he could not cross the Brandywine River without the Ferry card. On his previous turn, Frodo had drawn that card, but he had failed to roll the requisite wisdom of twelve or greater to keep the card (despite his already impressive wisdom score of four). His friends, perhaps sensing the uncertainty of the move, had managed to avoid the Ferry via Sarn Ford and Tharbad. Unfortunately, they too were stuck—although they had the Password card ("Speak, Friend, and Enter") to the Doors of Durin, no one had yet drawn the Doors of Durin card, which was required in conjunction with the password to open the door.

Across the table, a different Frodo, Sam, Merry, and Pippin, as well as their fellow Hobbit Fatty Bolger were working their way toward the Mines of Moria. Fatty drew an event token and everyone huddled around the board. What horrible future awaited the Hobbits?—"Orcs Attack: Group discards five 'fighting' symbols; otherwise, Sauron approaches ever closer to corrupting the team." Quickly counting up their cards, the group discovers they have just enough fighting symbols, but one member of the gang refuses to participate—it would exhaust Pippin's supply of cards. Cooperation turns to distrust as the Fellowship starts to dissolve. With no other options, Sauron advances: now, he is just one space away from Merry and that much closer to grabbing the Ring for himself and ending the game....

Although vastly different in scope, mechanics, and game play, the two games described above—*The Lord of the Rings: The Complete Trilogy Adventure Board Game* (*The Complete Trilogy*) and Reiner Knizia's *The Lord of the Rings*

(*LOTR*)—use similar strategies to represent the paratextual connections to the Peter Jackson-directed film series and the original J. R. R. Tolkien novels, respectively. In both games, cooperation is used as a play mechanic to advance the narrative. This cooperative mechanic lies in contrast to both a more traditional competitive style of game play and a more collaborative style of multiplayer game play in video games and MMORPGs.[1] For these two *Lord of the Rings* games, cooperation becomes a way of advancing through an already-determined narrative structure.

LOTR is based on the Tolkien book series, and has won numerous awards, including the Spiel des Jahres special award for *best use of literature in a game* and the *Games Magazine* Games 100 honor.[2] Such awards may help explain the popularity of *LOTR,* for as of 2007, Knizia's game had sold over a million copies.[3] Game awards like these often help spur sales, especially of paratextual games: "winning titles are almost guaranteed to see sales rise by 200,000 or 250,000."[4] As described by José P. Zagal, Jochen Rick, and Idris Hsi, *LOTR* is "extraordinary" and "the most popular collaborative board game ever."[5] Designer Reiner Knizia described the game as not so much a direct adaptation of the novels, but rather as a text that stayed "within the spirit of the book so that the players would experience something similar to the readers of the book."[6] In contrast, *The Complete Trilogy* is based on the film series directed by Peter Jackson. It has won no awards, and no scholarly work has been written on its game mechanics, rules, play, or intertextual relationship with the original text. On boardgamegeek, *The Complete Trilogy* has an abysmal rating of 3.32 out of 10 (with 19 votes counted); in contrast, *LOTR* ranks on boardgamegeek as one of the top 500 board games of all time, with almost 10,000 people voting. *The Complete Trilogy* is, despite its low rating, still reasonably popular, having sold over 120,000 units.[7] In the pantheon of board game literature, *LOTR* is a classic, while *The Complete Trilogy* seems destined to be forgotten, a game echoing Parlett's assessment of licensed board games as "essentially trivial."[8] A critical comparison between the two games, however, reveals useful nuances in understanding paratextuality and play.

Whereas in the first chapter of *Game Play* I focused on game *rules,* in this chapter I turn my attention to game *play.* For Salen and Zimmerman, the concept of play foregrounds "the player's participation with the game and with other players."[9] Different games create play in different ways, and the definition of *play* is so inherently ambiguous that it defies normative application: despite the fact (or perhaps, because of it) that we "all play occasionally, and we all know what playing feels like," we have little common definition of the term.[10] But we deploy the term in our everyday lives as if we all agree on its definition—we know it when we see it. Salen and Zimmerman define play as "free movement within a more rigid structure,"[11] and this definition is nicely broad enough to apply to playing games, watching cult media, experiencing paratextuality, and using digital technology.[12] That is to say, play is what happens when there are structures in place, but we have the flexibility to push against those structures. All play, as Johan Huizinga noted, "means something."[13] In this chapter, I argue that the play in paratextual board games means players can both inhabit a cult world and cocreate narratives within that world.

Both *Lord of the Rings* games reflect paratextuality differently, begging the question of what is "play" in a game that unveils a narrative with already-set parameters. Both *Lord of the Rings* games attempt to place players within the narrative structure of the original texts, but by integrating the mediating influence of cooperation, the games develop a more subtle paratextual mechanic. By harnessing gaps within the cult narrative texts, both games present opportunities for players to become involved with the story. Indeed, because both games demand knowledge of the original texts, there is a complex interaction built into these games' reliance on "texts and activities [that] may refer to the same fictional 'world' despite presenting themselves as different media."[14] Each game is neither pure extension nor pure adaptation; rather, each plays in and with the cult world it begets.

In both games, players must develop strategies, share resources, and enable social connectivity in order to vanquish the enemy. However, the differing manifestations of that enemy in both games reflect different concerns of the cinematic versus the literate versions of the *Lord of the Rings* tale. In the game based on the film, one player controls Sauron while the others control members of the Fellowship, creating an explicit hierarchy among the game players and forcing competition to develop in spite of the cooperative mechanic. In addition, the victory condition of *The Complete Trilogy* ultimately forces one player to be the winner. Even if everyone collaborates throughout the game, only one person emerges victorious. In Knizia's *LOTR*, the game only becomes winnable if *everyone* cooperates. Sauron is instead controlled by the game rules and the team wins or loses together.

This cooperative mechanic reflects the third principle of paratextual board games:

Principle 3: Paratextual board games create meaning from the tension between an authorial presence and audience play; this meaning is created between player, designer, and original text.

The first part of this chapter explores the concept of media convergence as a metaphor for understanding the different ways players can interact in each game. Convergence, the spread of media content between both producers and audiences, has been defined by Henry Jenkins as "both a top-down corporate-driven process and a bottom-up consumer-driven process."[15] Both a technological construct and a cultural mindset, convergence is a way of thinking anew about how producers and audiences enable content flow. Both *Lord of the Rings* board games deepen and extend our understanding of cross-media convergence by relying on the complex interaction between the original text's top-down "authority" and the game's bottom-up "play." All paratextual board games exist in a similar convergence between these two elements—reliance on an original text but deviation for gameplay mechanics—and here this convergence is actualized through the play with *The Lord of the Rings*. The notion of convergence reflects the fourth principle of paratextual board games:

Principle 4: Paratextual board games use play *as a specific mechanism by which players inhabit and make media their own.*

The second part of this chapter examines how both Knizia's *LOTR* and *The Complete Trilogy* serve as key exemplars of cooperative approaches to paratextual game play. I discuss the roles of cooperation and play within board games as they relate specifically to convergence culture, a manifestation of the contemporary new media environment.

Playing games/Playing media

If rules, as I described in the previous chapter, can best be understood as formal algorithms that guide the structure of a game, play can best be understood as the *experience of the game itself.* We can only understand game play through multiple contexts of actual experiences—a "social experience, or a narrative experience, or an experience of pleasure"—that envelop the game players.[16] Like the *Battlestar Galactica* games I discuss in Chapter 4, part of the fun of the game play lies in interacting with the other players. Play is always experiential and always lived. Board games generate play in the moment, but the instant the game pieces are put back in their box, the play of the game disappears.

Board games create a unique situation where the term "play" describes both the action that happens in the game and an "engagement with any fixed structure, something that both games and … stories invite."[17] We both *play* a game and play *with* a game. Paratextual board games like *LOTR* and *The Complete Trilogy* reflect this two-fold structure: there is the space of the game itself (the board, the table, the pieces) and the space of the cult narrative world, the space of Middle-earth. To watch *Lord of the Rings* is to be a part of a bounded cult franchise, but to play *Lord of the Rings* is to push against those boundaries, to become both a reaction to and a reification of the rules and restrictions, structures and shapes, of the cult world. Play is, at once, serious business and fanciful imagination.

Playing a paratextual board game thus requires existing within an already-extant space as well as within an imaginative space of the player's own creation: "play enables the exploration of that tissue boundary between fantasy and reality, between the real and the imagined."[18] The interaction between physical and virtual "playspaces" has led researchers Shanly Dixon and Sandra Weber to theorize a connective tissue between the act of imaginative play and the structured process of playing.[19] Players of the *Lord of the Rings* games play in the world of Middle-earth by codifying the boundaries of Middle-earth. In *LOTR*, all five Hobbits work together to take the Ring of Power from its hiding place in the Shire to Mordor and Mount Doom, where they must throw it into the fire and keep Sauron from using its power to take over the world. In *The Complete Trilogy*, the Hobbits are joined by the other members of *The* Fellowship of the Ring as well to complete this task, although in this game Sauron sends enemies after the group to defeat them in combat (there is no combat in *LOTR*, although dice rolling often simulates the uncertainty of encounters with game characters). Cult media offer this same sense of play, enacting a "philosophy of playfulness" within the media fan.[20] Fans engage in playful behavior, and push against the boundaries of the media text.

To remain open and "playable," however, the paratextual board game must address the closed nature of the narrative, begging the question of how one plays a narrative whose ending one already knows. Paratextual board games demand a flexible narrative structure, for knowing the ending of the game, especially a complex one based on an already-created media narrative, may undermine the freedom a player might have for creating a new ending.[21] In Chapter 5's *Star Trek: Expeditions,* the narrative develops throughout the game in a number of branching paths. In contrast, in Chapter 6's *The Hunger Games: District 12,* there must be a strict adherence to the underlying structure of the film for the game to "fit" within the text's story universe. Unlike a strict adaptation—wherein one might have read the book before seeing the film and is thus expecting, if not a precise matching of elements, at least some kind of fidelity to the narrative—a game invites player cocreation in the unfolding of the narrative. As French critic Roger Caillois has described, games must be a "free and voluntary" activity; that is, one must *want* to play in order to become part of the cult world.[22] In order to want to play, there must be some sort of uncertainty in the game: as Costikyan points out, the uncertainty described by Caillois is contained in the *outcome* of the game—who wins or loses should be uncertain. But Costikyan argues that uncertainty "can be found almost anywhere" in games, not just in the outcome.[23] Uncertainty can be less a focus on what *will* happen than on *how* it will happen. We know that the Hobbits *should* vanquish Sauron. If the game is won, we know that Sauron will be defeated. The uncertainty in the two *Lord of the Rings* games isn't whether or not they actually will, but rather *how* they will do so given specific win conditions. What specific mechanisms take them to Mount Doom? What characters follow them? In a way, playing a paratextual board game is like roleplaying fan fiction; the familiar characters and settings are there, but their relationships to each other and to the plot are variable.

All fictions create alternate worlds, vast structures with variable elements. While often fantastical, these other worlds can be closely related to ours, as Umberto Eco writes in an essay describing the cult world of *Casablanca*: the "completely furnished world" of the film becomes its defining characteristic.[24] This definition of "cult world" has been questioned by Sara Gwenllian-Jones, however, who writes:

> The existence and practices of fan cultures suggests that the opposite is true; films and television series achieve cult status not because they present "completely furnished" worlds but rather because the fracture and excess of their fantastic imaginaries draw the audience's attention to the fact that their diegetic worlds are invariably incompletely furnished.[25]

Fans see their interactions in the cult world as ways of "playing" in an extant universe: the "incomplete" nature of the world allows interaction in a way that augments a fannish connection to the text. Paratextual board games like the *Lord of the Rings* games present both the physical spaces of the narratives and some imaginative gaps that players/fans can complete. Through an examination of the play mechanics of the two *Lord of the Rings* games, a tie between the cult narrative and paratextual game becomes clear, revealing a convergence of author, player, and game as a constituent of paratextual game play.

Convergence, cooperation, and contemporary media

LOTR was one of the first popular cooperative board games designed for an international audience. According to Woods, *LOTR* was "the first time that such a complex European-style design was given wide exposure in the English-speaking mass market," and the fact that it has been re-released with subsequent editions speaks to its continued popularity.[26] The game quite successfully recreates the "sense of overwhelming dread as great and dark forces wheel around the heads of the players."[27] According to Knizia, the elements of cooperation required in the game become obvious not just because of links to the thematic elements of the book, but also because of the structure of the game itself. As Knizia describes, "even the most competitive players would soon realize that the game system threw so many dangers at the players that they would naturally have to support each other." Much like in the original novel, cooperation increases chances of defeating the evil Sauron. This play element is echoed by Zagal, Rick, and Hsi, who analyzed Knizia's game for its focus on collaborative game play. They demonstrate how "what is interesting about *Lord of the Rings* ... is how the tension between the individual rationality and the effect on the group is highlighted"—in other words, how the cooperative elements of the game actually reflect larger concerns within the culture of *The Lord of the Rings* in popular discourse.[28] Further, the cooperation mechanic becomes a prerequisite for the game's "replayable" nature, as playing the game multiple times influences future outcome.

In *LOTR*, a group of Hobbits work together to take the Ring of Power from its hiding place in the Shire to be destroyed in Mount Doom. In order to do this, the Hobbits have to travel through seven different stages, from the most benign (their home, Bag End) to the most severe (Mordor, home of evil Sauron). Along the way various events occur that require the Hobbits to use different skills (fighting, friendship, traveling, and hiding) to overcome great odds. By cooperating, players can combine their skills to great effect. In *The Complete Trilogy*, the Hobbits are joined by other members of the Fellowship of the Ring, including Gimli the Dwarf and Legolas the Elf. The many characters fight enemies across the expanse of Middle-earth, as Frodo carries the Ring to Mount Doom.

Reiner Knizia describes having written and designed *LOTR* as a way of understanding not just the literature of Tolkien, but also the half-century of popular culture surrounding it:

> for the *Lord of the Rings* Board Game I needed to develop a deep understanding of Tolkien's world, the underlying themes, and the motivations of the characters. This was not achievable by merely reading the book itself. I also needed to know what excited the fans, and what was at the center of their discussions.[29]

It is not that all fans of Tolkien's *Lord of the Rings* want cooperation and collaboration in their fandom or in their lives (far from it; fandom is often fraught with tensions and hierarchies), but rather that Tolkien's narrative is deliberately focused on the elements of communication and collaboration between different beings.[30]

While competition seems to be the focus of many games today, cooperative board games have a long and significant cultural history. Other paratextual games I discuss in this book are cooperative—*Arkham Horror* and *Star Trek: Expeditions,* for instance—and some use aspects of both cooperation and competition in the game play—*The Walking Dead: The Board Game* and *Battlestar Galactica,* for example. In a contemporary neoliberal context valuing individual self-interests over communal well-being, the play of contemporary games seems to be focused intensely on hierarchical values of winning and achievement.[31] Brian Sutton-Smith, however, describes how some of the earliest forms of play in human history were social and cooperative, and focused on inclusivity instead of one exclusive victor. This inclusive rhetoric foregrounds the experience of play as both feminist and communal, with an emphasis on the social context of cooperation instead of competition. For instance, sports games often value cooperative play instead of individual achievement (but a neoliberal sports mentality often tends to reward the individual player for the deeds of a group effort). Historically and culturally, cooperative play is common, especially when considering unstructured play like children's games. Indeed, Sutton-Smith points out that:

> empirical support for this [cooperative play], and therefore for the importance of distinguishing the rhetorics of community from those of power, comes from the anthropological record of the great dominance of cooperative forms of play over competitive forms in most earlier tribal societies. In smaller human groupings

where cooperation is essential for survival, it is more likely that cooperative games will be more important than competitive games.

One might well argue that large-scale cultural ideology has had less of a hand in the construction of games over time: after all, cooperative games in one form or another have been popular at different times, in different societies, and with different types of players. However, as Sutton-Smith contends, "escape from cultural rhetoric is well nigh impossible." Structurally, human play is always constructed within and around a particular societal and cultural moment. Any game "requires a gaming society, and any society has norms and hierarchies that interpenetrate the game"; for Sutton-Smith, "players enjoy participating in social play because it makes them a part of the collective social dreams" that undergird contemporary culture.[32] Games reflect the prevailing cultural economy. For my board game group in particular, a gaming society of sorts, the socialization of play is one of the most compelling elements. Whether we considered a game "good" or not, the social interactions we experienced helped make each session memorable (perhaps even more so when the games weren't very good and we all could laugh about it). Whether or not the game has a competitive mechanic, we cooperate throughout, often offering help and advice to players who are new to a particular game, or talking through rules for everyone in a supportive and encouraging environment.

In contrast, for Elias, Garfield, and Gutschera, cooperative interaction in games is "problematic" (and, in fact, they relegate its description to a footnote), arguing that "it is not a feature exclusive to cooperative games, and indeed it is possible in principle for a cooperative game not to have it." Such is the difference between cooperation as a design mechanic and cooperation as a social system. Comparing a cooperative game to a single-player game, where "the player plays more against 'the system' than against an imaginary opponent," Elias, Garfield, and Gutschera seem to deny the effect that interplayer communication can have on the outcomes of the game play.[33] But it is precisely this communication that reflects a contemporary ideological concern of paratextual board games in general, and of the *Lord of the Rings* game in particular: that of convergence culture.

A term for an emerging media ecology in which both consumers and producers become participants in the flow of media information, "convergence culture" serves as a paradigm for participatory media culture.[34] For Henry Jenkins, whose *Convergence Culture* has become a significant work of media studies scholarship, *convergence* describes the "flow of content across multiple media platforms, the cooperation between multiple media industries, and the migratory behavior of media audiences who will go almost anywhere in search of the kinds of entertainment experiences they want."[35] Looking through a convergence lens, content becomes "something that is increasingly shared with those who one used to work for: audiences. The culture of industry therefore can be seen as spilling over on to the creative process of consumption."[36] Paratextual board games reveal aspects of convergence, not just in the way they reflect active consumptive behavior, but also in the implicit interaction between the game and its antecedent media text. There must be a certain level of adherence to an original text and at the same time a deviance from that original text in order to create a unique gaming experience. In fact, this deviance lies at the heart of all paratextuality: as Gray notes, while a paratext is distinct from an original text, it must also be like that text, as well as part of that text.[37] Without these tenuous connections, the paratextual game would not have the same force of textual meaning undergirding it; with too strong a connection, the game would not allow enough freedom within the play mechanics to permit uncertainty to become part of the game experience. There must therefore be a "happy medium," a hypothetical sweet spot between the authorial intent of the original text and the original productivity of the players. Through this tension between these two concepts, the paratextual board game generates its unique play mechanics.

In terms of active consumptive behavior of paratextual board games, both the *Lord of the Rings* games highlight how collaboration reflects convergence ideals. For Knizia's *LOTR*, the convergent activity of audiences arises from the way players are encouraged to generate meaning *alongside* that of both Knizia and Tolkien. As Knizia details, "distilling an epic story into a game" means both incorporating "key parts of a story" and "presenting them in game form."[38] Players must both incorporate narrative elements from the original *Lord of the Rings* books (taken from "top-down" processes of story construction, both Tolkien's and Knizia's) and integrate their own gameplay narratives. The game is split between two boards; on one board, individual Hobbit markers move ever closer to Sauron. This "corruption" board is a representation of the individual Hobbit's mental state, and if overtaken by Sauron, the Hobbit is taken out of the game (Figure 2.1).

The other board is a representation of the events and stories that happen in one of four locations in Middle-earth. On this "conflict" board, the Hobbits are represented as a single group, participating in their fighting, traveling, hiding, and friendship activities (Figure 2.2).

Figure 2.1 The *Lord of the Rings* board with the corruption track. Photo by the author.

In one of our games, for example, my board game group gave the characters on the corruption board personalities perhaps unintended by Knizia, but no less a part of the game mechanics. We would speak in the voices of our characters, identifying when they were nervous, or excited, or brave; Sauron was single-minded and intent on destroying us. The conflict board allowed for more

Figure 2.2 The *Lord of the Rings* Mordor board with conflict tracks. Photo by the author.

cooperative discussion to occur between us all while making decisions as a group about how to progress, whom to save, and whom to leave behind. We became co-constructors of our narrative: this most dramatically manifested when our game literally depended on the results of one dice roll, which sadly, we lost.

The Complete Trilogy also functions as an example of convergence culture, especially as it relates to audience empowerment. Although the aesthetics of the game follow Peter Jackson's filmic version of the story, the actual game play differs significantly. In *The Complete Trilogy*, the game board is a giant map of Middle-earth. The game board itself is constructed from twelve interlocking pieces, which do not allow structured breaks as in Knizia's version (see Figure 2.3 for one of those pieces). While it is an enjoyable experience to join the pieces together—and the fact they "fit" with the game version of Jackson's *The Hobbit* series of films as well makes them particularly useful as paratextual tools—they ultimately do not shift or move and simulate a traditional immobile game board. The fluidity of the game is uninterrupted by breaks in the action, as characters might be constantly moving around the static board.

In one game we created a storyline wherein the Nazgûl inhabited the Shire, near Hobbiton, and destroyed all the escaping Hobbits. Aragon and Boromir were constantly getting into scrapes, and Frodo was antisocial and only wanted to mope. As Gray describes, citing Ellen Seiter, toys can become "generative of their *own* meanings," and as "'mass-media goods, these kind of toys actually facilitate group, co-operative play, by encouraging children to make up stories with shared codes and narratives.'"[40] The stories that our group made up during our *The Complete Trilogy* game play diverged greatly from those of Jackson's

Figure 2.3 A piece of Middle-earth. Photo by the author.[39]

films, but nevertheless were no less meaningful to our group; we became co-constructors of convergence meaning within the game.

Convergence, as Graham Meikle and Sherman Young define, relies on the underlying "tensions … between *contestation and continuity.*" They define contestation as the way in which communication practices can alter traditional meanings, while conversely, continuity highlights the maintenance of cultural rituals. Convergence happens when "new actors and old industries, contending modes of distribution and visibility, [and] complex assemblages of digital media" cohere.[41] Paratextual board games must retain some semblance of the original text in order to be identified with it. The sense of betrayal in *Battlestar Galactica: The Board Game* and the cutthroat diplomacy of *Game of Thrones: The Card Game* mirror similar themes from their respective texts. For *LOTR*, Knizia attempted to create continuity with the original books; he writes that "Tolkien's Hobbits were rarely in control of their situation. To reflect this, I introduced a general tile deck with a series of events that affected the players directly." At the same time, he had to reflect a contestation with the original in order to make the game *a game* and not just a turn-based story: "Apart from identifying the most interesting features and the most intuitive rules, an important focus of the continual playing and replaying was to balance the game."[42] Similarly, *The Complete Trilogy* includes continuity with the film series by using character photos from the film as icons for the playing pieces, through the various cards with images and text from the films, and through the overall narrative of the game, as players navigate through the different locations just as the characters do in the films. But it also demonstrates contestation through the different order in which events can occur, and through the fact that characters can act completely out of character compared to their cinematic counterparts. Indeed, although the game purports to be *The Complete Trilogy,* the characters that one can play as are solely from the first film; notably absent are any of the female characters (Galadriel and Arwin would be obvious characters from the first film, but Éowyn plays a major role in the third film, killing the Witch-King of Angmar, Lord of the Nazgûl). Also absent is Faramir, a major character from the second film; and even though Boromir dies in the first film, he remains a playable character throughout the game.

Convergence culture may be deemed a product of the Internet age, and indeed, "the advent of the Internet and online fandom has 'out-moded' the previous nature" of cultural capital related to production practices.[43] For Elana Shefrin, the Internet now "supplies a strong link" between artistic practice, power relations, and class difference. But convergence goes beyond technology and reflects a larger cultural paradigm shift. Board games by their very nature represent a convergence of player-generated meaning and authorial meaning. Paratextual board games take this convergence even further, uniting player, author, and cult texts as one. Perhaps the rise in the popularity of complex paratextual board games lies in the fact that they represent, at least in part, aspects of the convergence culture that we see around us.

Playing *LOTR* and *The Complete Trilogy*

This paratextual convergence manifests in two different ways within the games based on the *Lord of the Rings* franchise elements. First, we see this convergence evident in the feeling of community generated by both games. In Knizia's *LOTR*, the Hobbits can move individually on the corruption board, but they work together on the conflict board. While it is possible for a Hobbit to become "corrupted" and have to leave the game, rarely do the Hobbits work on their own. Conversely, in the cinematic *The Complete Trilogy*, the players all take turns, including the Hobbits, and the characters can find their own routes through the game board to defeat Sauron. While this is not like the film, the mechanic does offer players the freedom to either follow the film's narrative or not follow the film's narrative. Second, we see this convergence evident in the different styles of gameplay progression within each of the games. Knizia's *LOTR* game features definitive stages: there are four main conflict boards (Moria, Helm's Deep, Shelob's Lair, and Mordor), each of which references particular adventures in the original book series. The stages are represented in the instructions as well, which offer short synopses of these important narrative events. In contrast, *The Complete Trilogy* game play is broken into different turns between Sauron and the different characters. Both these breaks contradict the feelings of community that undergird both texts.

Community

Perhaps because of its popularity, Tolkien's original *Lord of the Rings* trilogy (1954–55, actually a sextet of books, two of which are contained in each of three volumes) has been read as an allegory from virtually every conceivable angle, with discussions of religion and racism coupled with connections to the Second World War (as well as the First World War) peppering many of them.[44]

Although Tolkien himself always denied an allegorical reading of his series, arguing "it is neither allegorical nor topical," the series has become both popular and influential in the world of popular culture.[45] In concert with the book series, Peter Jackson's award-winning trilogy of *Lord of the Rings* films (2001–03) has also had a profound effect on both popular culture and film. In the decade since Jackson's *The Return of the King* won the Academy Award for best film, the series has been the focus of countless readings as well, looking at the films not just as a series of adaptations but also as a site of cultural and social commentary.[46] In their relation to the board games that share their names, both the book series and the film series reflect similar diegetic concerns that both of the games attempt to manifest, albeit in different ways.

Perhaps the most overt diegetic characteristic of both the book and film series lies in their representation of the "fellowship" of the characters—one theme that is present within both texts is the idea of collaboration between disparate groups of people. In her analysis of the *Lord of the Rings* books, Jane Chance argues that the series depicts "the value of community."[47] The uneasy alliance of Hobbits, Dwarves, Men, Wizards, and Elves becomes a compassionate friendship among the allies as they battle the mighty Sauron and his forces of demonic evil, the unnatural Orcs, Uruk-Hai, Wargs, and Ringwraiths. By the same token, the evil forces themselves form a type of alliance—perhaps not as strongly bonded as our heroes, but certainly the antagonists collaborate in their attempt to destroy the Fellowship of the Ring in both texts.

Both *LOTR* and *The Complete Trilogy* aim to replicate this sense of community and collaboration. This replication is made most obvious in the text written on the box for *The Complete Trilogy* game, which details how one player plays as Sauron and the others "are The Fellowship" who must defeat him. *LOTR* does not advertise this collaboration on the box as obviously as the cinematic game, but on the first page of the instruction booklet, the gameplay mechanic is made quite clear: "It is the collective aim of the players to destroy the Ring ... without cooperation, there can be no success. There is no individual winner—the group scores points as a whole." Both games, therefore, take pains to connect the particular gameplay mechanic of cooperation to the underlying thematics of the books and films upon which they are based.

Zagal, Rick, and Hsi use Knizia's *LOTR* board game as an example of how cooperation can function within a board game environment. Their discussion focuses on the mechanics of cooperation and how those mechanics might apply to video game development. While an interesting and useful assertion in terms of digital play and video games, their assessment largely ignores the underlying paratextual connections between the game and the book series upon which it is based. At times, however, their discussion does hint at such relationships. For instance, in a narrative description of their own game play, they note how:

> the game was won; every player rejoiced. Pippin sacrificed his life to save Middle-earth. If such a moment of self-sacrifice is interesting as a story, it is even more engaging when you are the one to make the decision (in the game).[48]

By relating the ending of the game to the ending of a story, Zagal, Rick, and Hsi explicitly reveal the paratextual connection to the underlying novel, and also implicitly articulate the importance of this connection: that it reveals one of the reasons why cooperation may work so well for this game but fail in others.

Furthermore, for Zagal, Rick, and Hsi, a particular pitfall of collaborative games is allowing one player the ability to make all the decisions for the team. This can become "boring" as one player can dominate and not allow other players to interact, participate, or even influence the outcome of the game. *LOTR*, they argue, undercuts this pitfall by giving the characters:

> different roles and abilities so that optimal game-play depends on good coordination and decision making on the part of the players. *Lord of the Rings* gives different abilities to each of the hobbits so that each hobbit has a useful role to play at various points in the game.[49]

While "making a better gameplay experience" is certainly one *result* of this emphasis on differing abilities, the game's antecedent of Tolkien's books may reveal its impetus. This connection is something designer Knizia reveals as well: he writes that "more important [than the detail of the world] was the feeling of the world. The true focus of the book was not the fighting, but more personal themes—the development of each character's sense of self as they attempt to overcome adversity."[50] Indeed, although it is not laid out as succinctly in the books as done by Knizia in the game, all the main Hobbit characters *do* have different attributes that portend their eventual character arcs. Samwise Gamgee in the game has the attribute of being able to withstand Sauron's influence more readily than the other Hobbits: he is less vulnerable to corruption. In the books, it is Sam's stalwart, dogged determination that allows Frodo to throw the Ring into Mount Doom—without Sam's ability to withstand the influence of the Ring, Frodo would not have been able to succeed. In the game, Frodo is particularly good at using resource cards—he can convert any brown resource card into a "wild" card, which can be played at any time. There is an analogue for this in the books as well, as Frodo's ability to make use of resources like his sword Sting, the Mithril vest, and the light of Eärendil reveals a similar resourcefulness. And it is not just the surface abilities that match the original: each ability encourages players to make decisions that mirror those of the narrative too—Sam can protect Frodo from Sauron's corruption because he is more doggedly resistant.

Other characteristics, however, are less specifically relevant to the original book: Merry needs only two of three types of "life tokens" to complete a round, while all the other Hobbits require three each. The life tokens—"evidence that [the Hobbit's] heart is in the right place (Heart Life token), that darkness is not overtaking him (Sun Life token), and that he is resisting the corrupting influence of the Ring (Ring Life token)"—are more specific to the game world than they are to the original world of the novels, in which Merry has no special talents equivalent to them.[51]

This tension between the direct tie of different characteristics for each character within the game and each character's unique gameplay mechanic reveals themes from the book; and Zagal, Rick, and Hsi describe how Knizia used the progression of the villain, Sauron, to demonstrate how competitiveness in the Hobbits leads to ruin. The Hobbits are more than the sum of their parts, and "notably, Sauron achieves his best result (5 steps) when a Hobbit is corrupted to behave in a selfish, competitive manner."[52] At the same time, however, the fact that players take turns within the game but the characters of the Hobbits "play" in a pack contradicts the trajectory of the novels. That the game deviates from the novels is a design choice, and may not be as interesting as the fact that this deviation actually augments the convergence of book and game. For instance, the corruption board and the conflict board each reflect aspects of the narratives. Each Hobbit can move independently on the corruption board, but they all move as one unified group on the conflict board. This actually differs from the narrative of the books, in which the Hobbits are off doing their own things at different times. Merry and Pippin are absent from the scenes with Shelob the spider, for instance, although in Knizia's *LOTR* game they (as well as Fatty, a character who appears only briefly at the start and end of the books) may be part of the unit that tries to defeat the giant arachnid. But in terms of the convergence of the top-down corporate authority of Tolkien's *Lord of the Rings* books and the bottom-up consumer gameplay mechanics of the paratextual board game, the inclusion of these characters into a new scene can serve to augment and deepen the player investment in the narrative. If Merry and Pippin had to leave the game at Shelob's lair, simply because they were not part of the original novel, the game would be far less fun for those players (and make less sense in the game play overall).

The cooperation mechanic in *The Complete Trilogy* differs from the one in *LOTR*. Indeed, while the majority of the players attempt to cooperate in the game—a mechanic made obvious through the players' ability to share goods between characters if they are on the same space—the fact that one player *must* play as Sauron and control his dark forces makes the game more competitive. As the player playing Sauron also has at his or her disposal the ability to control hordes of different enemies spread throughout the board, the competitiveness of the game is further emphasized as the end of almost every turn results in a battle between characters. At the same time, moments from the game, especially those related to the movements of the non-Sauron characters, deepen a feeling of fellowship as the play commences. On each move, players have the opportunity to move not only their own character's playing piece, but also a character that is unclaimed by another player. In other words, on my turn, I could move both Frodo (who was the character I was playing) and Legolas, Gimli, Boromir, Faramir, Gandalf, or any of the other characters that were not being played by my friends.

This multicharacter turn allows the play to commence in a cooperative fashion: as a group we could decide to move Legolas (whom no one was officially playing) closer to particular enemies; Legolas's unique power is that he can attack enemies up to four spaces away from him. Collectively, those of us on the Fellowship side were able to make use of this particular skill on each turn, defeating Sauron's forces as each player moved.

The result of this multiple movement, however, is that characters end up scattered across the board in ways that deviate so completely from the trajectory of the films' narratives, they seem to follow a completely new story, one cocreated by the players themselves.[53] While Legolas may be in the Dead Marshes killing Orcs (a place he never approached in the film), Gimli the dwarf may spend many of his turns unused in Mirkwood, a location the character would avoid. Even Boromir can survive for the entirety of the game! Such deviance from the original film again coheres the players with the game. Like the film, the game offers characters a chance to explore Middle-earth in different paths. It is entirely possible, then, for players that play *The Complete Trilogy* to attempt to replicate the cinematic characters' journeys exactly. It is possible to emulate Frodo, Sam, and Gollum's journey to Mount Doom; Aragorn, Legolas, and Gimli's flight to track the Uruk-hai as they hope to rescue Merry and Pippin from the evil Orcs;

and Gandalf's transformation from the Grey Wizard to the mighty White. At the same time, however, it is also possible to play the game completely differently from what the original film trilogy offers: players can chart their own paths and journeys through the multi-stage game board, using the game play to write their own stories of the cult world. Such play between the top-down authority of the cinematic narrative and the bottom-up freedom to enact consumer-created narratives drives the convergence within these two games.

Gameplay progression

One element of the *Lord of the Rings* books and films that is difficult, if not impossible, to replicate within the confines of a board game is the expansive world and long-form narrative enacted by each original text. Tolkien's trilogy is, collectively, over a thousand pages long, and that is not including *The Hobbit*, *The Silmarillion*, or any of the other works that take place in the lands of Middle-earth. The Peter Jackson film series comprises three films which, when originally released, formed a block over nine hours long, and when re-released on special edition Blu-Ray, formed an extended version over 12 hours long. Pat Harrigan and Noah Wardrip-Fruin describe the *Lord of the Rings* narrative as "vastly deep" with emphasis placed on the world's extent, character continuity, and multicharacter interaction.[54] Both versions feature a similar "overarching shape and sense of the story," but the dialogues, details, and even transitions between scenes are different, as, according to Jim Smith and J. Clive Matthews, "the demands of the [cinematic] medium have occasioned every departure" from the original book.[55] When designing a game that will last for less than a quarter of that time, game designers must navigate the key plot elements necessary to keep the narrative on trajectory with character simplification in order to expedite the story.

In each of the *Lord of the Rings* paratextual board games, the tension between the games' structure and the original text's structure reveals a dissonance within the progression of the narrative. Ludic narrative is a complicated issue, just as adaptation of a narrative from one medium to another is.[56] This complication forces Britta Stöckmann and Jens Jahnke to ask:

> How can a fixed story, which develops in a linear, unrepeatable way from a certain beginning to a certain ending, be transferred into a medium which, by definition, has to be not only repeatable, but at the same time changeable and open to decision-making, so as to offer a new experience every time the game is played?

Such a narrative adaptation is possible, although "turning a board game into a novel means transferring a story from a changeable medium into a fixed one and vice versa, a board game representing a novel has to assimilate the essence of the book's story."[57] Assimilation requires a play with structure.

In Knizia's *LOTR* game, specific and definitive stages in the game play match similarly structured stages within the narrative trajectory of the novels. There are seven separate stages in the game, each one depicted as a ringed icon on the corruption board. At three of these locations, good things happen to the Hobbits: at Bag End, they get cards to help them on their quest; at Rivendell (home of the Elves), the Hobbits receive more cards; and at Lothlórian (home of Galadriel, mightiest Elf in Middle-earth), the Hobbits earn more cards and have the option of recovering from Sauron's corrupting influence. These three locations match similar locations in the books, as the Hobbits make their way through Middle-earth toward Mordor to destroy the Ring.

However, there are four stages in the game where bad things happen to the Hobbits, and these are represented by the four separate conflict boards, each of which corresponds to a particular series of events in the books: The Mines of Moria, Helm's Deep, Shelob's Lair, and Mordor. At each stage, the Hobbits must complete tracks like the Battle of Balrog in the Mines of Moria and the Fight Against Shelob in Shelob's Lair. They can also claim friends and help through other tracks, like the Friendship track on each conflict board. The point here is not just that the game matches scenes and chapters from the books, but also that after each of these seven stages, there is a deliberate break in the action. Each conflict stage is difficult to complete and the Hobbits do not all necessarily emerge out of it unscathed. Often, one or more of the Hobbits will have become slightly more corrupted and closer to dying, and many times making it through a stage will require sacrificing cards or will depend simply on the roll of a die.

Making it through a stage in the *LOTR* game, therefore, becomes a stressful event. This kind of "eustress," or positive stress event, mirrors the feelings of excitement generated by reading stimulating chapters of the book, and the emotional reaction of readers at a particularly harrowing experience in a book may find a counterpart in the game's play.[58] Only by delineating the different stages so concretely—literally switching game boards to indicate a shift in the story, in the same way that one might close one book and open another—does the game realize such a break, matching in tone the emotional highs of the novel.

In contrast, there are fewer gameplay breaks within *The Complete Trilogy*, and it is harder to anticipate the structure of the game: is one complete turn a stage? Is it when the Sauron player moves? Sauron's turn would seem to indicate a shift in the game play, but because he can attack any character in the game, one could theoretically have a turn every time Sauron moved at the expense of others' turns. Such indeterminacy of breaks undermines the structuring of the narrative in the *Lord of the Rings* film, which as Smith and Matthews assert, is very closely aligned with that of the book series.[59]

In the static yet mobile board and the indeterminacy of the stage given Sauron's movements, *The Complete Trilogy* game denies the connection to the film that it is trying to generate. That is, the game may aesthetically match characters and situations from the films through the character cards and tokens, but given the actual game play, the lack of structure forces players to imagine the game in a different type of world: one determined by a different set of rules. This is playing with the story. As Stöckmann and Jahnke note, this doesn't have to be the case: "though game and literature are different media diverging in certain respects, they perfectly complement one another, when it comes to telling a story.[60] But with *The Complete Trilogy*, the denial of specific narrative moments from the film force a different reading out of the game's story, one created not just by authorial figures, but by the convergence of players as well.

"What to do with the time that is given to us..."

As convergence manifests in multiple ways in the contemporary media environment, it is important to recognize how paratextual board games constantly negotiate the tension between remaining tethered to an original text while branching out for original gameplay elements. This convergence allows for unique methods of interacting with classic texts. Paratextual games can offer a playful introduction to a media text, but they can also allow players to revisit and reimagine that media text. For example, in the next chapter I examine two games based on *The Walking Dead*, each of which encourages players to encounter the narratives afresh.

Convergence culture, while a key shift in contemporary media studies, is not without its criticism. One of the major issues with the utopian ideals of a convergence culture lies in the fact that human beings rarely exist in perfect harmony with each other or within the culture they reside. Although my game group tended to get along during the games, tensions would occasionally arise, especially when discussing the finer points of some of the more arcane rules of these complex paratextual games. As Gary Alan Fine writes in *Shared Fantasy*, his discussion of role-playing games as social worlds, the social structures inherent within game systems reveal that:

> not only does a social structure exist that incorporates players' natural interactions with each other, but a social structure also exists in the [game] world, as characters form adventure parties, and these parties must negotiate a social order.[61]

In terms of *LOTR* and *The Complete Trilogy*, although the players may not have the type of freedom Fine describes in relation to RPGs to develop character attributes (thus becoming interpolated into their characters' social and ideological situation), there is still a sense of character hierarchy.[62] This hierarchy may stem from the book series (the player using the Fatty Bolger piece in our group was ridiculed because the character is relatively minor in the books compared with the other Hobbits, he doesn't actually go on the quests, and his name is Fatty) or from the different attributes each character has in the game (in *The Complete Trilogy*, the Merry character is substantially more powerful than the Pippin character, even though the two Hobbits are actually quite similar in the film series; thus, playing Pippin may come with inherent value and hierarchy judgments). It could also stem from the different levels of Tolkien knowledge each of the players in my group brought to the table. But at the same time, as Jane Chance writes, each character necessarily has different characteristics within the book series as well, so perhaps the convergence here is a way of enveloping different elements of the book with the game.[63]

A common criticism of licensed board games regards the way that individual media corporations make use of convergence for financial reasons, seemingly taking advantage of fan audiences. Shefrin's analysis of the participatory fandom surrounding Jackson's *Lord of the Rings* franchise, and its contrast with George Lucas's *Star Wars* franchise, reflects a significant shift in the way fan cultures are alternately courted and placated by studios:

> *Lord of the Rings* fans have been actively courted by Jackson and New Line Cinema throughout all aspects of authoring, casting, filming, and marketing the trilogy. *Star Wars* fans, however, have been doubly offended by the actions of Lucas and Lucasfilm: on the one hand, their desires to be "consumer affiliates" in the cinematic production process have been generally ignored; on the other hand, their roles as "illegal pirates" of corporately-owned intellectual property have been overtly emphasized.[64]

Convergence, as much as it demonstrates the continued and growing power of audiences to construct their own meaning out of media texts, also reminds us that conglomerated media corporations still hold much power in the way they oversee franchises.

For *The Lord of the Rings*, the Tolkien estate and New Line Cinema seem to have had little hand in the production of these paratextual board games. In a discussion at Capricon 2014, a science fiction convention in Chicago, game designer Kenneth Hite noted that, beyond finding authorized images, media corporations tended to let game designers have free rein in creating paratextual board games.[65] Perhaps this is for the best, as each game provides different insights into how paratextuality functions when translating a filmic or novelistic text into a ludic medium. One of the key lessons that paratextual board games reflect in this system, as demonstrated by these games, is that communities have the power to perform their own versions of media franchises. According to Salen and Zimmerman, the social aspects of games are often the most important: "As players mingle with each other inside the magic circle, their social interactions highlight important aspects of a game's design. Meaningful play can be framed as *social phenomena*."[66] The *Lord of the Rings* franchise has, over its half-century of popularity, generated entire communities of audiences, fans, and consumers. Both the films and the novels continue to excite thousands of fans. That the paratextual board games based on these texts can represent a convergence of community and consumerism through the metaphor of collaborative game play reveals just one of the many important media elements contained in the relationship between paratextual board games and their original texts.

Transmedia Pathos and Plot in
The Walking Dead

You can't think forever. Sooner or later, you gotta make a move.
                                        The Governor, *The Walking Dead*

Glenn glances over his shoulder as he makes his way through the hexagonal landscape surrounding Atlanta, Georgia. His backpack, lighter than it was before he used the last of his ammo to blast a couple of Walkers, clings to his sweaty shoulders. Glenn tries to control his breathing in case the Walkers hear, so he slows—decides to walk two spaces instead of three. Although tired and hungry (he ran out of food three turns ago), he continues onward to the mall, ever vigilant to avoid the line of hungry zombies following his every footstep. He checks his fuel level, ready to run at a moment's notice....

Meanwhile, across the table, Lori runs circles around her campsite, seeking shelter and supplies at various stops along the way. She is just ten steps away from her final destination, when a Walker pops out of the sewer and attacks her. Her defenses down, and with too few supplies to use, Lori succumbs to her undead assailant and falls. As she dies, she can feel the change coming ... her body and mind shifting to turn her into a zombie....

Glenn and Lori are two characters from the graphic novel series *The Walking Dead* that also exist in the television adaptation of the series. Both *Walking Dead* versions tell a similar story set within a zombie apocalypse. Unlike the cult world of Middle-earth in *Lord of the Rings*, the world of *The Walking Dead* is much more based in a contemporary reality; like the Lovecraftian world described in Chapter 1, it is a world like ours, but different because of the appearance of single-minded, undead antagonists. This world extends to multiple paratextual products, as diverse as books, action figures, jigsaw puzzles, video games, clothing, and even pet accessories (for the canine fans). As paratextual board games, both the *Walking Dead* games use the same characters and diegetic elements, such as food and guns, to reflect their antecedent text. But both games use their zombies in different ways, creating distinctive approaches to paratextuality.

As I have been discussing in previous chapters, paratextual board games offer unique perspectives on contemporary media theories. The paratextual relationship developed between board games and media products augments contemporary notions of media complexity and cohesiveness. In this chapter, I want to examine more specifically the narrative complexity that a paratextual relationship engenders—as Adam Brown and Deb Waterhouse-Watson ask, "how do the more 'conventional' narrative perspectives of film and television source texts translate into board games?"[1] Or, rather, more generally, if board games offer moments of "playful" escape, then how can they "fit" into larger paradigms of narrative storytelling?

In 2011, both Z-Man Games and Cryptozoic Games released these board games based on *The Walking Dead*, one for the graphic novel series and one for its television adaptation, respectively. Both games reference their core text in the artwork and both develop from an explicit association with the requisite text of each medium. The game based on the graphic novel, *The Walking Dead: The Board Game* is a complex game using multiple dice, cards, and character options to develop a play experience that, I argue, transmediates the emotional pathos experienced by the characters in the graphic novel. I am using the term "pathos" to refer to the emotional appeal that a text can make to its reader. Pathos is generated by affective actions happening to a character in a media text, the feeling of connection between character and player. In its attempts to transmediate *pathos*, the graphic novel board game (here abbreviated as WDGN) develops gameplay *affect*. I am defining "affect" as the way that emotions are generated through the game. In this sense, the WDGN generates unique player pathos, opening up the definition of transmedia storytelling to include player affect as a constituent element. In contrast, *The Walking Dead Board Game* is a relatively simple board game played to mirror the *narrative* experience of the show. The fact that the television board game (here abbreviated as WDTV) reflects the narrative trajectory of the television show presents an *adaptation* of the narrative rather than a transmediation of pathos. In other words, each game based on the *Walking Dead* franchise approaches the source material differently, WDGN taking a character-centric approach, and the WDTV taking a narrative-centric approach. This seemingly minor shift heralds a major change in studies of transmediation and paratextuality.

The existence of these two board games, each based on the same larger narrative structure but developed for two different media, offers a relevant opportunity to investigate alternate versions of transmediation (the spread of narrative information across multiple media texts) and adaptation (the translation of one media text into a different medium) within nominally similar media texts. However, in our rapidly converging media environment, the relationship between games as ancillary products to a narrative core franchise generally *problematizes* conceptions of transmedia narrative coherence. Rarely can media-based board games influence transmedia narrative development. If games are not narratively consequential, can they even be considered transmediated? Transmedia games require the active participation of the audience as well as key attributes of the core medium. In other words, while players of games must actively generate their own meanings from the game, each paratextual game benefits from the particular affective experience of the original text as well. But this process relies on a conception of transmedia that develops interactively from both author and audience, both creator and player. This notion of interaction development leads to the fifth principle of paratextual board games:

Principle 5: Through player/text interaction, paratextual board games can transmediate pathos and affect better than they can transmediate narrative.

A structural analysis of narratives reveals that different aspects of a narrative can be transmediated in different ways, rather than from a strictly story-oriented perspective. Some of these aspects include static existents, like character, setting, or plot. Other aspects would fall under what Marie-Laure Ryan calls a more dynamic category, including the development of character relationships.[2] For example, Christy Dena notes that a cross-media franchise might develop a character more thoroughly than a core text would have time for, by offering more time across the multiple outlets for character development.[3] Splitting transmedia narratives into their constituent elements reveals multiple ways that stories could be spread across outlets. Jason Mittell has shown how different types of transmediation can function in television texts, including what he terms "What Is" transmedia and "What If" transmedia on television. "What Is" tends to focus on expanding the storyworld through augmentation—adding additional paratexts to explain a central narrative. The television series *Lost*, with ancillary products like jigsaw puzzles, video games, and DVD extras all focusing on one overarching story, represents a "What Is" type of transmediation. In contrast, "What If" tends to pose "hypothetical possibilities rather than canonical certainties, inviting viewers to imagine alternative stories and approaches to storytelling that are distinctly not to be treated as potential canon."[4] In this case, paratexts offer possibilities not explored in the original text, running parallel to it rather than augmenting it. Fan fiction could be considered an example of "What If" transmedia, as the work of fans would not be considered canonical but does open up new possibilities to read the narrative. Although both the *Walking Dead* board games exemplify Mittell's conception of "What If" transmedia stories, the comics-based game deepens the world through *pathos* while the TV-based game deepens the world through *plot*. Both games play on their connections to their core text, but do so in radically different ways.

By participating in the games, the player experiences a level of pathos engendered by the larger the *Walking Dead* narrative structure. Each game approaches pathos differently, and the relationship between the players and the characters becomes less grounded in the overall the *Walking Dead* narrative than in the relationships between the characters themselves. The players find themselves discovering that same connection. This is transmedia, but it is not a general transmediated narrative—it is a transmediation of affect, of deep and experiential emotion. This connection between player and character affect establishes a sixth principle of paratextual board games:

Principle 6: Paratextual board games rely on mixing familiar characters and unfamiliar characteristics to facilitate player investment.

First, I will discuss transmediation as it has traditionally been applied to narrative. In trying to transmediate the television narrative, the WDTV ends up downplaying the character-based affect generated by the television series in favor of focusing on plot-driven narrative adaptation. Then, I will discuss what I term "transmedia pathos," an emotional connection between transmediated texts, as it applies to the graphic novel and the game based on it. As Kevin Veale points out, "the affective dimension of something refers to a spectrum of subjective things that we feel but that we are less conscious of than our emotions."[5] In other words, the game based on the comic does not replicate a narrative situation, but rather places the player in the same situations and with the same type of pathos as the comic book characters. Finally, I will conclude with some observations about the future of transmedia and what this might portend for further studies of paratextual board games.

Transmedia pathos

In the previous two chapters I have looked at the way *rules* and *play* can govern modes of game design and mechanics in terms of paratextual board games. In this chapter, I examine *culture*. Salen and Zimmerman consider these three overarching schemas as "not merely a model for game design," but also as a representation of "a way of understanding any sort of design."[6] As we have seen, rules govern the algorithmic functionality of games (*Arkham Horror*), and play structures the way the players interpret the narrative (*The Lord of the Rings*). Culture is, in turn, a way of understanding the larger context in which the games sit. For contemporary paratextual board games, Salen and Zimmerman's discussion of culture as "in a context, a surrounding cultural milieu" highlights the contemporary media environment as conducive to this paratextual relationship.[7] More specifically, a contemporary focus on transmediation as it appears across both scholarship and creative practices highlights how paratextual board games fit into today's media culture.

Transmediation describes the spread of narrative information across multiple media outlets. While board games most overtly problematize narrative *coherence*, they also expand, deepen, and augment the narrative world through individual player associations with the core text. Chapter 5's *Star Trek: Expeditions* is a great example of this. The game does not mimic the plot of the 2009 film, the text upon which it is based. Rather, it introduces a *new* narrative that deepens the players' understandings of the *Star Trek* universe. In traditional interpretations of transmediation, media scholars have tended to examine these outlets' relationships as being based in narrative storytelling. Although often associated with digital media,[8] transmediation can also be traced to Greek myths and Biblical stories as well as literature like Cervantes' *Don Quixote* and Lovecraft's mythos (see Chapter 1).[9] The term "transmedia storytelling" was posited by Henry Jenkins to describe a narrative network where "integral elements of a fiction get dispersed systematically across multiple delivery channels for the purpose of creating a unified and coordinated entertainment experience."[10] As he later writes:

> In the ideal form of transmedia storytelling, each medium does what it does best—so that a story might be introduced in a film, expanded through television, novels, and comics, and its world might be explored and experienced through game play. Each franchise entry needs to be self-contained enough to enable autonomous consumption. That is, you don't need to have seen the film to enjoy the game and vice-versa.[11]

But narrative is itself composed of many attributes, and a detailed investigation of those attributes reveals the many and varied ways that texts can cohere in a transmediated fashion—for example, through audience participation, emotion, and interactivity. As Edward Branigan notes, viewer emotional response to a narrative often develops from interpreting multiple associations between these dynamic elements.[12] In the *Walking Dead* graphic novel, the character of Jim becomes emotionally relevant (and thus uses affect to generate pathos) because the story of his family—killed in front of him by zombies at the start of the outbreak—extends his past life into his present predicament.[13] As I will show, the two *Walking Dead* board games use different mechanisms, including game mechanics, character identification, and aesthetic connection, to generate affect through the game play and increased player pathos.

Both games are based in the *Walking Dead* universe, in which reanimated corpses walk the Earth and (slowly) chase the protagonists. In WDGN, the characters inhabit a geographic area surrounding Atlanta, Georgia, and can use resources like guns to kill hordes of zombies or food to heal after being attacked. Players can also run away from zombies, which they end up doing most of the time. The end goal of the game is to scout three locations—for example, the airport, the football stadium, the motel, the campsite—and complete different challenges at each location. Challenges include killing a set number of zombies while maintaining a certain level of supplies. Often, one player has to have more supplies than other players do in order to complete a location. WDTV imagines a different type of *Walking Dead* world, as the characters from the television series walk through the streets of Atlanta encountering zombies and fighting them. Players fight zombies using supplies they can find, including guns, ammunition, and melee weapons like axes. If a character succumbs to zombie attack, he or she turns into a zombie and can attack the other players.

Both *Walking Dead* board games attach to their original text in multiple ways. For Marie-Laure Ryan, two different types of transmedia storytelling exist.[14] "Snowball" storytelling consists of a core narrative that becomes so popular—for example, *Star Trek, Star Wars*—that it inspires multiple products to be created after its release. That is, the core narrative grows over time as new products are added. *Star Trek* started as a single television series, but over time (and without a deliberate game plan set in motion from the start) has developed into multiple television series, films, graphic novels, toys, and other franchise elements, including games *Star Trek: Fleet Captains* and *Star Trek: Expeditions*. Alternately, "system" storytelling describes transmedia narratives that are deliberately designed to use more than one medium to tell one story—*The Matrix*, as described by Henry Jenkins, is a good example of system storytelling as it was deliberately designed to tell an expansive story over multiple texts.[15] Both types of narratives involve transmedia extensions, or elements that fans collect to increase their encyclopedic knowledge of the story.[16] As indicated in Jenkins's original quotation, board games are complicated extensions to transmedia franchises, as they build what Christy Dena might call a "storyworld," neither providing a "primary source of information about characters [or] setting," nor playing "a direct role in the unfolding plot." Paratextual board games do not necessarily develop an overarching story, but they do allow "the fictional world to be accessed in the real world through character identification."[17] In short, games generally develop *worlds*, not *narratives*.

Both the *Walking Dead* board games could be described as "snowball" storytelling, as each game uses particular locales, characters, and design features from its requisite core text. Robert Kirkman's comic *The Walking Dead started* in 2003 and was developed into a highly rated cable television series in 2010. *The Walking Dead* television series is quite deliberately an adaptation of the graphic novel, as evidenced by the first season, which follows the first few issues of the comic relatively closely (although, as Craig Fischer describes, there are important differences that shape our understanding of each, including the development of Shane's character in the television series instead of his rather abrupt death in the graphic novel).[18] As it has progressed, the show's narrative has increasingly diverged from that of the comic series.[19]

As a corollary of transmedia storytelling, adaptation describes how one narrative is translated from one medium to another. In the conclusion of the book, I will talk more about ludic adaptations and the way paratextual games like *Doctor Who: The Interactive Electronic Board Game* adapt the "feeling" of the original show. "Adaptations," as Linda Hutcheon notes, "are everywhere": they have a special relationship with their antecedent text, as there is always a trace haunting the adaptation.[20] An adaptation, as film critic Dudley Andrews describes, remakes and matches an original text's "sign system to prior achievement in some other system."[21] Adaptation is the translation and reproduction from one system to another. But just because the story may be borrowed does not mean the adaptation necessarily lacks originality: according to Deborah Cartmell, adaptation will always "rewrite the story for a particular audience."[22] Part of the pleasure of adaptation comes, Hutcheon argues, from "repetition with variation, from the comfort of ritual combined with the piquancy of surprise."[23] In the case of a board game adaptation of a television or graphic novel narrative, this pleasure lies in noting specific aesthetic similarities as well as in recognizing moments of balance between adherence to a narrative and departure from it.

We recognize familiar characters and scenes—an image of Carl on a card or a scene of the protagonists attacking zombies—as an aesthetic connection to the original text, but the gameplay mechanics allow us to play with that narrative world in ways unanticipated in the original storyworld. In the WDGN, we travel to locations, the airport for instance, that the characters in the graphic novel do not. A ludic adaptation can never precisely reproduce the "sign system" of the original narrative; rather, only a limited set of signs can be adapted. Indeed, Carlos Scolari notes that transmedia storytelling "is not just an adaptation from one media to another. The story that the comics tell is not the same as that told on television or in cinema."[24] And as Robert Brookey argues, the adaptation of film to a video game rarely matches the style and tone of the original, reducing the adaptive narrative to a few key plot points.[25] Board games make adaptation even more difficult—while a board game can include the same representations of characters, locations, and props as the original text, it will rarely match precisely the events as they occurred on screen or on the page, given the fluidity of game play. And the two *Walking Dead* games make this adaptation more different still, as the WDTV is itself an adaptation of an adaptation.

Board games are rarely analyzed in terms of transmediation, although many canonical definitions of transmedia describe *video* games as one of the main nodes in the storytelling network, perhaps because of the convergence of technologies video games engender.[26] As I discussed in Chapter 2, many franchises that fit within a transmedia paradigm have vast environments and worlds for the characters (and the audience) to explore.[27] Video games model this paradigm because they "fit within a much older tradition of spatial stories."[28] This hyperdiegetic sense of narrative—that there is a sense of more world than can be experienced in any one text—fits the spatial organization of video games, which tend to have this type of expansive world.[29] Indeed, in 2012, Telltale Games' video game based on the *Walking Dead* franchise was released as a hyperdiegetic extension to the series: it details the first few weeks of the zombie infection (scenes both the television series and the graphic novel have left deliberately vague). In contrast, the physicality of board games tends to limit them to nonhyperdiegetic roles in narrative, as the expansive worlds of video games (or of cult narratives generally) are difficult to replicate in physical and tangible spaces.

If video games reflect a more spatially oriented focus on transmediation, board games complicate this narratological notion. As Markus Montola notes, video games and other "virtual worlds have more in common with ordinary life than with board games."[30] And as Zagal, Rick, and Hsi have shown, while video games involve complex interaction with multiple technologies, contexts, and mechanics, "the nature of board games implies a transparency regarding the core mechanics of the game and the way they are interrelated." Yet, as I discussed in the previous chapter, Zagal, Rick, and Hsi actually use board game mechanics to generalize about video games, and it is relevant that they focus specifically on an analysis of the *Lord of the Rings* board game—not seen in a transmediated relationship with the core text, but rather as a "themed" spin-off of the books.[31] The *Walking Dead* board games—especially the WDGN—reflect the application of the game to "ordinary life," as the ethical decision-making that must occur to progress within the game finds voice in the lived experiences of the players. As seen in a connective relationship with a core text, board games can generate new dynamics within narrative interaction; as Wilson illustrates, focusing on things that board games are good at, like face-to-face communication and tactility, allows board game designers to give each game a unique identity, "a certain feel."[32] Transmediation allows individual texts to develop sections of the storyworld, each one "contributing to a larger narrative economy."[33]

For Ryan, a storyworld transmedia franchise develops through a "static component that precedes the story, and a dynamic component that captures its unfolding."[34] These static components include characters, items, rules, or other underlying existents. The dynamic components include physical events that change the items or mental events that give those items significance. Static elements remain stable from one text to another. *The Hunger Games: District 12* features Katniss Everdeen. *Arkham Horror* will include the town of Arkham. It would be unusual to have a *Walking Dead* board game that did not in some way feature zombies. Dynamic components can change the trajectory of the particular iteration of the narrative within the specific text; in the comic, as I mentioned, antagonist Shane dies very early on in the narrative, but in the television series, Shane survives far into the second season. The dynamism of Shane's existence clarifies and separates the two iterations, lending weight to Shane's death in both. Similarly, the way zombies are dealt with in both games highlights how this static element can become dynamic. In the WDGN, the zombies spawn after every move and continue to swarm the board. In the WDTV, the playable characters themselves can transform into zombies when they die in the game. Rather than populating the board, zombies become playable characters themselves.

Translating a television series or a graphic novel to a board game form requires what Ryan calls "transmedial adaptation"—the use of those static elements in combination with interactively generated dynamic components.[35] Both the *Walking Dead* board games make use of static elements adapted from the prerequisite text, including the main characters who have to find supplies and clear locations of zombie infestation and their encounters with the undead along the way. The WDGN dynamic component is original to the game; it places those characters in new situations that further develop the affective relationship between the player of the game and those characters, transmediating that text's pathos. In contrast, the WDTV's dynamic component—the situations that each character/player encounters—mirrors moments from the television program. The WDTV does not develop its dynamic elements, focusing instead on reflecting the plot of the show.

It is not my intent here to get mired in the "narratologist/ludologist" debate within game studies, which (in simplified form) tends to examine games as either narrative based or play based.[36] Greg Costikyan summarizes this debate as a "culture class" between those who "view story as perhaps important but tangential to understanding the nature of games, and those who view it as essential."[37] That said, rather than getting hung up on one way to view games or another, I agree with Zimmerman—it is not determining *whether* narrative is part of a game, but understanding *how* it interacts with ludism that is important.[38] As Ryan writes about the transmediation of *Star Wars* from film to game, "its plot is one of countless stories that tell about a fight between good and evil. What makes the *Star Wars* storyworld distinctive is not the plot but the setting."[39] As I will show with the *Walking Dead* board games, such interactions can indicate either transmediation or adaptation, depending on the relationship between the game mechanics, character interaction, and appearance of the game.

The Walking Dead zombies and playing *Walking Dead*

Both the *Walking Dead* board games approach the interactive, generative participation of the game players as a constituent part of the ludic experience. On the surface, it would be relatively easy to ascribe value to one or the other game—it's a "good" game because it is only sort of like the television show, but a "bad" game if it is too much like the television show: the "uncanny valley" of transmediation, or the pejorative "pasted on theme." Such determinations might be useful for a critical conversation about ludology and the "ludological dissonance" that narrative-based games engender.[40] However, it is not my intention to argue that one game is "better" than the other; rather, the evaluative judgments I use allow me to probe deeper into the mechanisms of transmediation itself. After all, the effectiveness of transmediation as a concept must somehow relate to the effectiveness of transmediation as a narrative form.

Participation and interactivity are integral to any game (see Chapters 6 and 8), but they are even more so when discussing the relationship between paratextual elements of a narrative franchise. This is an inherently difficult proposition, as Montola suggests:

> play is a temporary and ever-changing social process that can only be analyzed as a whole in retrospect. Participants obtain different pieces of information during the play, and no participant can ever accumulate all the information related to a game.[41]

Yet, it is necessary to assume standard attributes in order to generalize about the mechanics of the games for the players. There are some standard elements in *The Walking Dead* that make this analysis slightly easier. *The Walking Dead* relies on audience affect, what Kyle Bishop terms "dramatic pathos," to engender a connection to the characters.[42] Both the comic book and the television series reflect this, as Jay Bonansinga notes: "the spiritual center of the comic series—a human story laying out amid all the gore—translates well to the intimate confines of television."[43] Zombies may be the most obvious characters from *The Walking Dead*, but they are not necessarily the titular characters: the "walking dead" are also those humans left alive *after* the outbreak.

The generative process of game-based pathos emerges from player empathy for characters. Empathy is what allows players to feel emotion within a fictional world and for fictional characters. As Salen and Zimmerman show, the complex relationship between game player and game character generates affect in game players by giving them "permission to play with identity."[44] This pathos translates particularly to the WDGN. Indeed, while many of the same characters are present in both games, only the close connection between the player and the character in the comic-based game engenders a transmediation of affect. In other words, the WDGN generates *transmedia pathos* through the character attributes and the player investment in the unfolding of the game.

In order to examine the salient differences between the two games, I will focus this analysis on three elements: the gameplay mechanics, the player/character interactions within the game, and the artwork of the game. Through an investigation of these elements, I will show how the WDGN functions through transmedia pathos and how the WDTV functions through plot adaptation. The point of this comparison is to illustrate how transmediation can be enacted through board games, but only by tapping into what Celia Pearce describes as "Aristotelian notions of empathy"—the feelings we have for characters.[45]

Mechanics

The game mechanics of the WDGN allow for creativity in how one plays the game through more random elements and more freedom to choose options, in contrast to the WDTV, which focuses more on replicating story experiences from the show. Through the gameplay mechanics, the WDGN's individual player actions can affect the outcome of the game. For instance, whether or not a player chooses to ally himself or herself with another character, like in *The Lord of the Rings: The Complete Trilogy,* may influence whether or not the two characters survive. As Chris Klug describes, one of the "tools for evoking player emotion" in board games "is the ability of the player to directly manipulate, understand, and experience game systems themselves."[46] This allows players to become invested in their own choices while not remaining tethered to the plot of the comic. Conversely, the WDTV offers a more closed system that limits player interactivity through forced choice. For instance, players do not have the opportunity to choose an ally themselves, nor do they have the choice of, say, which locations to visit. These non-choices induce players to experience a set narrative, akin to watching a television episode. The freedom to make complex decisions within the WDGN encourages an affective relationship between players and characters, highlighting a transmediated connection with the original text. Conversely, the WDTV features a more static, less interactive game; players have fewer options and follow a more predetermined route through the game. With fewer opportunities to make choices, players have less agency in the construction of the game play, and may become more passive in their play. Elias, Garfield, and Gutschera describe the way different games engender different player costs, including one of work.[47] More mainstream and popular games often require less work, while more complex games require more player agency. In the WDTV, such dynamics encourage passivity in the players and engender a closer reflection to the original text.

Specifically, the differences in the game boards themselves offer a useful heuristic by which we can learn the mechanics of the game. In the WDGN, the game board is expansive and multi-spaced. Like with the board of *The Lord of the Rings: The Complete Trilogy,* each space of WDGN is hexagonal and players can move in any of the six directions (Figure 3.1). Players can choose to move up to three spaces at a time, or additional supplies allow more movement if deemed necessary. After a player moves off a space, however, zombies populate that space, and the board gradually becomes filled with the undead. The game is highly randomized, in terms of both objectives and game play. The players have 13 objective locations, only four of which are open at a time. As soon as one location is cleared of zombies, another is randomly selected. When encountering zombies, players roll multiple dice—sometimes as many as 10—in order to defeat or survive the attack. Supplies can be found throughout the game, and can be used in multiple ways. For example, if one finds fuel in the game, the player can use it to either travel *further* or travel *silently* (avoiding the spawning zombies). A player wins once he or she has cleared three locations of zombies.

Players can interact with other players in various ways—some randomly selected cards force player interaction, either through fighting or through ethical decision-making. In one memorable moment from a game my group played, my opponent drew a card that asked him to decide whether or not I gained supplies—if I did, he would also get supplies but I might be closer to winning. Players, however, can also cooperate (as discussed in the previous chapter), working together to defeat massive numbers of zombies, especially useful when walking past the hordes created by the ones that spawn on vacated spots. In short, at each point in the game, players are encouraged to make decisions that impact not only their own character's survival, but also the survival of other players. Players can follow multiple paths, and become invested in what others are doing. In no way does this mirror the *narrative* of the graphic novel—the specific scenes and adventures that take place in Kirkman's books are not mentioned, and only the static elements of the series exist in the game. The dynamic elements are those created by the players themselves, using their own decision-making to affectively design their play experience.

The WDGN encourages players to revel in their own created world of *The Walking Dead*, effectively transmediating the *feeling* that one gets from the comic. Following the exploits of the survivors of the zombie apocalypse, the graphic novel is more akin to a melodramatic soap opera than to a horror story.[48] For example, in the comic, protagonist Rick is knocked unconscious before the zombie apocalypse, and awakens after it had reached its zenith. Setting out to find his family, he eventually encounters them in the woods with a group of other survivors and learns that his wife has had an affair with his best friend,

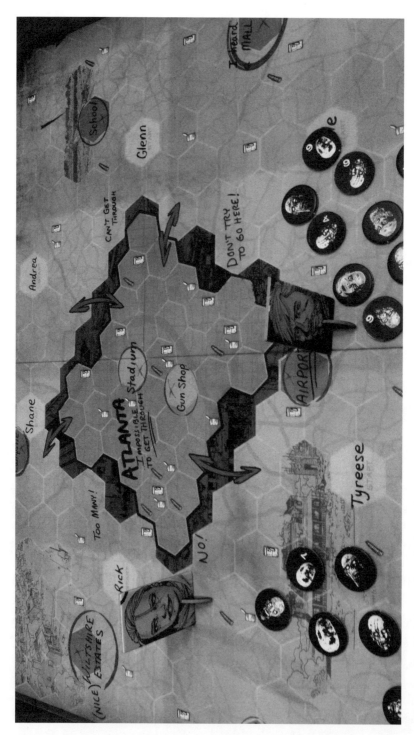

Figure 3.1 Section of game board. *The Walking Dead Board Game* ©Z-Man Games 2011. Photo by the author.

Shane. Although some of the narrative involves killing zombies, the majority of the graphic novels' violence depicts characters fighting against each other, as character Negan demonstrates with his barbed-wire-wrapped baseball bat. Other melodramatic scenes depict characters, like Rick and Andrea, falling in love; others, like Tyreese and Carol, having intense sexual relationships; and families, like Rick and Carl, trying to remain together.[49] For example, the characters of Glenn and Maggie provide a lot of melodramatic story to follow, as they meet and fall in love, and eventually must deal with Maggie's depression and Glenn's death. As Bonansinga notes, *The Walking Dead* graphic novels tell the story "from inside the characters, and the power comes from an accumulation of detail."[50] The nature of comics as a medium invites audience connection.[51] This feeling of being connected to the characters and situations, of having an emotional stake in their survival, is what is transmediated in the board game. As a component of narrative, this describes a participatory and interactive element of pathos, rather than a specifically formalistic element of plot.

The game board for the WDTV is quite different from the WDGN, and illustrates how the WDTV attempts adaptation rather than transmediation. In contrast to the hexagonal spaces of the WDGN, the WDTV has a linear board—squares connected in a particular path. Players can move forward or backward, but must progress in one direction or its reverse. The objectives of the game are also static—at each corner of the square board are four locations that must be traversed. At each objective, characters must defeat zombies, a task that relies on the "supply" cards one has drawn in the past. Supply cards have numbers on them, and players must play a higher number than the number of zombies that are attacking, itself generated via drawing an "encounter" card. A player wins if he or she moves to each of the four corner locations and survives the zombie attacks.

The WDTV encourages players to follow situations that exist in the television show. For example, encounter cards have specific scenes described from the show written on them, and so each encounter references a specific event from the show. The "Out of Reach" card features a still image of Merle from the television series stretching to grab a gun, just out of his grasp. This card alludes to a scene in the first season of the show when Merle is handcuffed to a pipe and attacked by zombies. In this, the WDTV does not present the game as "new narrative"; rather, it adapts narratives that already exist on the show. The static nature of the game and the relative inflexibility of player choice in how the game progresses means that players are not particularly emotionally connected to the story—it has already played on television, and we are playing it on the tabletop. The WDTV functions as adaptation, not transmediation, through its particular game mechanics.

Character

All of the paratextual games I describe in this book generate emotional connection to their text through the application of pathos in character development. In most games, specific attributes of the characters, as I described in the last chapter in relation to *The Lord of the Rings*, help to make the characters unique and, thus, stand out more. This pathos is obvious in the two *Hunger Games* games that I describe in Chapter 6. In *District 12*, all players play as Katniss and because there is no differentiation between them, less pathos for the character is generated. In *Training Days*, each player plays as a different Tribute with wildly different characteristics. Despite having no name, the player's character seems more "real." In terms of WDGN, this pathos connection helps to engender a sense of transmediation within the franchise. In contrast, the WDTV subordinates character development in favor of narrative progression. This subordination helps to develop a sense of adaptation within *The Walking Dead television* franchise.

In an online interview, Keith Tralins, creator of the WDGN, reveals how he designed the graphic novel game to focus less on narrative and more on character interaction and empathy:

> Our approach to the game was really focused on creating an experience based on "The Walking Dead." It is Robert Kirkman's world, and this is a chance to play in his world, with his rules. It is actually about finding a safe haven from the zombies…. Just like in the book … [characters are] usually only fighting zombies to defend themselves, get to where they have to go, or secure a location.

As Matt Morgan elaborates:

> the game's mechanics encourage player actions that are in line with the subject matter and theme. This is what separates rich gaming experiences from abstract strategy, and where the label "pasted on theme" is applied to games which fail in the endeavor.[52]

The idea of a "pasted on theme" reflects a pejorative reading of games that are created simply for synergistic reasons. In contrast, the creator of the WDTV,

Cory Jones, notes how the WDTV was developed to capture the narrative of the television series: "The goal for me was to play up [character] tensions, because it seems the drama lives in the tension."[53] Character pathos seems less the focus than following a series of events to structure a single narrative. It's not that affect is completely effaced in the WDTV as opposed to the WDGN, but the emphasis on adapting static narrative elements of the television series precludes the transmediation of the dynamic narrative elements. The WDTV seems focused on constructing an adaptation of the series while the WDGN seems to develop a transmediated approach to character affect.

Video game and literacy scholar James Paul Gee has noted that this affective relationship coheres player to character, creating a "projective identity" that exists between game diegesis and player control.[54] As audiences feel emotional attachment to characters, the empathy for those characters can translate as the character moves from one medium to another. Characters are what Ryan calls static elements, but the particular pathos engendered by characters can be dynamic; indeed, one element that Ryan elides in her structural analysis of transmedia narrative is the audience, and the particular affect generated by audiences of a cult program.[55] Steven E. Jones notes the pleasure that audiences can feel at piecing together a transmedia "puzzle":

> part of the allure of such cross-platform "intermediation" is the viewers' or players' pleasure at following the "hacks" or media repurposing created by the game, seeing different media crossed and re-crossed in order to use the network as the platform for a larger, unstable, paratextual structure.[56]

But here Jones is writing about the affect experienced nondiegetically, the "pleasure in experiencing the media crossings in real time and physical space." Rarely is affect itself discussed as an element of narrative that itself can be transmediated.

To understand games as part of a transmedia franchise, then, game characters need to do more than just tell the story; they must illustrate relationships. In *The Walking Dead* comic and television series, many characters interact differently when allied with others. For example, in both texts Rick tends to be more protective and violent when near his son Carl; for example, in both the comic and the show, when Carl is kidnapped and threatened with rape, Rick kills all of the attackers. This characteristic is mirrored in the WDGN, as each character has a special ability that is only tuned when a *relationship* is shown. For example, if the player holds the character card for Rick, he or she only gets her special power (an extra roll of the die and an ability to experience additional fatigue) if Carl is also part of the players' team. Similarly, if the player holds the character card for Patricia, a minor character in the graphic novel, the special power (an extra roll of the die) is only provided if Otis, another minor character, is also part of the players' team; in the comic, Patricia and Otis are in a relationship. This focus on character-dependent traits illustrates a particular complexity in the pathos of the WDGN and the fluid mobility of character types across the game.

In contrast to the WDGN, the WDTV does not devote as much attention to character development as it does to narrative fidelity. For example, the WDTV features only six characters from the show, and no special relationships are revealed in the game play. In an interview with Morgan, WDTV creator Cory Jones describes: the "interplay between the characters themselves … that's a hard abstraction in some ways and very dependent on who plays what character. I didn't want to create a situation where I pick my character because you picked a certain one."[57] The creators of the WDTV seem to have adapted the semantics of the show as a way of generating corporate synergy and franchisability.[58] Characters are given less "freedom" in the WDTV than in the WDGN; they have fewer attributes and players have less of a chance to make decisions based on those attributes. Fewer creative interactions with the characters reify the character's original nature from the television series, rather than augment it through player collaboration.

The WDTV includes an attribute not in the WDGN: players commonly lose their encounters before securing all the objectives. When this happens, the player's character is turned into a zombie for the rest of the game. The play changes and the zombies attempt to attack the other players. When two players are turned into zombies, the game shifts again as all players form two teams—Team Zombie and Team Survivor. The objective for Team Zombie is to defeat the other players. The objective for Team Survivor is to secure the corner locations. Because of this fundamental switch of character, the reliance on any one particular character isn't as meaningful as it is in the comic game. Jones describes the character shift as:

> When you die, you become a zombie. You are still playing on the board, but your hand goes away and is replaced with new zombie cards.… You are playing against the remaining players and trying to kill them, so we emulate the strange dynamic from the show where some of the characters do die and they have to be put down.[59]

The WDTV forces a change in characterizations, reducing the empathy a player has for a character. A zombie loses all the cards, abilities, and powers gained throughout the game—to play as a zombie means giving up the character one has worked for. If you are playing as Rick and you change into a zombie, you no longer care if *the character* Rick wins because he no longer exists in the game. The disappearance of identity may be a good philosophical debate for zombie-themed media,[60] but it reduces the level of investment one might have in their character. If all the attributes disappear, there is no incentive to develop. In other words, although both games have you playing as a character, the time spent in becoming emotionally invested in the WDGN character reveals closer ties to winning the game while the WDTV reduces the incentive for viewing the character in a more complex way.

As zombie scholar Brendan Riley suggests, the work of any zombie text lies in defining what it means to be a person; a key component of media-based board games is the way that character and player interact in a form of avatarism.[61] That is, zombies themselves always straddle the line between "human" and "inhuman." The horror of the tale isn't just that hordes are attacking, but that such zombie hordes represent the intimate loss of humanity. In the WDGN, the players are people, the living, the survivors. In the WDTV, in contrast, the endgame loss of humanity is adapted literally—the players *are* zombies, blindly following the formulated rules and randomly generated cards. For all intents and purposes, each character is the same in the WDTV, making the game a narrative and philosophical adaptation rather than transmediation.

Art work

Within both of the games, artwork functions to connect the games to the core text. For example, in the WDGN, all the art is original—and was commissioned and created by Charlie Adlard, the same artist for the majority of the comic books.[62] All the art draws on the same aesthetics as that in the comic. The presence of new artwork within the game builds player affect, encouraging a greater consumption of the elements (cards, game board, inserts) of the game as an addition to the storyworld of the comic, not a replication of it. As Morgan notes, all the artwork:

> stays true to the look and feel of the comic book. The first and most obvious way
> it goes about this is by embracing the black and white color scheme. While not

completely devoid of color, the game's style is a bit jarring for the average gamer. However, for fans of the comic, it is a spot on design choice.[63]

Conversely, all the artwork of the WDTV is constructed of either advertisements for the show or still images from the show. For example, on a scrounge card, there might be a still image of Darryl holding an ax, although Darryl is not available to "play" as a character. The artistic elements of the game (mainly on the cards, but on the character information boards as well) encourage players to reconnect to the original text by reflecting the original text. Each image adapts scenes from *The Walking Dead* television show through replication, not through origination. Character quotations from the series are added to the images, further reifying that connection. Players are not creating their own stories; they are reliving stories that already exist within the world of the television series. In this way, the WDTV adapts the television show; it does not transmediate.

There are similarities between the games that augment their respective textual structures. The cover of each game mirrors that of the other, both seemingly based on promotional material for the AMC television series (Figure 3.2). The advertisement helps to sell the connection between the graphic novel and the series, showing not only the similarity between them (characters share clothing, poses, and diagrammatic relationships) but also that one "reflects" the other. Notably, however, the antagonist zombie at the center of the image is from the television program—both groups of survivors appear to be aiming at the televisual undead, reifying the television series as the more viscerally authentic (as would befit an advertisement for the television series). Yet the connection between the comic and the television show is made explicit through the direct reflection of the two images.[64]

The two board games came out in 2011, a coincidence noted by Morgan, writing on the *MTV Geek!* Blog.[65] The image from the television series that

Figure 3.2 Original 2010 advertisement for *the Walking Dead* TV series ©AMC 2010.

graces the cover of the television game box was created in 2010.[66] Bringing together all the main characters from the first season of the television show, it prominently features protagonist Rick Grimes, pointing his gun toward the left, his son Carl behind him to his right, and his wife Lori behind Carl (Figure 3.3). Other characters—including Shane, Dale, Andrea, Amy, and Glenn—are also depicted. The comic version features a mirror image of its cover as taken from the television advertisement. Protagonist Rick is holding his gun in his left hand (in the comic, his right hand has been severed from his arm) while his son Carl peeks from behind Rick's back on his left. Shane, separated from the group slightly on the far right, mirrors his distance from the group on the left in the WDTV image. An exception to this mirror image is Amy. In the original advertisement (Figure 3.2), she is mirrored on both sides; she is the closest character to the centered zombie. In the WDTV cover, Amy is placed identically, on the far left of the box. In the WDGN cover, however, Amy has been moved, now also on the far left of the box. Crucially, then, Amy is the only character placed similarly on both images—and Amy is the only character that

Figure 3.3 The *Walking Dead* board game covers. *The Walking Dead: The Board Game* ©Cryptozoic Entertainment 2011. *The Walking Dead Board Game* ©Z-Man Games 2011. Photo by Katie Booth.

dies at the same point in both the comic and the television series. Canonically, the character experiences the same things in both texts as well.

Examining the aesthetics of each of these board games allows us to interpret not only how the games are being marketed and sold to audiences but also how they are being positioned within the media franchises themselves.[67] Investigating the aesthetics of games is important in and of itself: as Flanagan notes, "the play experience has, for thousands of years, been intertwined with aesthetics."[68] But for paratextual board games, aesthetics help define the connection to the original text even more strongly. The WDTV reveals a close connection to the television program, mirroring images that have already appeared or are reappropriations of those that might have referred to different elements within the show. Similarly, the WDGN hews close to the aesthetics of the original graphic novel, but augments those aesthetics with original drawings, as if the game reflected the spirit of the comic.

Interestingly, just as I was completing revisions on this chapter, Cryptozoic released a third *Walking Dead* board game, *The Walking Dead: The Best Defense Board Game*, based on the television series. *The Best Defense Board Game* offers a melding of the types of paratextuality and adaptation I have described in this chapter through the cooperative mechanisms of the game play. As mentioned in the previous chapter, designer Reiner Knizia emulated the cooperative, character-based pathos in *The Lord of the Rings* rather than the narrative of Tolkien's books. As he describes: "more important [than the story] was the feeling of the world. The true focus of the book was not the fighting, but more personal themes—the development of each character's sense of self as they attempt to overcome adversity."[69] *The Best Defense Board Game* mimics this sentiment by having the players cooperating to defend themselves by defeating the zombie hordes. However, the personal affect developed in the television series is mirrored in the game by forcing each player to act as the "leader" of the group in alternating turns. The leader must make decisions that affect the other members of the group but is often in the dark as to what the other players may need to do. This rotating hierarchy generates feelings of transmedia pathos via the cooperative mechanics of the game play; that is, players have to cooperate instead of competing but may sometimes have to inadvertently work against the group as a whole. Much like in the television series, where characters have multiple motivations propelling their actions, to be an effective survivor in this game, one must play it as a paratext, being both part of, and apart from, the group.

"You can't think forever..."

If transmedia storytelling is becoming a major marketing and creative aspect of television entertainment and the digital media environment, then it behooves scholars and game players to examine any other avenues it begets. This includes both focusing on ancillary products that are not normally considered narratively significant, like paratextual games, and delving more deeply into aspects of narrative storytelling. As we refine our understanding of transmediation, it becomes a critical foundation of contemporary media studies, allowing new opportunities and creative potentialities in media production.

Board games can become part of the transmediated media environment, but must be designed to augment more complex aspects of the media franchise than just the plot. Remediating the plot of a television series, *The Walking Dead* board game based on the television show becomes an adaptation, an ancillary product that, at least in appearance, seems to exist as promotional item rather than an expansion of a storyworld. In contrast, *The Walking Dead* board game based on the graphic novel series becomes part of a transmediated experience, drawing on the pathos of the characters' adventures as depicted in the comic. The game, while drawing on the aesthetics of the comic, maintains a unique identity that focuses on player affect and emotionality.

Splitting transmedia narratives into their constituent elements reveals multiple ways that stories could be spread across outlets. As Henry Jenkins, Sam Ford, and Joshua Green describe, this split allows producers of transmediated stories "to prolong audience engagement with media texts in order to expand touchpoints."[70] On one hand, media producers find transmediation to be a lucrative franchising endeavor. Derek Johnson's analysis of media franchising points out that this "inter-industrial franchising ... across the social and industrial context of multiple media industries" helps to fuel the production of multiple ancillary products across media.[71] The media industries find within transmediated products a profitable structure.

On the other hand, it is not just the media industries developing transmedia outlets. Jenkins, Ford, and Green see transmediation as intimately tied to viewer engagement, stressing "the importance of relationship building" between producers and audiences.[72] Audiences are an integral part of transmedia franchises. When audience pathos is removed from the game/text transmediation, more than just empathy is lost. The potential to deepen and enrich the storytelling world is lost as well. In any cross-media transition, according to Jennifer Cover:

> an audience might take bits and pieces from several related narratives told in multiple media in order to form a full view of a particular story. As audiences, we increasingly decide which versions of stories to accept ... while each medium gives us certain advantages, certain affordances that shape the telling of the story, texts work together to form a more complete view of a storyworld, characters, and even plotlines.[73]

In this view, transmediation isn't about the renegotiation of storytelling elements, but rather the interactive mechanisms by which audiences construct and develop those stories outside the realm of authorized interpretations. Integrating board games into this interactive space allows more empathy and pathos to grow within transmedia franchises. For a board game to emulate the plot of another text is adaptation; for a board game to produce emotional connections akin to those of another text is transmediation. Board games *can* transmediate, but not through story; rather, they transmediate through character and player affect.

Part Two

Understanding Media

4

Battlestar Galactica and Spimatic Meaning in Games

So say we all.

Admiral William Adama, *Battlestar Galactica*

The four ships circled each other, each pilot warily surveying the space around him. Each had flown from the *Galactica* on a routine training mission around a black hole and a purple planet. All was going according to plan until the *Galactica* sighted a disabled and abandoned Cylon Raider floating in space. The Cylons—robotic enemies of the human race, perpetrators of the destruction of the human homeworlds—were nowhere in sight and so the abandoned ship represented a chance to study this metallic species, to learn more about the enemies that threatened the continued existence of humankind. For each of the pilots, the mission suddenly changed—instead of routine training, each pilot would now simulate combat, as each was encouraged to fight the others to acquire the Cylon vessel (using only a simulation of combat, of course). Now in competition with each other, the four Viper pilots must use all three commands at their disposal—turbo thrust, force field, and laser torpedo—to bring the Raider back to the *Galactica* hanger deck....

Thirty years later, and across the table, another *Battlestar Galactica* appears. Only this time, the Cylons have not abandoned a disabled ship in outer space—instead, they are planting spies on board the *Galactica* itself. The Cylons have evolved, and now can create robots that look—and act—like human beings. For Admiral Adama, leader of the Human fleet, these Cylons represent a dangerous type of traitor: one that cannot be identified. Cylon spies might attempt to disrupt the workings of *Galactica*, reduce the food or fuel supply, or siphon the morale of the crew. To make matters even worse, many of these Cylon spies do not even know they are Cylons. President Laura Roslin until recently thought that she was a human, but she draws a card halfway through the game that reveals her true identity as a Cylon sleeper agent. Roslin looks around the board at her colleagues, people who were once her friends but are now her worst enemies....

Each of these games is based on a different television series named *Battlestar Galactica,* and each reflects a changing perception of space, time, and performance as they manifest in paratextual board games. Parker Brothers' 1978 *Battlestar Galactica* (*BSG78*) is based on the original 1978 television series. It is a relatively simple game, aimed at children between the ages of 7 and 14, and with a suggested playtime of 30 minutes. Developed as a family-friendly game, *BSG78* couldn't be more different from the complex gameplay mechanics and rules that must be learned to master Cory Konieczka's *Battlestar Galactica: The Board Game* (*BSG08*), a thoroughly immersive, narratively rich game that is based on the 2003 *Battlestar Galactica* remake. Involving player deception, cooperative action, and simulated combat, *BSG08* is expansive and expressive. A quick comparison of the rule books helps illuminate the contrast between the games: Parker Brothers' 1978 *Battlestar Galactica* rule "book" is a pamphlet, one double-sided piece of paper. Konieczka's *Battlestar Galactica: The Board Game's* rule book is a 32-page-long tome, augmented with online frequently asked questions, rulebook expansions, and errata corrections.

It is somewhat misleading, therefore, to directly compare these two games, as each is designed for different audiences, at different historical moments. However, examining each game for its paratextual connection to its antecedent text reveals much about the way paratextual games have developed into specific sites of performative mediation. In the first section of this book, I explored how Salen and Zimmerman's three primary schemas for understanding the critical impact of games—rules, play, and culture—manifest within and are complicated by paratextual board games. In this section, I look at specific characteristics that help to deepen our understanding of paratextuality in the contemporary media environment. I want to look not just at some primary schema for critiquing games, but also at the widely diverse array of contemporary game characteristics that help explain the contemporary playful media landscape.[1] To that end, this chapter focuses on two additional principles of paratextual board games as they manifest within the comparison between the two *Battlestar Galactica* board games.

Principle 7: Just as a media text takes place within a specific spatial-temporal environment, paratextual board games mirror this space/time amalgam via the board and the pacing of the game play.

Games transport players, giving them a different "sense of time and space": both *BSG* series highlight the unique spatial and temporal elements of outer space as a science fictional—genre environment, while these games mimic this spatial and temporal awareness via their play mechanics.[2] Moving beyond games, Bruce Sterling's conception of the "Spime"—a digital and physical trace of an object through both time and space—reflects a cyborgian presence within contemporary media technology which, in turn, links space and time in a digital context. As I explore later in this chapter, Spimes are physical objects that "begin and end as data." In Sterling's rather poetic words, Spimes are:

> manufactured objects whose informational support is so overwhelmingly extensive and rich that they are regarded as material instantiations of an immaterial system.... They are designed on screens, fabricated by digital means, and precisely tracked through space and time throughout their earthly sojourn.[3]

In other words, seeing an object as a Spime means taking into account the temporal structure that guides the object's development as well as its physical presence in the world.

By playing as specific characters with separate motivations, players help create a social aspect of role-play. This is reflected in the eighth principle of paratextual board games.

Principle 8: Paratextual board games can offer players the opportunity to mirror characteristics of particular characters within the specific spatial-temporal environment of the media text.

The original television show follows the remnants of humanity as they escape the Cylons, a deadly race of alien robots. The *Battlestar Galactica* must escort civilian ships carrying the last survivors of a massacre as they search for a world named Earth that houses the mythical thirteenth tribe of humankind. The reboot show tells a tale similar to the first, but with the added complication that the Cylons are able to replicate sentient models that look like and can mimic human physiology. For the characters as well as the audience, these humanoid robots problematize traditional notions of "personhood," as they develop personalities, human traits, and even biological compatibility—one of the major plot points of the reimagined series is that the offspring of a human and Cylon would lead humankind to its eventual salvation—forcing a reconception of what it means to be human.[4] The show's questioning of the nature of humanity manifests in the board game as well; its emphasis on robotics, sentience, and the ethical consideration of machines reveals a close correlation with our world today.[5] In terms of the board games, *BSG08* highlights this cyborgification through its use of moral decisions and player memory. By mirroring the characters' moral and ethical quandaries surrounding what it means to be human, *BSG08* asks us to question our own place within an automated digital media environment that encourages us to become Cylonic in our own lives.

Traditionally, board games have been seen to create a critical distance between theme and subject matter, to facilitate the development of what Huizinga calls the "magic circle," a space where the culture of the game supersedes the culture of "real life."[6] But paratextual board games also ask the reverse: reflecting a more integrated take on the magic circle, they require players to integrate their "real world" and diegetic concerns within the game space as well. We can see this in the way that, for example, knowledge of the different families in Chapter 7's *Game of Thrones* helps players understand the complex relationships depicted in the game. In terms of *Battlestar Galactica*, the moral issues brought up by a game like *BSG08* offer us a certain perception of contemporary culture. The specific mechanics that facilitate this understanding are encapsulated in the game board and the character role-play. Generally, as people play games, they "lower their barriers and reveal their true personalities."[7] When playing *BSG08*, however, players must not only keep hidden their true personalities, but might also have to play the role of the Cylon traitor.

To illustrate the way space and time come together in these games, I first look at the *Battlestar Galactica* games as specific moments in their diegetic universes. Next, I focus on the relationship between the characters in the game and the players of the game as key to creating meaning within that universe. Ultimately, playing a game that asks individuals to role-play, cooperate, and mistrust extends theories of paratextual board games beyond the schemas of rules/play/culture, and augments intimate connections to the contemporary media environment. The combination of computational thinking and emotional role-play remakes all players into cyborgs. Ultimately, even though only one or two players are Cylons within *BSG08,* we *all* become "Cylons" in the digital media environment.

Space and time in paratextual games

All paratextual board games create a sense of place. For *Star Trek: Expeditions,* as I describe in the next chapter, it is the planet Nibia. For *The Lord of the Rings,* it is Middle-earth. Not all places are fictional: the *Walking Dead* games take place in Atlanta. Both *Battlestar Galactica* board games attempt to replicate the "feel" of their requisite television program, but each does so using different game mechanics and aesthetics. In the case of *BSG78*, the specific game board aesthetics seem to draw the player into a *spatial* understanding of the cult world of *Battlestar Galactica*. For *BSG08*, the mechanics of game play, including the hidden Cylon mechanic and player interaction, highlight a more *temporal* understanding of the unfolding of the serial narrative of *Battlestar Galactica*. While both of these methods approach an audience's understanding of the "essence" of *Battlestar Galactica*, they hinge on a single premise: the player must be seen as a co-participant within the narrative itself in order to draw the player into the cult world of the show. Players of these games must navigate both their own player choice and the demands of the game itself in order to complete the play session. The mechanics and aesthetics of the game, as a collaboration between a technology and the individual, highlights both what is uniquely *algorithmic* about the human experience and what is distinctively *human* about technology.

In *BGS08*, players play as characters on board the *Galactica*, which is on the run from the Cylons. During each turn, a number of events happen that players must solve together. Events are solved by players contributing numbered cards to a pile; if the appropriate number is reached, then the event is solved. Each event might cost or provide one of four resources—food, fuel, population, and morale. Additionally, Cylons might attack or board the ship, and one (or more) players are "hidden" Cylons, sleeper agents that can attempt to subvert the card-number system and sabotage the ship. In *BSG78*, alternately, each player plays as an unnamed pilot fighting over a Cylon Raider. Using three strategies—turbo thrust (an additional role), force field (making another player lose a turn), or laser cannon (entering a firefight with a player)—each player attempts to haul the Raider back to Galactica.

According to Karl Bergström, Staffan Björk, and Sus Lundgren, effective game creation happens when the game *play* mirrors a particular game *design*. In other words, and in reference to *BSG08* specifically, "the close connection between the game and the TV-series can … result in a very strong emotional immersion … as players identify with their characters and the humans' goal to save humanity."[8] Indeed, both *Battlestar Galactica* series offer similar narratives, but approach them in vastly different ways. Lincoln Geraghty describes the new *Battlestar Galactica* as a "vindication of a show long gone"—the "reimagined" series is vastly more critically acclaimed, and he describes it as "far more a product of modern television programming than it is a throwback."[9] In discussing the differences between the two series, C. W. Marshall and Tiffany Potter argue, however, that "our familiarity with the earlier work informs how we interpret a given episode, and our analyses are the richer for it."[10] Interestingly, my game group's understanding of the two board games based on these shows is also richer for having played both: we found playing the *BSG08* game to be narratively satisfying in part because of the paucity of narrative in the *BSG78* game, and we enjoyed comparing the detail on the miniatures in *BSG08* to the ones in *BSG78*.

Instead of narrative exploration, the *BSG78* game highlights a spatial awareness of the original text. This is particularly relevant in keeping with the original text's focus on deep space: as Geraghty notes, the original 1978 series tended to draw "upon space exploration as a narrative template."[11] Typically (and usually pejoratively) seen to be a *Star Wars* "knock-off," the original series used the metaphor of humankind escaping the Cylons as a chance to depict space battles.[12] However, as Geraghty points out, "thanks to production values that promised groundbreaking special effects but instead delivered the same recycled fight sequences week after week," the show died prematurely.[13] These space battles often fell into a traditional trap of deep-space science fiction stories: the uniplanar depiction of space. Space is rarely conceptualized as three dimensional, as the spaceships all tend to orient in the same direction and attack each other from one plane. In her *Screening Space*, Vivian Sobchack calls this an "excess of surface," wherein the "hyperspace" of science fiction "is proudly two-dimensional—even in its depiction of three-dimensionality."[14] Such flattening of space ignores scientific realism for the aesthetics of familiar Earth-bound combat, where foes face off on the same dimensional plane.

The *BSG78* game cleverly mirrors Sobchack's excess of surface via its two-dimensional game board (Figure 4.1). The basic game play follows four Vipers engaged in mock combat to capture a Raider. At each corner of the game board, the *Galactica* sits in a different color matching the color of the player's Viper. The damaged Cylon Raider starts the game in the central space of the board. Each Viper starts on its similarly colored *Galactica*; and it is this color coding that provides the "third dimension" of space. The colors do not depict four different versions of the spaceship, but rather illustrate a three-dimensional spherical curve in two dimensions. Imagine that each corner *Galactica* is actually the same ship, the board curved into a sphere with the *Galactica* and the Cylon Raider at antipodal points. However, instead of being able to travel through the sphere (as the Vipers would in normal space), due to the limitations

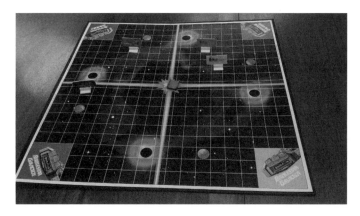

Figure 4.1 The *Battlestar Galactica* game board. *Battlestar Galactica: A Parker Brothers Game* ©Parker Brothers 1978. Photo by the author.

of the representation of three-dimensional space in a two-dimensional form, the Vipers are only able to travel on the outer edges of this sphere (except via the magic portal of the black hole, which, upon entering, the player can move to any other black hole space on the board—through the sphere, as it were). Aesthetically, this game board links the spatial economies of the original *Battlestar Galactica* television program with the spatial realities of board game play. In actual game play, these economies thus put the player in the same plane as the pilots (pun intended), who are trapped in the same science-fictional two-dimensional "excess of surface" as those in the original text. This spatial player/ character collusion invites identification with the media text and encourages immersion within the cult world.

In contrast, the *BSG08* game does not attempt to mirror the spatial environment of the original reboot text, focusing instead on the temporal unfolding of a narrative. The game board for *BSG08* depicts the *Galactica* in the center of the board and the Presidential ship *Caprica One* off to the side. Cylon Basestars, Raiders, and Heavy Raiders can attack around the board while the human civilian ships are positioned behind *Galactica*. Rather than a true spatial positioning of the ship, locations are marked in approximate areas, in line with the direction playing pieces are moved around the board, thus focusing on a temporal awareness of narrative rather than a spatial awareness of the ship (Figure 4.2).

BSG08 focuses on the temporal development of the narrative. This temporal awareness fits within the scope of the paratextual connection to the original text as well. The reboot *Battlestar Galactica* series uses "temporal displacement" to develop narrative complexity: flashforwards and flashbacks indicate changes in

Figure 4.2 The main section of the *Battlestar Galactica* game board. *Battlestar Galactica: The Board Game* ©Fantasy Flight Games 2008. Photo by the author.

an audience's understanding of events, while moments of unsure temporality limit audience knowledge.[15] The show's narrative trajectory also seems focused on temporality: episodes like "33" revolve around time passing in fixed amounts, and the series hinges on an uneven sense of temporal closure, what Glen Creeber calls a "flexi-narrative," in which episodic and serial narratives combine within "a complex exchange of narrative and character" development.[16]

Geraghty also alludes to this temporal complexity, arguing that the show uses both flashforwards and flashbacks to build up "audience expectation and contribute … to the must-see appeal of the series as a whole … [they] gave *Galactica* an epic quality."[17] Part of this epic quality comes from the narrative revelations throughout the show. Because some Cylons in the reboot appear human, there is a tension surrounding which characters will betray the others. Adding to the tension, many of these Cylons are "sleeper agents" who themselves do not know whether they are human or Cylon. Robert W. Moore describes this "question of personhood" as the central theme of *Battlestar Galactica*, a narrative hook for viewers.[18]

The *BSG08* board game mirrors this tension within the game time via a specific mechanism, the hidden Cylon mechanic. At the beginning of the game, players are randomly dealt a "loyalty" card. These cards identify if a player is or is not a hidden Cylon agent. If the player is a hidden Cylon agent, he or she may choose to remain hidden in order to try and surreptitiously sabotage the ship by depleting fuel, food, morale, and/or population, the four resources on the ship. The human players must try to keep these constant, or even increase them. The Cylon player(s) try to disrupt them or reduce them. These resources are lost throughout the game play, and there is a temporal countdown feeling as they tick ever further down to zero on the board. It is possible that no player will be dealt a Cylon loyalty card in the first round of the game; there is a second round of loyalty card dealing during which there will definitely be one hidden Cylon card dealt. This means that the first round may contain a sleeper agent, a player who doesn't even know if he or she was a Cylon, but is "activated" for the final few rounds.

The gameplay mechanic of the hidden Cylon in *BSG08* thus resembles the temporal structure of the original show's narrative, in the same way Knizia's *Lord of the Rings* parallels the book's structure. The tension in the game arrives from not knowing who the Cylon is, and, for those who are not the traitor, waiting for the Cylon to reveal himself or herself. Like the television series, which increases tension both by hiding the character's true loyalty and by postponing narrative closure via cliffhangers, the *BSG08* board game replicates this feeling of uncertainty by increasing suspicion and fear among the players. Bergström, Björk, and Lundgren specifically describe *BSG08*'s gameplay design aesthetic through its "dynamical patterns [of] Communication and Collaboration using the mechanical patterns teams and mutual enemies in combination with asymmetric abilities."[19] That is, players must play cooperatively but also defensively in order to "out" the Cylon player as Cylon. The game offers different playing styles depending on the role that one is fulfilling. Players that are playing as the Cylon can engage in what Lewis Pulsipher calls "turtling," or sitting "on the sidelines, avoiding conflict, while other players fight a debilitating war." Other Cylons might actively reveal themselves in order to deal the most devastating, overt damage. In contrast, players that are not Cylons may try "sandbagging," or "pretending to be worse off than you are, to somehow disguise how well you're doing," to hide their success from the traitor.[20] Deception is a key element of the game.

A side-effect of both this spatial and temporal structure for each game is that the players must inhabit these various aspects of the original text in order for the game play to function. That is, in *BSG78*, players must subscribe to the spatial rules—"you may move your Viper horizontally and vertically, but *not* diagonally," indicating a two-dimensional playing field—in order to mimic being part of the television series, while in *BSG08* players must act the way their loyalty card prescribes in order to further the temporal structure of the game.[21] Although players do have the freedom to move and act as they see fit, the demands of the games determine most of this activity; players themselves become pawns in the larger paratextual connection between the games and the cult worlds. Players in either game have to integrate their own decision-making into the rules of the game—as they do with *Arkham Horror* or *A Game of Thrones: The Board Game*—turning themselves from players into active co-participants in the development of each game's game play.

To this end, the players' relationship with the game can be said to be Spime-like. As mentioned above, the Spime is a technosocial construct first developed by futurist and science fiction author Bruce Sterling. A portmanteau of *space* and *time*, the concept of the Spime defines a trackable entity, a "protagonist of a documented process. It is an historical entity with an accessible, precise trajectory."[22] A Spime is both the digital and the tangible moments of an object's life. In an age when we can follow the history of an object from its very (digital) conception to its final (physical) destruction, the tangibility of an object describes only one portion of a much longer cycle. For example, when I purchased the 1978 *Battlestar Galactica* board game from eBay, my copy of that game did not begin and end with the physical object. Instead, from the publisher's first design notes, to the seller inputting data into eBay's servers, to the (eventual) barcode associated with the game when I donate it to my school, that game becomes part of a process that integrates digital and physical into one—a Spime. And it is a personal Spime—it defines just *that* copy of the game, *that* digital imprint. In addition, any meta-information recorded about the production of the game— the type of paper used, the fonts, marketing, or even the publisher's website— becomes part of the book's Spimatic identity. That game's existence as I play it is just one part—often the shortest part—of its Spimatic life cycle. A Spimatic examination of game play would see the interactive participation of the player at multiple times in the temporal process as generative of production. Spimatic game play doesn't describe just one way of experiencing this relationship: as every Spime is unique, so too is every player's interaction in this cycle. Applied to the mechanics of paratextual board games, players' journeys throughout a game, their narrative and gameplay trajectories, become Spimatic as they must begin and end their experiences of the game as moments both immaterial and material. The paratextual board game becomes just one node on the player's individual journal through the franchise.

In *BSG78* players are both comrades (all are from *Galactica*) and competitors. But in *BSG08*, cooperation between players is predicated on suspicion and fear. The "traitor mechanic," as Linderoth describes it, means that "the motives of anyone suggesting a specific strategy can be questioned"—players are uncertain about the loyalty and allegiance of the others.[23] At the same time, individual players may be aware that their own allegiance can shift: the second dealing of the loyalty cards can change the state of the player. Just as the Spime is an unstable entity, and can be seen to develop through multiple instantiations, so too are the players' roles within *BSG08* mutable within the game's structure.

This Spimatic cycle, defined by and inclusive of the physical object at its heart, can be applied to the development of the play of a paratextual board game. Starting from the position of pre-knowledge going into the game, based on the players' variable experiences with the original text, the paratextual board game develops and adds to the cult text depending on both the previous knowledge of the player and the ongoing play during the game. For instance, in Chapter 8's *Doctor Who: The Interactive Electronic Interactive Board Game*, players' knowledge of the first series of *Doctor Who* may help structure their play. Playing *BSG08* with no working knowledge of *Battlestar Galactica* (as in the case of one of the players in my board game group) created a different player journey through the game than it did for me (having spent years watching and writing about the show).[24] Applying the concept of the Spime to paratextual board games thus allows us to note and augment the saliency of player activity and knowledge within the game play, and the perception of consumption and play as separate *practices* shifts to see them as one cogent and chronological *process* instead. Paratextual board games are uniquely positioned nodes in a network of player activity.

As a concept, the Spime expands on the technological infrastructure of human discourse; yet, it has traditionally been associated with technological developments. To that end, the concept of the Spime has been usefully applied in the past to multiple aspects of technology.[25] But the Spime could also usefully be applied to issues of culture as well as to issues of technology—culture and technology not being opposed so much as complementary. As James Allen-Robertson and David Beer note, focusing solely on technological infrastructure ignores much value in "resonance between [the Spime] and the range of debates that are occurring in sociology and across the social sciences with regard to possible viable future directions" of cultural research. They take a meta-approach to the Spime in their study, viewing the Spime as an *idea* that can be traced throughout space and time, effectively giving a Spimatic trace to a nonphysical object. In the same way as Allen-Robertson and Beer treat ideas as "objects that can be followed and visualised along their lifecourse," a Spimatic reading illuminates the patterns of process and progress of nonphysical entities, like the experience of game play.[26] This ascribing of autonomy to both physical and digital objects augments notions of game participation.

By following a player's Spimatic journey with a paratextual board game—from his or her introduction to Lovecraft, through his or her playing *Arkham Horror*, and finishing with his or her return (re)read "Call of Cthulhu"—one could theoretically see the birth of a new form of creative product, one formed not just from corporate control and organization, but also from player involvement in the creation of narrative meaning, a hybrid system of production and consumption.[27] For Sterling, such cyborgian opportunities develop through time. He calls our current society "synchronic," which places:

> high value on the human engagement with time. We human beings are time-bound entities. So are all our creations.... So we are not object, but processes. Our names are not nouns, but verbs. Our existence does not precede time or postdate time—we personify time.[28]

For players of *BSG08*, as well as for the characters within the *Battlestar Galactica* reboot, this focus on time and temporal structure highlights the continual process of *becoming*.[29] Just as the Spime represents a technosocial structure wherein digital machines can communicate and act autonomously, so too does *Battlestar Galactica* highlight how machines can be autonomous entities. As Geraghty notes, this "inherently American" fear of automation manifests in science fiction texts that examine cyborgs, robots, and automated technology.[30] The Spime as a mode of paratextual game play is both a representation of that fear and a metaphor for understanding how to combat it. Particularly relevant to *Battlestar Galactica*, Sue Thomas notes that the Spime makes us all *cyborgian*:

> So, a spime is a phenomenon that exists at various times either virtually, as data, or materially, as physical object, or both, depending upon its cycle? Well, we can easily grasp that notion because today we are very accustomed to sometimes inhabiting cyberspace with our virtual personae and manipulating virtual materials such as emails, images, and other items; and other times inhabiting physical space such as streets, fields, and houses and manipulating physical materials such as bottles, books, and furniture.[31]

In many respects, paratextual games themselves force players to become cyborgian; as Berland notes, "tabletop boardgames encourage or require ... players [to] engage in computational thinking, [and] they require that players talk about their computational thinking and engage in the social aspects of computational literacy."[32] *Battlestar Galactica* constructs different ways of looking at what it means to be a person versus what it means to be a cyborg, as examining player interaction becomes a key attribute both of the shows and of the games.[33]

Playing human, playing Cylon

The Spime offers us a technological metaphor for understanding the interactive relationship between the paratextual board game, the cult media world, and the game player. Specifically in terms of the two *Battlestar Galactica* shows and their paratextual board games, this relationship can be seen in two related areas: player interaction as a style of game play that reflects the characters of the shows, and memory as a game mechanic that exposes the relationship between the game system and the human player.

Like *The Walking Dead: The Board Game*, the *BSG78* game relies heavily on competition as player interaction. Players not only race to try to reach the damaged Cylon Raider, but also engage in simulated firefights and forced landings in order to take the Raider from each other. This combative player engagement is ironic given the background of the game itself, which describes the combat within the diegetic world of the game as simulated based on the cooperation of the *characters* (the game is thus a double simulation, as the actions *players* take simulate the actions that the *characters* take, which themselves are simulated). That is, the nameless Viper pilots within the diegetic world of the game are supposedly on the same "side" in the war with the Cylons (they are all from *Galactica*) but are ordered to, as the rules state, "*simulate* actual combat conditions."[34] The mission that appears to be a practice run becomes competitive. Thus, instead of fighting the evil Cylons, players must fight their supposedly cooperative fellow humans.

One way that absence of cooperation among players makes a connection between the cult world of *BSG78* and the game itself is through the three types of action cards players can use. Throughout the game, players face off against each other by spinning a spinner and moving that number of spaces. However, players have nine cards at their disposal to use in any way they see fit: three "turbo thrust" cards, three "force field" cards, and three "laser torpedo" cards. These cards roughly match the three abilities that Viper pilots have in the original *Battlestar Galactica* television series, indicated by the three buttons on the Viper's yoke (Figure 4.3).

Figure 4.3 Yoke of a Colonial Viper. *Battlestar Galactica* ©Universal TV 1978.

To block one of these commands, opposing players have three "evasive maneuver" cards, which negate the effect of the force field or laser cannon. Players can use these cards at any time to countermand the Command orders of their fellow pilots/enemies. Because there are so few evasive maneuver cards in relation to the command cards, players have to remember what their opponents played and how many of a particular type they might have left.

From the standpoint of player interaction, the game quickly loses the sense that all players are on the same side, leading to a more competitive sense of fun. The competitive nature of the game means that players are soon pitted against each other rather than working together, as might be seen in a more contemporary cooperative game (like *BSG08* or *Star Trek: Expeditions*), despite the underlying connection between characters. This player competitiveness-instead-of-cooperation ends up distancing the player from the cult world of *Battlestar Galactica* (1978). Instead of investing the players within the Spime—itself constructed from the interaction between the game/narrative/player elements—the *BSG78* game turns the players into faceless entities.

In contrast, the *BSG08* game relies most heavily on a cooperative player interaction, with a dash of competition implied by the hidden Cylon mechanic. Players must recognize that they are on the same side, but also may not be able to trust one or two people to be truthful in their interactions. The game sows mistrust among players, as all *actions* in the game are observable, but the *motivations* of the players/characters are unknown. Like the collaborative disease-prevention game *Pandemic*, *BSG08* "encourages important collaboration and active listening skills," as players must focus on each other's playing styles and dialogue to try to figure out which of their teammates could be a Cylon.[35] This directly mirrors one of the main themes of the show, that Cylons might be hidden among the crew because they are indistinguishable from the humans, and emphasizes the digital hybridity of human identity in the twenty-first century. Indeed, the notion of what it means to be human or robotic in *Battlestar Galactica* (2003) takes on additional meaning in the age of digital technology, as our everyday interaction with machines is making a more complex ethical intrusion in our understanding of humanity. Techno-philosopher David Gunkel argues that we need a new ethical stance on machines:

> What is happening right now in this new century, the 21st century, is that machines more and more are moving away from being intermediaries between human beings and taking up a position as an interactive subject. So the computer and other kinds of machines like the computer—robots, machines with Artificial Intelligence (AI) and algorithms—are no longer just instruments through which we act, but are becoming "the other" with whom we interact.[36]

In other words, as machines become more autonomous, it will become necessary to stop viewing them as free of ethical concerns. For the Cylons in *Battlestar Galactica*, the ambiguity around the nature of their humanity takes the central focus. The additional element that the hidden Cylon in *BSG08* is also a fellow game player adds an unexpected level of emotional attachment and immersion in the game.[37]

This theme of attachment, like many of the underlying ideas of the 2003 *Battlestar Galactica* television show, is continually present within other games as well. Like the transmedia pathos that is developed in *The Walking Dead: The Board Game,* or the material attachment to *Star Trek: Fleet Captains* that I describe in the next chapter, the attachment in *BSG08* highlights what game developer and artist Mary Flanagan calls games' abilities to open "a window on the values, hopes, and beliefs" of a particular culture at a particular time. One particular theme is that of hybridity. As we have seen in the previous chapter, games do not just emerge from a culture but rather help to illustrate what is happening in a culture at a particular moment; in her book *Critical Play,* Flanagan uses the example of board games of the nineteenth century, which illustrate a "country facing immigration, urbanization, and the rise of industry. The middle class, with growing incomes and expanding leisure time, encouraged children to play games to develop thinking skills and for moral instruction."[38] The original *Battlestar Galactica* did not attempt to create ambiguity in the binaries established: Cylons were bad, humans were good. *Battlestar Galactica* (1978) has been discussed as a show heavily influenced both by classic Westerns and the Mormon faith, both of which are equally binaristic in their depiction of good versus evil.[39] For Geraghty, the show "relies on familiar themes of the Puritan Errand and the belief in a divine mission." He goes on to note that:

> This *space opera* role-play replicated the American colonial experience as played out between Puritan settlers and Indian inhabitants, yet it also alluded to the Mormon faith's particular belief in ... God. Similarities between the twelve colonies' search for Kobol and the journey of Joseph Smith to re-establish Eden in America recounted in the Book of Mormon may not have been coincidental, as Glen A. Larson ... was a Mormon.[40]

For Marshall and Potter, the newer *Battlestar Galactica* "explicitly engages current American culture," but does so "using devices that draw upon a wide range of mythic tropes and religious traditions."[41] In this way, the show is a hybrid form of literary allusion, destabilized narrative, and participatory audiences.[42] Rather than coming down on one side of a political debate or the other, the 2003 *Battlestar Galactica* series tends to resist "strict antitheses" and instead embraces multiplicity and other views.[43]

The *BSG08* game works in a similar algorithmic fashion as does *Arkham Horror*, but instead of *unstructure,* the players' focus on rules allows a strict adherence to the "procedural rhetoric" of the game.[44] This procedural rhetoric creates an argument within the game's structure, and by following the rules, players follow that argumentative structure. One consequence of this procedural rhetoric, then, is that in order to follow the rules, players must subscribe to the automated processes that rules allow. While playing as a Cylon, no matter how much one may be tempted to help the human characters and save *Galactica* and humanity, the game functions best (and as planned) if the Cylon works against the group. This performative aspect of the game, as Kurt Lancaster argues, cannot happen without rules: "rules ... situate players in prescribed rules and demarcate what kind of fantasy they will play."[45] The game prescribes meaning to players' actions: the player, despite having the freedom to choose what cards to play and what moves to make, must ultimately subsume his or her own actions to the actions of the game. In effect, this turns the player from an autonomous agent into an algorithmic structure unto himself or herself.

Here, since the show has a "renewed focus on the fundamental nature of what it means to be human," the argument about the nature of humanity becomes crucial to understanding how the game functions as a Spimatic node within a continuum linking the cult text, the paratextual game world, and the player.[46] For players, choice is prescribed by the game's mechanisms, and the game mechanisms are prescribed by the cult text upon which it is based. The Spime functions precisely because these elements enjoin and engender a particular trajectory through time and space while experiencing the idea of *Battlestar Galactica*.

Yet, although generalizable, individual player interaction is highly personalized. The use of memory within (and without) the game highlights this personalization of the Spime, especially as it demonstrates familiarity (or unfamiliarity) with the cult text. There are multiple steps required to navigate any round in *BSG08*. During a player's turn, he or she will draw particular skill cards based on the character they are playing. Each character has particular skills—Admiral William Adama has three Leadership skills and two Tactics skills; Sharon "Boomer" Valerii has two Tactics skills, two Piloting skills, and one Engineering skill. Players collect as many cards as they have skills, and each skill is color coded. After drawing the skill cards, players can move to another location on the ship (largely, it doesn't matter how one gets there, once again de-emphasizing the importance of "space" in *BSG08*) and complete an action like repairing the ship or destroying a Cylon Raider. Finally, the player draws a "crisis card" that usually invokes a particularly difficult aspect of the *Battlestar Galactica* universe and narrative that the group collectively has to try to combat. Some of these cards need many skills to overcome the crisis; players secretly play any number of their skills to try to defeat the crisis. The Cylon player can try to disrupt the skill check by playing cards that count against it.

Both Event cards and Skill checks reference particular moments from the show, focusing on players' specific viewing memories; for instance, event crisis cards display moments such as "Rescue Caprica Survivors," in which Starbuck travels back to the planet Caprica to try to rescue any survivors. Like with the *Babylon 5* role-playing game Lancaster describes, so too does *Battlestar Galactica* embed "tropes from the television series in order to ensure that players become transported to the same imaginary environment."[47] Losing one fuel and one food but gaining population makes sense in the context of "Rescue Caprica Survivors"—when Starbuck went back to Caprica, she did expend food and fuel, but did add to the population as well. If she had not gone, the crew would have lost morale. The same type of narrative connection occurs in other games, like the *Game of Thrones: The Card Game*, when character attributes are drawn from the television series.

The Cylon attack cards also reference specific moments, but narratively may not make sense in the context of the particular game as it is being played. In this case, memories of the show (as well as memories players may have of other elements within the game) may complicate the Spimatic connection between the text—game player. For example, the Cylon attack card "Thirty-Three" references the episode "33," which I mentioned earlier in this chapter (Figure 4.4). In that episode, *Galactica* is being hotly pursued by the Cylon fleet. Despite using its Faster-than-Light (FTL) jump capabilities, which should hypothetically allow it to escape, *Galactica* could not evade the Cylons. This meant that the crew of *Galactica* had to reset the FTL and jump as quickly as possible—and the fastest they could make it was 33 minutes. Of course, as the FTL jumps are physiologically disruptive, the fleet and crew could get no rest during this flight, leading to tension and drama.

The "Thirty-Three" card illustrates this close narrative connection to the show with its "special rule," named *Relentless Pursuit*. Unlike other Cylon attack cards, once this card is resolved, it is kept in play. This means that the Cylons, as in the episode, would continue to attack as long as it was in play. However, the other part of the special rule seemed to counter the very threat posed by the episode: "If this card is in play when the fleet jumps, shuffle it back into the Crisis Deck." For those in my game group who had never seen *Battlestar Galactica*, this statement made little difference: once we jumped to evade the Cylons, the card was over. But for those in my game group with a memory of this episode, this additional aspect of the rule made no sense. If the card was referencing a particular narrative moment, why would it contradict that moment by having the Cylons leave *Galactica* alone once the ship had jumped? That was the whole point of the attack, after all.

The individual memory of the relationship between the game, the cult text, and the player acts as a personal variant within the Spime of *Battlestar Galactica*. In my group, two of us knew the show and were surprised at the card; two did not know the show and played as if nothing was amiss. To resolve this, we turned to another cyborgian aspect of the paratextual board game, the Internet forum.

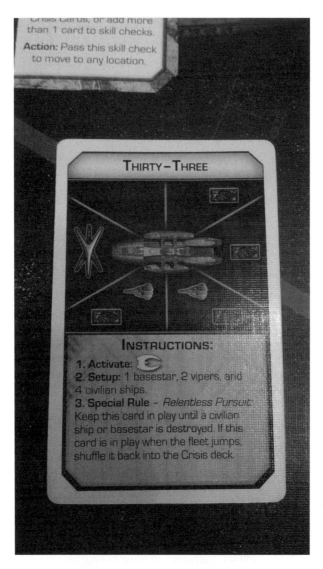

Figure 4.4 "Thirty-Three" Cylon attack card. *Battlestar Galactica: The Board Game* ©Fantasy Flight Games 2008. Photo by the author.

Individual players have particular experiences with a game that others may not, leading to moments personalized with the text. There exist online hundreds of spaces for players to ask and answer game FAQs, or frequently asked questions that can interact with the game mechanics, facilitating new rules or changes to the game.[48] My group searched for FAQs about this particular card—the search results reveals scores of posts of people asking the same questions that we did.

In another personalization of the game Spime, then, many of these answers connected the cult text to the game via their own player-generated solution to the issue. One person writing on *boardgames.stackexchange.com* came up with three different interpretations of the card, each of which was defended with reference to the show.[49] Comments on the page agree or disagree with the different interpretations, and some offer additional "house rules" solutions, such as "you shuffle thirty-three into the top 3 cards of the crisis deck. This makes things quite a bit more difficult." On boardgamegeek, Milan Rancic (username MilanGM) altered the appearance of the card and changed the rule—from "shuffle it back into the Crisis Deck" to "put it back on top of the Crisis deck," which means it will be drawn over and over again. He has uploaded a .jpg of the new card so that others can shuffle it into their decks (Figure 4.5).

Unlike video games, which have algorithms that are impossible to change—or, at the very least, are far more difficult for the average player to change—board games offer the opportunity to manipulate and change the rules underlying the game—who among us hasn't changed a rule in a game to make the game harder or easier at times? An exemplary instance of this is the culturally used rule in

Figure 4.5 Fan-made "Thirty-Three" Cylon attack card. *Battlestar Galactica: The Board Game* ©Milan Rancic 2010.

the game *Monopoly* that instructs players to put the money collected by the bank via community chest or chance cards into the "pot" in the middle of the board to be collected by the player that lands on "free parking." Such a rule does exist not within *Monopoly*'s "official" rules but rather within the "house rules" played by many households.

Yet "house rules" also change the fundamental structure of the game—playing with the revised "Thirty-Three" card may make the game more akin to the original show, but it also changes the game itself from what the designers intended. Such manipulation reveals another hybrid aspect of the paratextual board game: not just that playing the game by the rules turns players into Spimatic cyborgs, but also that it provides them the ability to change the system itself. The game is not as powerful as those playing it; in this respect, the audience can take control of the narrative through their Spimatic connection within and around the system.

"So say we all..."

In the pilot episode of 2003's *Battlestar Galactica*, Admiral William Adama invokes a mantra to unite the survivors of the Cylon massacre: "so say we all." It is a saying replete with meaning. Indicative of a group mentality, the mantra coheres the fleet, the civilians, the government, and the military into a single unit. They are all united, all acting as one. The *BSG08* game also asks its players to unite, to act as one. But as in the pilot episode, when Sharon "Boomer" Valerii is revealed to be a Cylon sleeper agent, so too do players of *BSG08* have to contend that "we all" do not "so say" exactly the same things. However, rather than through out-and-out combat, it is through dialogue with the other players, skillful listening to conversation, and observational memory that players are able to discern which of their friends is actually a hidden agent. As Lancaster describes, understanding the character one is playing in the game means "verbally interact[ing] with each other."[50]

The notion that one can be both a teammate and a traitor is highlighted in the *BSG78* game as well, although in that game the diegetic need to pit solider against solider confuses, rather than augments, the gameplay mechanics and player interaction. Simulating combat, the game does not offer the same opportunities for player cohesion between cult narrative and paratextual board game. This cohesion, which I have identified as Spimatic in this chapter, relies on the individual player being able to make connections between these objects.

Examining paratextual board games through the lens of the Spime allows us to see them not as separate entities, but rather as one continuous correlation: here, the *idea* of *Battlestar Galactica*. BSG08, in this vein, is just one node within the larger, but individual, understanding of what *Battlestar Galactica* can be. If, as in the previous chapter, the transmediated aspects of paratextual board games manifest through player affect, then it is this affect that coheres the multiple parts together. As Sterling notes of the development of the Spime:

> technocultures do not abolish one another in clean or comprehensive ways. Instead, new capacities are layered onto older ones. The older technosocial order gradually loses its clarity, crumbles, and melts away under the accumulating weight of the new.[51]

In this case, the Spime of *Battlestar Galactica* as a whole is built by not just our experiences with one aspect of the text/game, but rather with all of them together.

For Kurt Lancaster, the *Babylon 5* role-playing game allows players to "immerse themselves in this same kind of wonder as found in *Babylon 5* … [it] configures players" within the game space to act and participate in certain ways.[52] As the paratextual board game illustrates, the generative potential of player performance within the game does not just happen at specific moments of reception, but rather becomes emblematic of the entire process of interpretation. Players are always-already imbricated within the game/text system, from start to finish. New concepts in technological development, including the Spime, can be usefully applied to noncorporeal procedures, like media creation and game play. Applying the theories of the Spime to paratextual game play portends a more emotive, affective *process* of interpretation. Just as the Spime exists through both space and time, so too do these *Battlestar Galactica* games parallel the spatial and temporal situations of their requisite texts, and in doing so, they draw their players into that world.

Mutability and Materiality in *Star Trek*

A balance of power—the trickiest, most difficult, dirtiest game of them all, but the only one that preserves both sides....

Captain James T. Kirk, Star Trek

The planet Nibia is in crisis. Rebel forces have taken control of the capital. An energy reactor powering the planet has ruptured, throwing the citizens into a panic. And to top it off, both the Klingon Empire and the United Federation of Planets have sent emissaries to try to negotiate a treaty with the unaligned world. The Federation team, consisting of Captain James Tiberius Kirk, Commander Spock, Dr. Leonard "Bones" McCoy, and Communications Office Nyota Uhura, beam down to the planet. Only by working together can the group hope to solve all three crises at the same time. While Kirk is using every point of his *Diplomacy* and *Command* status (currently at a high level of 10) to negotiate with the Nibian President, Spock is helping to rebuild the power generator with his *Analysis* and *Engineering* skills. As a fellow science officer, Dr. McCoy is lending support to Spock, while Uhura is putting all her *Stealth* power to good use fighting the rebels. With these crises on their hands, the officers will need to muster as many supplies, additional crew members, and resources as they can in order to save the planet from ecological disaster, find out who is leading the rebel forces (spoiler alert: it is the Klingons), and usher in a new wave of peace and prosperity for the Nibian people by allying them with the Federation.

Elsewhere, across the table, flotilla of Federation ships approaches a fleet of Klingon destroyers. Already having placed control influence on a number of sectors, the Klingon fleet is attempting to amass more control by constructing a Starbase along the Federation border. The *IKS Maht-H'a* is at Yellow Alert and is in danger of being destroyed by the combined forces of the *USS Enterprise* (NCC-1701-A) and the *USS Enterprise* (NCC-1701-E). Scarred and battle-weary, the *Maht-H'a* plays one crew card to end her turn, hoping that K'Ehleyr (Commander Worf's one-time flame and emissary to the Federation) will protect her from the dual assault. Still, as they say, "*batlh Hegh!*"[1]

Both of the games described above allow players to explore new worlds, help them to seek out new life and new civilizations, and ask them to boldly go where few games have gone before: into the realm of clickable miniatures. With a half-century lifespan, the *Star Trek* franchise is particularly well-suited for paratextual board games that invoke different eras, different characters, and different narrative structures. Indeed, in the fifty years since the original series premiered, over thirty different *Star Trek* paratextual board games have been published, from complex war games (e.g., Greg Costikyan and Doug Kaufman's 1985 *Star Trek: The Adventure Game*) to relatively simple spin-and-move games (e.g., 1992's *Star Trek: The Final Frontier*). These original paratextual games attempt to place the player within the universe of *Star Trek*. Part of the reason so many games have been developed is the large narrative world of *Star Trek*, which has continually expanded since 1963. The premiere of a new series, for example, *The Next Generation* (1987), or a new film, for example, *Star Trek II: The Wrath of Khan* (1982) helps to spur developers to release games. The expansive *Star Trek* franchise allows players to become part of "a brand, a world, and a set of characters that exist across clothing, toys, videogames, a film, ads, books, comics, DVDs, CDs, and many other media platforms."[2] These paratextual games deepen the experience of the *Star Trek* world and facilitate player immersion in the *Star Trek* franchise.

In this chapter, I look at how both Reiner Knizia's *Star Trek: Expeditions* and Mike Elliott, Bryan Kinsella, and Ethan Pasternack's *Star Trek: Fleet Captains* integrate and manipulate characters and characteristics within two parallel *Star Trek* universes. Each game is based on an iteration of *Star Trek*. *Fleet Captains* is based on the "Prime Universe" franchise made famous by Gene Roddenberry in the 1960s, and *Expeditions* is based on "Alternate Timeline" franchise constructed as a reboot by J. J. Abrams in the 2000s. The game based on the Prime universe, *Fleet Captains*, integrates all the original *Star Trek* iterations (*Star Trek*, *The Next Generation*, *Deep Space Nine*, *Voyager*, and *Enterprise*) in one game world, eliding both the temporal differences between series (the original series took place about 70 years before *The Next Generation*) and the larger cult plots of the shows (in the game, as I will discuss, the Federation is fighting the Klingon Empire, a plot specific to the original series and tangential to *The Next Generation*, rather than *Deep Space Nine* or *Voyager*). As I will discuss later in this chapter, while integrating aspects of all the series, *Fleet Captains* does not concentrate as heavily on *Star Trek: Enterprise* (2001–05). Potentially, as I describe, this could be because *Enterprise*, as a prequel, sits in an uneasy relationship with the other series, and creates its own "Prime" universe narrative, complicating the cohesiveness of the *Star Trek* whole. *Fleet Captains* centers on the conflict between the Federation and the Klingons, and each player controls one fleet of ships, broken into different flotillas, that battle each other in an expanse of unexplored space. This "best-of" the *Star Trek* series serves as an acknowledgment of the reach and influence of the original universe of *Star Trek*, celebrating rather than extending the series.

In contrast, *Expeditions* is a cooperative game based on the Abrams movie series, and features characters who have a number of differently themed missions to accomplish. Given the film's emphasis on a Romulan enemy, it is telling that the game concentrates on the more traditional Klingon enemy—the game's narrative seems to jump past that of the original film to follow a more serialized storyline (see Chapter 7). Much like in the film, each of the main characters has unique attributes and particular strengths; the characters can combine their strengths to accomplish their missions. While cooperation is certainly a theme within the 2009 film (all the characters have to learn to work together, despite their differences), the film is much more focused on space combat, so a more competitive mechanic in the game might have seemed more appropriate for connecting the paratextual board game to the film. The fact that the game is largely cooperative, therefore, is an important factor in how the game connects to the larger cult world and how it recreates the "experience" of *Star Trek*. *Expeditions* extends the narrative in time as well as in space, opening up unexplored possibilities and adventures for the new crew of the revamped *Enterprise*.

Both games manifest similar aspects of paratextual board games as they connect to the *Star Trek* franchise. First, utilizing the WizKids HeroClix system, a "flexible game system ... that aims to simulate the action" of the game's requisite text, both games feature miniature figurines of people and ships to model elements within the *Star Trek* universe.[3] For both *Fleet Captains* and *Expeditions,* the HeroClix figures mirror the characters and ships from the *Star Trek* universe and make use of a mutable base that "clicks" into different positions. Each position indicates a shifting set of attributes to simulate power loss (clicking down) or healing (clicking up). The collectible nature of HeroClix turns many WizKids games into "starter sets," with booster and expansion packs released with additional models that add to the game play, collectability, and narrative developments within the world of the game. As Geraghty describes, the physicality of the objects helps cohere the object to the player.[4] This focus on materiality within the paratextual board game world leads to the ninth principle of paratextual board games:

Principle 9: The materiality of the game pieces in paratextual board games facilitates fan interaction with the game as a system while also externalizing the game as an additional episode within the media franchise.

In the case of *Expeditions,* the figures of Kirk, Spock, McCoy, and Uhura (and Scotty, Chekov, and Sulu in the expansion pack) offer an opportunity for players to interact with the world of the game while also expanding the storyworld via external identification. Like "feelies"—video game artifacts, and collectibles described by Ian Peters—these HeroClix figures "serve as an extension of a game's fictional world."[5] Using the figurines allows players to see Kirk, Spock, McCoy, and Uhura on the planet, and to perform new episodes within the *Star Trek* franchise. In contrast, the numerous HeroClix model ships in *Fleet Captains* (there are 24 ships in the base set, with an additional 24 included with both the Romulan Empire and Dominion expansion packs) not only give players the chance to try out different combinations of ships, but also encourage a sense of collection: as Geraghty describes of fan collecting, the value of a particular object may not be "based on quality, condition or rarity but is found in the fact that such items can help to complete [the fan's] collection."[6] At the same time, the very materiality of these pieces lends tactile and sensual pleasure to the game: opening the pieces and clicking the bases becomes pleasurable in and of itself, in contrast to the ethereal and emotional pleasures the original media text might generate for fans.

Second, in contrast to their material components, both games also use highly mutable elements as an aspect of their game play. The replay value of the games is high because of the randomized nature of the game board (in *Fleet Captains*) and the missions (in *Expeditions*). In *Expeditions,* for example, each of the three missions the players attempt to complete have different narrative paths, potentially leading players in different directions each time the game is played. In *Fleet Captains,* the entire game board is constructed by laying hexagonal cards at random, producing different pathways through the game that can radically change the engagement of players with the game play. The mutable elements of each game suggest randomization within the play, and lead to the tenth principle of paratextual board games:

Principle 10: Mutable elements randomize game play while also reinforcing the paratextual game structure.

In the previous chapter, I discussed how the *Battlestar Galactica* games highlight the automation and cyborgification of the digital world through a Spimatic analysis of the interactive mechanics within the game. Principle 10 extends this discussion by approaching Axel Bruns' notion of "produsage" from the standpoint of user-created game play. Produsage is the intersection of production and usage within a digital environment, and looks not just at the way individual texts become converged online, but also at how nothing is ever *finished*—everything is always *in process*.[7] Similarly, each of these *Star Trek* games is never just *a* game; each is always a game *in process*. I can never point to any one play session as the quintessential "*Star Trek* paratextual board game experience" and this is crucial to the relationship the games have with their requisite texts. The world of *Star Trek* is also always *in process* and never seems complete: as a franchise of multiple iterations, the series includes narrative gaps that facilitate additional moments of narrative building. *Star Trek* is one of the most franchised television series, with an original series spawning three sequel series, a prequel series, six original series films, and four new series films, as well as the addition of three alternate timeline reboot films with their canonized graphic novel series, and that's not counting the ancillary products and spin-offs, including the animated series, the novels, the comics, and all the fan-created productions.[8] Although similar in terms of structure and aesthetic elements, the additional iterations of the *Star Trek* franchise make it harder and harder to characterize "*Star Trek*" as any one particular entity. The franchise, as Geraghty points out, "continues to change and adapt for a new audience."[9] By examining, first, the materiality of the games and then, the mutable aspects of each of the games, I demonstrate how the series and cult world of *Star Trek* is continually changing and shifting, mutable in its textuality.

Playing (with) multiple *Star Trek*s

Although both games use similar components, the game play of *Fleet Captains* and *Expeditions* are quite different from one another. In *Fleet Captains*, each player controls an armada, using those ships to explore space, to build Starbase stations, and to engage in battle with the other players' ships. The player who earns 10 victory points, by completing missions, surviving encounters, or building Starbases, wins the game. In contrast, *Expeditions* follows the adventures of Kirk, Spock, McCoy, and Uhura on the planet Nibia, where they have to solve three major crises happening at the same time. By exploring the planet and uncovering different missions, the characters attempt to use their resources, crew, specialized knowledge, and any artifacts they may find (each of these is worth a certain number of points) to help solve the crises and help the Nibian people.

Both *Expeditions* and *Fleet Captains* embrace a sense of materiality in their gameplay and HeroClix components. This materiality serves to cohere the players to the franchise universe. Here, I am defining the materiality of the game as the specific tactile interaction players can have with the individual pieces within the set. Many paratextual board games reflect a concern with materiality—in *Battlestar Galactica*, the Cylon ships are molded plastic models, and the characters in *The Lord of the Rings: The Complete Trilogy* appear as miniature versions of the actors from the films. There are multiple types of pleasures associated with this materiality. As Raph Koster notes, "nobody actually interacts with games on an abstract level exclusively ... delivery is important."[10] For Michael G. Robinson, the pleasures of the HeroClix system are specifically threefold:

> The first is competition.... While it is not the only game to ever do so, HeroClix thus offers a superhero fan a second appeal, the opportunity to manipulate favored characters and to play out favorite scenarios. The third appeal to players is collectability, a feature obviously encouraged by WizKids in the booster distribution system.[11]

The first HeroClix figurines were based on Marvel and DC comic characters, but additional franchises have since used the system. For *Fleet Captains*, the clicks can change the power distribution of the ships, so, for example, the USS *Enterprise* could reroute power from the sensors to the main engines if she needed to traverse a greater region of space with a few simple clicks. Alternately, during a battle, the *Enterprise* could channel all her power to weapons and shields. In *Expeditions*, there are two types of HeroClix: characters and ships. The clickable base on the character figurines indicates a reduction in effectiveness, usually as a result of in-game fatigue or damage. For example, the character of Dr. Leonard McCoy initially starts the game with a "command" power of 8, a "science" power of 10, and an "operations" power of 8. Were he to take two "clicks" of damage, he would be reduced to 7 command, 9 science, and 8 operations. The other HeroClix figures in *Star Trek: Enterprise* are the ships orbiting the planet Nibia, the *Enterprise* and a Klingon Battle Cruiser. Throughout the game, combat between the two ships produces damage, indicated by turning the Clix base to the right, resulting in a reduction in power for shields and both long-range and short-range weapons. If either ship clicks down to a zero marker, it is destroyed; the destruction of the *Enterprise* results in a game loss.

Because the pieces are inscribed within a game structure, they take on additional significance not just as toys, but as aspects of delimited play. Unlike traditional feelies (e.g., a toy Batmobile included with a Batman video game), these HeroClix pieces create diegetic consequences. One could play with the figurines in whatever way one wanted—having the characters kiss or the ships join forces, perhaps—but in order to play the game correctly, one must use the figures in the prescribed, authorized way. Robinson notes this double standard, arguing that "as an evolving game system, HeroClix challenges players' identities as superhero fans. With elements beyond their control, fans must negotiate with WizKids if this game is to be the basis of their community."[12] Gray describes this as "self-serving hypocrisy of media firms that hype their licensed toy lines, only to clamp down on other types of paratextual play."[13] Indeed, there is nothing stopping players from using the game pieces however they want, but fitting the game within the paratextual spectrum of the original media text means being beholden to the original design of the game and thus the original design of the cult world. Espen Aarseth argues that the player is "created" by the instructions of the game, hailed into existence as a particular type of player desired by the game. But rather than being limited to this interpellated existence, active players can make use of ruptures within the game system in order to enact "transgressive play." Transgressive play "is a symbolic gesture of rebellion against the tyranny of the game, a (perhaps illusory) way for the played subject to regain their sense of identity and uniqueness through the mechanisms of the game itself."[14] The aforementioned "free parking" rule in *Monopoly* is an example of transgressive play, but there are others—for instance, using nonsanctioned words in *Scrabble* or allowing oneself to get eaten by zombies in *The Walking Dead: The Board Game*.

Transgressive play becomes a meaningful aspect of HeroClix games because the appearance of the figurines can engender personification of the characters. In early writing about board games, Erving Goffman describes how the specific shape of the piece is irrelevant to the playing: they "illustrate how participants are willing to forswear for the duration of the play any apparent interest in the aesthetic, sentimental, or monetary value of the equipment employed, adhering to what might be called *rules of irrelevance*."[15] Jesper Juul argues against this position, noting that "the relation between rules and fiction in the games … is *not* arbitrary."[16] He terms this relationship concept "half-real," noting that video

games in particular are constructed of both *rules* and *fiction* at the same time—
that is, video games have real rules guiding the action within fictional worlds.
Board games complicated this notion of the "half-real"—paratextual board
games even more so. The appearance of the pieces in a paratextual board game
takes on even more significance than in a video game, I would argue, because
although one is still playing within a fictional universe, there is a tangibility
and materiality to the game that more firmly places it within the real world of
the player. As Peters notes here about video game feelies, they "raise questions
about how we immerse ourselves in fictional worlds on material, narrative, and
cultural levels, encouraging scholars to further explore the intersection between
the virtual and the real."[17] If video game feelies permit players to feel a certain
connection to the virtual world on their television and computer screens, then
the HeroClix figures become material connections to the diegetic world itself.

For Robinson, HeroClix is not about the pieces themselves, but about the
way the combination of pieces becomes "representative of the person building
them"—the character I choose to play in *Expeditions* helps to fashion my own
identity as game player (Figure 5.1).[18] This is made even more overt with booster
packs, as more HeroClix characters can be added to the player's roster.

This identification is particularly telling with HeroClix, as different types
of miniatures help to engender different types of identification. Playing as a
particular character may help players identify more with the actions; playing as
an entire ship abstracts the game play. As Costikyan notes: "Getting players to
identify with their game position is straightforward when a player has a single

Figure 5.1 HeroClix Spock, Uhura, McCoy, and Kirk, flanked by a Klingon Battle
cruiser and the *Enterprise*. *Star Trek: Expeditions* ©WizKids 2011. Photo by Katie
Booth.

token; it is harder when he controls many. Few people feel much sadness at the loss of a knight in Chess or an infantry division in a wargame."[19] For *Expeditions*, it might be relatively easy for a player to identify with Spock or Uhura; for *Fleet Captains*, because the ships are mutable and replaceable, there may be less identification with the specific model and more with the general idea of the *Star Trek* universe. At the same time, there may be more opportunity to imagine yourself as an admiral of an actual fleet. More open identification loses specificity, but gains imaginative play. Other types of material identification may take different directions; in *Doctor Who: The Interactive Electronic Board Game*, players move both their own piece and a number of plastic Dalek pieces, forcing identification with both protagonist and antagonist.

Indeed, for *Fleet Captains*, the multi-series identification might be the major paratextual connection. As Matt Hills describes about *Doctor Who*, one of the foremost ways that a media franchise celebrates an anniversary is through uniting multiple iterations of the franchise at once.[20] For *Doctor Who*, this usually means "multi-Doctor" stories like the 20th anniversary "The Five Doctors" or the 50th anniversary "Day of the Doctor," which featured all fourteen actors to have played the part on television. For Hills, the "spectacle of seeing many Doctors on screen—an unusual special effect, to be sure—apparently works against narrative," becoming a celebration of the longevity of the series instead. I would argue that in the case of *Fleet Captains*, the spectacle of seeing many *ships* at the same time, each from different iterations of the show, takes on new significance in the board game realm. Rather than subsuming narrative at the expense of spectacle, the game paratextually references narrative within the framework of the play, turning narrative itself into a spectacle (of figurines and models). That is, the game itself is already a spectacle, and the narrative exists paratextually within the media franchise. Each ship manifests different meanings within the larger franchise: perhaps seeing the *USS Reliant* from *Star Trek II: The Wrath of Khan* fight against the Klingon *IKS Korinar* from *Deep Space Nine* takes on new significance because of the relationship the individual player has between these two texts. There are pleasures beyond narrative and beyond spectacle within paratextual board games: pleasures of play, pleasures of connection, and pleasures of performed materiality.

In this sense, HeroClix is both a game system and a system of representational fandom for a particular media text. The figurines represent not just the characters, but also the experiential pleasure of role-playing as the character within the game system and the diegesis of the narrative. We can "be" Frodo,

Adama, Kirk, or the Doctor. Many paratextual board games use icons or images of characters as tokens for movement—*Arkham Horror* had different characters with particular attributes, *The Lord of the Rings* used familiar characters from the books and novels, etc. But the HeroClix system goes one step further to allow tactile manipulation of the figures. In this way, the characterization of the miniatures becomes part of the pleasure of the game, not just as a way of living within the original media text, but also as a way of living through these characters themselves.

One way HeroClix manifests these pleasures is through its affordances of clicking. An affordance, defined by J. J. Gibson as the actionable properties between the world and an actor, describes the interaction an object facilitates in its users.[21] Buttons are great for pushing. Handles are good for pulling. That is, an affordance is the usable relationship between some sort of object and some sort of action upon that object—the mechanisms of that object that lead to an interaction. Donald Norman has applied the concept of affordance to technology, describing how the specific properties of a technology can facilitate or hinder the use of that technology.[22] Affordances can be deliberate or inadvertent. For example, while one affordance of my keyboard is the way I can press down on all the keys in different orders or even simultaneously, another is that it has rather pointy edges that might make a good weapon should the zombie apocalypse break out: while I doubt that the designers of my keyboard deliberately designed it to bash in zombie brains, the fact that it *can* means that it can be *used* in that manner.

The affordances of an object help structure the type of interaction around the object. For HeroClix, there are pleasures in the clicks: the pleasure of feeling the heft of the figurine in your hand, the pleasure of manipulating the game structure by adjusting character attributes, and the simple pleasure of the affordance of the device working well. For Robinson, the tactile pleasures of HeroClix manifest not just in the clicking, but in the actual miniature. He describes an instance in his board game group when a new game arrived in the mail and "the opening [of the box] became not just a commercial purchase but also a social event involving his friend, his brother, and his wife (who does not play the game)."[23] There are many similar online videos of people "unboxing" games. Similarly, my own experiences with my game group mirror Robinson's—when I opened the *Fleet Captains* box to reveal the 24 different miniature ships, all hands reached forward to play with them (Figure 5.2). *Expeditions* was even more tactile; the minute the character figurines emerged, some fantasy role-play occurred (which mainly involved characters making out with each other).

Figure 5.2 Klingon ship facing the fleet. *Star Trek: Fleet Captains.* ©WizKids 2011. Photo by Katie Booth.

Miniatures have a long history in board gaming, and for Jon Peterson, "the acquisition, customization and adornment of the miniature figurines themselves is painstaking."[24] For many fans of HeroClix, collecting the different figures becomes part of the pleasure of the game. Indeed, as Geraghty points out in his discussion of fan collectors, all collecting involves an element of play: Playing within the ludic spaces of popular media texts provided by the "ironic imagination"; play associated with how individual fans are able to express their own identity and fantasies through "enthrallment" with a favourite film or television series; the "enduring fandom" of life-long play within the fictional world provided by a global franchise like *Star Wars* or *Star Trek*; literally playing with the toy objects from childhood, making them new again; or collecting rare and authentic Hollywood memorabilia, playfully displaying them to distinguish accrued cultural capital.

Collecting the miniatures for a HeroClix game becomes part of the act of playful consumption, as "objects are dynamic and their stories never fully told as history, and collectors construct new narratives of ownership and meaning."[25] The *Star Trek*—themed pieces of the game, like the *Star Wars* toys described by Jonathan Gray, "contribute to the storyworld, offering audiences the prospect of stepping into that world and contributing to it."[26] The materiality of the pieces ties into the original cult programming, as players can use the pieces to imaginatively enter into the cult world through identification with the character, as "part of the attraction in these games is that gameplay is tied directly to the overarching narrative of the original source text."[27] In this way, the ethereal nature of the television or filmic text can become material through the paratextual interaction of the players during the game.

Mutability in space

All games rely on a sense of randomness to engender continued play. As I described in Chapter 1, randomness allows a type of *unstructure* to manifest in games. Unstructure is the sense that randomness itself can be generated via structural means, undercutting the binary between structured play and nonstructured chance. In *Arkham Horror,* unstructure stems from the complicated set of rules that govern the world and the unpredictability that occurs when those rules are placed in concert with one another. In *Battlestar Galactica: The Board Game,* this occurs through procedural rhetoric. In contrast, both *Expeditions* and *Fleet Captains* engender a different type of unstructure, one that emerges from the variable components comprising the game play. While every game will play differently each time, both *Fleet Captains* and *Expeditions* highlight mechanics and components that increase their replay value; the hundreds of thousands of combinations of cards in *Fleet Captains* and the branching narratives of

Expeditions allow a different reading of the paratextual connection between the game and the original cult media text, as they highlight the continual revision and modification that occurs within the *Star Trek* world.

Both games hinge on a sense of randomness. For game designer Greg Costikyan, "randomness can be useful. It is one way of providing variety of encounter."[28] That is, by varying and distributing elements within a game in a random way, the "replay value" of a game increases because the outcome can be influenced by the different random elements. Replay value is a type of affective capital generated by a game's ability to be entertaining despite having already been played. Replay value can be enacted in multiple ways. Some games have a high replay value because of complex human interactions at the heart of the game. Whether one is a Cylon or not in *BSG08*, what set of cards one gets in *Game of Thrones: The Card Game*, whether one has different character abilities in *The Lord of the Rings*—these change the way the game can be played and thus influence the different outcomes. Some games have a high replay value because of a large amount of randomness with the components, as demonstrated by the twenty-four ships, fifty "galaxy" cards, four hundred "command" cards, fifty "encounter" cards, and seventy-six "mission" cards in *Fleet Captains*, each of which may or may not be used in any particular gameplay session.

Conversely, a game with a low replay value may simply use more luck than personal choice within the randomness: in *BSG78*, players use a spinner with a one in six chance of hitting any particular number. The outcome is still random but the mechanic is stolid. "If a game has inadequate variety," Costikyan goes on to write, "it rapidly palls."[29] A game without randomness quickly becomes stale: the outcome is either assured or is never truly in doubt. As demonstrated by Alain d'Astous and Karine Gagnon, a board game's replay value is often tied to stimulating players' imagination.[30] Of course, replay value is culturally and contextually determined—my board game group particularly enjoyed *BSG08* although many groups may not have done so—and the relationship between replay value and actual replay may vary. Games must therefore be mutable in order to be entertaining to a mass audience. Additionally, as expensive as many of these paratextual games can get, the affective replay value is often linked to economic value. *Fleet Captains* costs $80, a hefty price for a game that, without a significant amount of replay value, might just sit on a shelf.

As I mentioned above, one consequence of a game's mutability is the fact that it becomes difficult to point to any iteration or gameplay session as indicative of *the game* itself because a sufficiently randomized game will vary with each session. Each play session—an "episode" of *Expeditions* or *Fleet Captains*—does not describe the whole experience. This focus on the game play as constantly "in-progress" rather than as a stable product relates to Axel Bruns' notion of produsage, or the "collaborative and continuous building and extending of existing content in pursuit of further improvement." Bruns identifies one of produsage's key characteristics as "necessarily remain[ing] continually unfinished, and infinitely continuing."[31] So, too, are paratextual board games in an "infinitely continuing" process, both within the unstructure of the random elements within the game and via their interaction with the original cult text.

Fleet Captains is not based on any one *Star Trek* text, but rather on the corpus of texts that compose the entirety of the *Star Trek* Prime universe. As a multiple text franchise, *Star Trek* has, as Johnson points out, "engaged in world-sharing across multiple historical moments and industrial contexts." By building a franchise through the accumulation of hundreds of hours of televised and filmed material, millions of published words, and scores of ancillary products, *Star Trek*, according to Johnson, is the product of a "negotiated identification" that can mean many things in many different contexts.[32] For Johnson, multiple voices have shaped the *Star Trek* franchise, from producers, to fans, to creators of licensed products. Although Gene Roddenberry is credited with creating *Star Trek*, it is impossible to assign his particular authorship to the many iterations of the franchise. Authorship in a franchised text is fractured, yet must be asserted as a discourse to make the text coherent.[33] This shifting authorship means that the *Star Trek* franchise is always in process; it is always being constructed at any moment through any number of lenses. Even the production of an entry in the franchise, while constrained by the rules of the cult world, strives for originality: as Johnson notes, "In making those claims to creativity … these producers often pursue textual strategies of difference that make the multiplication of franchising not a replication of sameness, but a more reflexive and iterative process."[34] In other words, each series in the franchise is positioned as original and new but must maintain ties to the larger structure to be relevant for the franchise itself.

Fleet Captains relies on this in-process aspect of produsage throughout the game. First, as I noted above, the sheer number of variable game components is staggering. Representing the original universe of *Star Trek*, the game compiles ships from various eras. The original series movie *Enterprise* (NCC-1701-A, from *Star Trek IV, V,* and *VI*) can be played alongside the *Defiant*, from the television series *Deep Space Nine*; the *Voyager*, from the television series *Voyager*; the *Excelsior*, from the films *Star Trek III–VI* and the *Voyager* episode "Flashback";

and even the later model *Enterprise* (NCC-1701-E), from the *Next Generation* films *First Contact, Insurrection,* and *Nemesis.* Second, because each ship is a HeroClix, players can decide how to distribute the ships' power by turning the dial on the bottom of a piece to determine whether, for example, shields, engines, or weapons should have more power. Each click of the HeroClix changes the game because of the unstructured element. Third, the ships in a player's fleet are determined by the draw of cards from a shuffled deck. Fourth, expansion packs like *Romulan Empire* or *Dominion* can add additional ships, cards, and missions to change the game.

The typical *Fleet Captains* game board itself is constructed from 27 randomized tiles, creating a representation of space.[35] Each tile is laid face-down, hiding its contents until a ship either scans the area or lands on it. Locations run the gamut of many different *Star Trek*—themed spatial anomalies or encounters. They can be anything from empty space, meaning there is nothing there, to a Protostellar Nebula, which automatically cloaks ships, to the classic Class M Planet (Class M planets in the *Star Trek* universe are habitable, Earth-like planets).

In addition, each location tile includes an "encounter" chance—if this occurs, the player must draw one of 50 random Encounter cards. Like the *Battlestar Galactica* cards, or the cards in *The Walking Dead: The Board Game,* these cards are sufficiently related to aspects of the *Star Trek*—universe to resonate with fans of the series. There are numerous Encounter cards that can have positive or negative effects on the game play, and often the use of these cards depends on the particular settings on the HeroClix base of the ship that engages the encounter. For example, the Pakled Encounter card requires a level 10 Weapons check, which means that the player must roll a die and add that score to his or her ship's HeroClix weapons score.

The various command cards that players possess complicate the mutability of the game spaces, pieces, and encounters. Each player has the option of ten 10-card decks, each with particular strengths and weaknesses. For example, the Captain Kirk deck provides additional support on combat missions, but does not provide many crew members; in contrast, the Evasive Maneuvers deck provides fewer combat options, but more operational help in terms of shields and scanners. Players choose 4 of these 10-card decks to use for any particular game; the additional 60 cards are not used in that session (but could be used in future sessions). In many ways, playing through one game session of *Fleet Captains* is different from any other play session: there is enough variation between locations, encounters, Clix, and command cards that mutability in game content is assured. *Fleet Captains* "continues to evolve and improve" and demonstrates that "that there is no reason to ever declare a game 'final.'"[36] New cards are constantly drawn and each new game brings new combinations of locations and commands. New ships are added to the fleet. New orders change the narrative of the game. As Sharp notes, "the fact is games are not going to be good at explaining a single position or a set of facts in the same way a documentary film or a pamphlet or poster might."[37] Indeed, games offer a variable, multiple, and mutable understanding of produsage within a paratextual context. Here, this mutability allies itself within the larger framework and context of the *Star Trek* franchise: the differences between the various *Star Trek* outlets come to the fore within the game's focus on multiplicity and mutability. *Star Trek*, the game seems to argue, is what one makes of it—if one wants to play with just ships from the films, one can. If one wants to embrace all spin-offs, one can do that. *Fleet Captains* reveals the produsage at the heart of all paratextuality, as any paratextual product opens new narrative gaps as it performs narrative completion.

Interestingly, there is one exception to the inclusion of the *Star Trek* Prime universe in *Fleet Captains*, and that is the almost complete absence of *Star Trek: Enterprise* in the game's content. As I mentioned earlier, *Enterprise* is the only prequel in the *Star Trek* canon, a show that premiered in 2001 but took place before the start of the original series. By depicting the early days of the founding of the Federation, *Enterprise*, Geraghty argues, also reinscribed a "revisioning" of the history of *Star Trek* itself—"it is trying to refashion *Star Trek*'s universal history by making it part of a very specific American mythic history."[38] In a small way, *Enterprise* attempted what J. J. Abrams more grandly did later—reimagining a different *Star Trek* for a different era. So while the game itself represents the Prime universe, *Enterprise* seems to sit uneasily in a limbo between Prime and Alternate. The only mentions of *Enterprise* in the game are two Klingon Raptor-class ships from the show and one Location card, which mentions the *Enterprise* crew. These small mentions relegate *Enterprise* to an inconsequential narrative blip, a historical footnote. Even the Location card reflects a historiographical look at *Enterprise* within the *Star Trek* universe.

Expeditions uses its own type of mutability. Whereas *Fleet Captains* has the entire *Star Trek* Prime universe with which to construct its fleets and accoutrements, *Expeditions* is based just on the 2009 film, which creates and takes place in an emergent alternate timeline. The film opens with a rupture in the fabric of space, when a renegade Romulan goes back in time and changes the course of history—the Prime timeline is changed and the audience is plunged into a fresh, new timeline. Any minor discrepancies between the original series and this new series can thus be canonically swept away, allowing for a fresh start on the franchise, what Johnson calls "a release from creative deference."[39]

Paratextually, this fresh start means that *Expeditions* is more subdued in its use of mutability. There are still multiple avenues for the game's plot to traverse, but there are far fewer randomized elements in *Expeditions* than there are in *Fleet Captains*. The mutability of *Expeditions* comes through most obviously in its storytelling devices. Whereas *Fleet Captains* uses specific elements—locations, encounters, crew—to create unstructure within the game, *Expeditions* uses a branching narrative outline, which reveals different pathways and outcomes depending on the player's actions and game mechanics: players are given options but do not get to choose the content of those options.[40] The three narratives at the heart of *Expeditions* each have four different outcomes, depending on how successful the game group is at solving the previous issue. One narrative involves the crew of the *Enterprise* helping to repair faulty power generators; another follows the crew as they investigate the planet's parliament and attempt to negotiate their joining the Federation; a third joins the crew as they attempt to stop an armed uprising by rebel forces. These forking-path narratives create different stories each time the game is played, as one narrative path contradicts the others. These narratives "juxtapose alternative versions of a story, showing the possible outcomes that might result from small changes in a single event or group of events."[41] For example, following the "rebels" narrative can lead down a number of paths, outlined here (Figure 5.3).

The first card gives two options: if solved on or before day 7, the better of the two options, players move to card 2A; if solved after day 7, the worse of the two options, players move to card 2B. Similarly, cards 2A and 2B give a two-tiered solution, leading to card 3A (best case), 3B (good outcome), 3C (moderate outcome), and 3D (worst outcome). Finally, each of the final cards (3A–D) offers four options for conclusions, each of which depends on mutable elements—the timing of the solution (on or before a particular day) or the number of crew involved in the solution.

An additional mutable element of the game, the "Captain's Log Supplemental" cards, serves a similar purpose as do the location tiles in *Fleet Captain*. Each Supplemental card is placed on a location, but there are fewer locations than

Figure 5.3 Branching narratives. *Star Trek: Expeditions.* ©WizKids Games 2011. Photo by Katie Booth.

there are cards. This means that different cards might be placed each time the game is played, increasing the mutability of the game and providing more replay value.

There are fewer Supplemental cards in *Expeditions* than there are location tiles in *Fleet Captains*, creating less mutability overall in *Expeditions*. This lessened mutability applies to the relative dearth of "text" manifest in the Alternate timeline depicted in *Star Trek* (2009). Although technically part of the *Star Trek* canon—the film is positioned to be at least tangential to it, using the figure of Spock (Leonard Nimoy; Zachary Pine) as a crossover icon between universes— there have been far fewer content hours produced of the alternate universe to play with in the paratextual game. When *Expeditions* was released in 2011, there had been only one film produced (by Paramount Pictures) and two four-part graphic novel series published by IDW. The same year that WizKids published *Expeditions*, a new graphic novel series was announced by IDW, and two years later the sequel film (and graphic novel) was released by Paramount. Indeed, while the Prime universe of *Star Trek* not only had hundreds of hours of footage, but also had created gaps between series. These gaps are both temporal—the 70 years between the original series and *The Next Generation*—and spatial—*Voyager* depicts a ship lost across the galaxy. These gaps help create what Matt Hills refers to as a "hyperdiegesis," or "the creation of a vast and detailed narrative space, only a fraction of which is ever directly seen or encountered within the text, but which nevertheless appears to operate according to principles of internal logic and extension."[42] *Fleet Captains* offers a chance to fill in those games using the mutability of the text; *Expeditions* has less hyperdiegesis to work with (there are fewer gaps) and therefore lacks the mutability of its HeroClix counterpart.

"A balance of power..."

For Salen and Zimmerman, building on Johan Huizinga, the *magic circle* describes the border between the in-game reality and the out-of-game reality.[43] Board games offer an exemplary way of seeing the magic circle, for there is literally a stage upon which the game is set. Paratextual board games, however, complicate the concept of the magic circle because they exist as both game entities and narrative entities, the world of one spilling over into the world of the other. In some respects, video games break this "magic circle" by creating an alternate world in front of the player. Some video games, like the *Skylanders* system, integrate physical components to help bridge the gap between game world and player world, and others, like Bogost's *A Slow Year*, turn the paratexts of the game itself—the box, the cover art, the game cartridge—into meaningful components as well.[44] But board games like *Expeditions* and *Fleet Captains* complicate the magic circle even further, for the use of mutability and materiality within both games highlights the interaction of the players as co-participants within the construction of a cult text/magic circle. There are multiple "realities" at play within a paratextual board game: the game reality, the cult world reality, the "real" world reality. The tangibility of the objects makes the connections between these realities more "real," but it also concretizes play within specific parameters. The mutability of the texts allows for greater replay value, increasing the cultural and economic capital of the games, and at the same time inscribing differences from the original text within the framework of the game itself.

Fleet Captains highlights the always "in-process" aspects of the *Star Trek* franchise, as the material elements create a seemingly never-ending style of game play.[45] Highlighting the expansive Prime universe of *Star Trek*, *Fleet Captains* reveals the inability to create one particular text out of the many gaps and lacunae within the franchises' hyperdiegesis, a type of "world-building" that produces "emergent creative behaviors among users of the production resources constituted by and contained within those worlds."[46] In other words, the design of the narrative world is shaped by ongoing, collaborative sharing of elements common to all franchise outlets.

6

The Hunger Games and Fan Paratextual Participation

May the odds be ever in your favor.

Effie Trinket, *The Hunger Games*

Of all the Districts in Panem, *District 12* was the poorest. Its residents had to scrounge for every bit of their food, clothing, fuel, and medicine. Katniss Everdeen was made painfully aware of this situation during round 10, when her meager collection of resource cards had to be given to the Capitol. One food, one clothing, and one fuel went into the discard pile. It was either that or add another Tessera into the Glass Ball—increasing her chances of being called for the next Hunger Games. Although she still possessed seven resources, the next instruction told her to discard down to six, so she reluctantly gave up her last medicine as well. Things looked dire for the young woman—but the same thing had happened to her fellow Katniss Everdeens, scattered around the board....

Weeks later and across the table, all the Tributes from all the Districts met for the first time during their *Training Days*. The actual Hunger Games were a week away, but each of the Tributes had to demonstrate strength, agility, cunning, and charm for the judges. Importantly, training also offered the opportunities for Tributes to make allies—one doesn't survive the Hunger Games without at least a few. The female Tribute from District 8 desperately needed to win some more approval: only by winning +50 approval by the end of the third day would she have the support of the judges. She placed her bets and then crossed her fingers, hoping that the roll of the die would be in her favor....

When my board game group sat down to play both *The Hunger Games: District 12* and *The Hunger Games: Training Days* I asked each person a question: "What do you think a game based on *The Hunger Games* would be about?" Everyone answered the same: the game would take place *during* the titular Hunger Games, and we would each play the part of a District Tribute competing for his or her life. This is not an unfair assumption. Suzanne Collins's popular *Hunger Games* trilogy (2008–10) takes place in a postapocalyptic North America in which the land is uninhabitable except for 13 Districts and one Capitol, which controls the economy, flow of goods, and entertainment. Three quarters of a century ago, an uprising led to tyranny, and the Capitol instituted an annual event known as the "Hunger Games," wherein a boy and a girl from each District would compete to the death in a televised event. The entire country, Panem, watched the games. The victor would be hailed as a hero but the losers would just be dead children. Besides being the title of the series (and the first book), the Hunger Games are also the centerpiece of the novels, as the heroine Katniss Everdeen volunteers for the Games in the first book (to save her sister Prim), is drafted into them in the second (*Catching Fire*) and uses her knowledge of them to defeat the President of Panem in the third (*Mockingjay*). The film series of the same name follows roughly the same plot—the adaptation of the first novel is quite faithful to the book's narrative.

To my group's surprise, neither of the paratextual board games based on these series focuses on the actual Hunger Games. While *District 12* is paratextually related to the first film, *Training Days* is a paratext for the first book. But both games delve more deeply into select scenes from each of those narratives that remain underdeveloped in both versions. *Training Days* spends time focusing on Katniss's training, fleshing out the training day scenes, adding context, characters, and story to the already present narrative. In contrast, the game *District 12* elaborates upon the day-to-day life of subsistence in the District in a way that the film simply does not accomplish.

In her book *Fan Phenomena: The Hunger Games*, Nicola Balkind notes that Lionsgate, the film company that made *The Hunger Games,* released a number of official video games based on the film, including *The Hunger Games Adventures, Panem Run,* and *The Hunger Games: Girl on Fire* for mobile devices.[1] These video games function as paratexts to further develop the world of Panem. Furthermore, Balkind describes some of the alternate reality games released by Lionsgate promoting the film, including *The Capitol PN,* that facilitated fan role-playing within the world created by Suzanne Collins. However, no mention is made of the official board games that were created for the book and the film series. Both *The Hunger Games: District 12* and *The Hunger Games: Training Days* are produced by the same company, WizKids games. *District 12* arrived on the shelves in 2010 to mark the publication of the final book in the trilogy (although the game focuses on just the first book) while *Training Days* was released in 2012 to coincide with the film's release date.

The games act not only as paratexts, but also as types of professionalized, mass-marketed simulation of participatory fandom, emulating a type of "filling in the gaps" mentality that structures much academic writing about fandom and cult media texts.[2] Like *Star Trek: Expeditions* or *The Walking Dead Board Game*, both *Hunger Games* games flesh out different aspects of the narratives. In doing so, both games use forms of transmedia storytelling to ask the players to perform the role of "fans" of the *Hunger Games series*. *Training Days* encourages players to become "active fans" through the cocreation of a narrative with both the game designers and author Suzanne Collins by offering flexible characterizations of unnamed, ancillary characters. As I described in Chapter 3, this type of "What If" transmedia encourages fan exploration of noncanonical work. Through this open-endedness, *Training Days* creates a narrative hyperdiegesis that allows fans to fill in ludic and narrative gaps. *District 12*, alternately, encourages players to become "passive fans" by presenting a complete narrative with few gaps, closing off interpretations of the narrative by fitting the game concretely into the cinematic narrative. This type of "What Is" transmedia, as described by Mittell, focuses on expanding the storyworld through matching plot details.[3]

In this chapter I extend my previous discussion of "produsage" in board games to investigate the notion of media fandom as it applies to contemporary paratextual culture. Many contemporary readings of new media invoke fan participation as a key trait.[4] In contemporary new-media participation, fandom becomes a recognized and emulated structure of media consumption.[5] The two *Hunger Games* paratextual board games reflect an industrial version of participatory culture within media fandom, highlighting the nature of both creative fan play and structured game play as they apply to game characters. Paratextual board games represent the participation of fans as they help to enlarge and perform a cult text's boundaries.

This connection between gaming and fandom highlights an eleventh principle of paratextual board games:

Principle 11: Paratextual board games harness the affective power of fandom to help generate player interaction within the game.

Further, I interrogate the ways paratextual board games can embody fandom and further expand fan literature by looking at how the *Hunger Games* fan culture is playfully invoked in these two games. I examine the two *Hunger Games* paratextual board games as exemplars of the mainstreaming of participatory fandom. This examination reveals a twelfth principle of paratextual board games:

Principle 12: Paratextual board games can either allow players to create their own stories or discourage players from doing so within the larger narrative framework of the text, depending on the structure of the game's narrative elements.

In the rest of this chapter, I focus first on the way fans of *The Hunger Games* are courted by the two games, and then on how the games themselves develop as a type of fan text. Although both games invoke *The Hunger Games*, they each invoke different aspects. In *District 12*, each player plays as Katniss Everdeen. During our board game group's play of the game, there were four Katnisses running around the board. Linking the game to a protagonist in this way delimits the narrative, as players know that Katniss *will* become a Tribute, both from the film version and also because she is the only character on the board (albeit in multiple iterations). For players invested in the *Hunger Games* narrative, there is no character uncertainty. In addition, players may find it more difficult to identify with the character, as *everyone* is Katniss. Simultaneously, a fannish freedom to articulate players' own versions of characters becomes less emphasized as the game closes off narrative gaps. The game becomes akin to what obsession_inc, an influential fan author, calls an affirmational fan—one who interprets the source text as canonized and embraces producer-centric ways of reading the text.[6] Affirmational fans are more likely to be courted by the media industries as they read the text *as writ*. In contrast, *Training Days* provides a relatively blank slate for players to create their own stories within *The Hunger Games,* echoing a more transformational view of fandom. A transformational engagement with the source text "aggressively alters and transforms the [material], changing and manipulating it to the fans' own desires."[7] Players have more freedom to ally with different individuals and to strategize for different skills than what the book offered. *Training Days* seems to offer more opportunities for fannish creativity, allying itself with fan-readings of the text.

Participatory fandom and *The Hunger Games*

One of the key themes of *The Hunger Games*, both the novel trilogy and the films, is the power of an individual to enact social change.[8] In many ways, this theme echoes in contemporary scholarship about new media and fandom. Indeed, the participatory nature of the *Hunger Games* diegesis has spawned fannish participation outside the novels and films: a plethora of fan-made texts exists online, and as Jen Scott Curwood notes, these fans are not just producing art, they are also "critically engaging with the text-based story in affinity spaces."[9] An affinity space, a term borrowed from James Paul Gee, is where individuals can interact and learn using common activities. Affinity spaces engender community participation through mutual interest.[10] As Dean Schneider demonstrates, *The Hunger Games* as a cult text attracts young readers to online affinity spaces through peer involvement: not wanting to be left out of the loop, teenagers create their own spaces online to discuss, comment, and focus on the book series.[11] These online affinity spaces are "more participatory, collaborative, and distributed" than traditional print-based practices. And, as participatory fandom becomes more common, "media paratexts" like board games "extend and enhance young adults' experience with literature" like *The Hunger Games*.[12] *The Hunger Games* is not particularly unique in this respect: *Harry Potter* has found numerous online spaces as have other young adult series like *Twilight* or *Divergent*.[13] These online affinity spaces reflect a similar play within and around the media that the *Hunger Games* paratextual board games engender.

In *Training Days*, players play as Tributes from each of the Districts in Panem, each with different abilities, including strength, charm, agility, and cunning. By allying themselves with other Tributes, characters can develop their abilities, which aids them in winning challenges. Players use tokens to bet on challenges. Each win brings more approval from the judges, and the player with the most approval at the end of the game wins. In contrast, *District 12* tells a story of the deprivation within Katniss's District in Panem. Characters wander around the board collecting resources like food, clothes, medicine, and fuel. At various times, however, the rulers of Panem demand that players give up their resources; if they cannot, they have to put a token in a pile in the center of the board for each resource they lack. At the end of the game, a token is randomly drawn from the pile and this player loses the game.

As fandom has migrated to online affinity spaces for the distribution of fan fiction, fan videos, and other fan-made texts in the social media like animated GIFs and digital cosplay, it has become more visible and more mainstream.[14] This means not only that fans are finding more avenues to connect with each other and that more niche communities can flourish, but also that mainstream media corporations are able to appropriate fannish attitudes and characteristics for commercial gain. As Roberta Pearson notes, digital media have provided not only more freedom for fans to create but also more opportunities for the media industries to shape that fannish creation into particular, industrially acceptable molds. She gives the example of the *Star Trek: New Voyages* fan-produced web series, which "are as faithful as possible to the old voyages," as well as citing Suzanne Scott's discussion of "authorized" *Battlestar Galactica* fan videos that "might constrain even the textual work of narrative speculation."[15] Both *Star Trek* games and both *Battlestar Galactica* paratextual games similarly encourage players to "practice" fandom in a particular, authorized way. Just as fans are becoming more participatory, media producers are appropriating some specific elements that define fannish identity.[16] This "mainstreaming" of fandom is a characteristic of contemporary paratextual board games that ask players to take on the roles of fans via connections to the original media text.[17] By invoking aspects of fandom via mechanisms like transmedia pathos, character identification, and role-play, paratextual board games like *The Walking Dead Board Game* reveal the participatory culture at the heart of paratextuality.[18]

As exemplars of an active audience, fans have served to clarify and represent larger concerns within a "participatory culture" for fan-studies scholars.[19] By examining the emotional attachment that individuals can feel for a media text, the creative work that fans engage in, and the communities that develop around media texts, fan studies attempt to engage in a sociocultural critique of audiences and to analyze the activities of fan communities. At the same time, fan researchers need to be cautious to avoid making "fandom" and "participatory culture" synonymous. As Leora Hadas has noted:

> while the logic of participation might seem to mirror the logic of fandom …
> they are not one and the same; … even an interpretive fannish community
> cannot be seen apart from its own norms and ideals; and … the loose and open
> nature of participatory culture as idealized in the Web 2.0 model might, in fact,
> clash with these ideals as much as it might clash with the wider cultural model
> of production it is threatening to replace.[20]

As she goes on to show, while some fans may embrace the emancipatory model of participation and utopian egalitarianism in Web 2.0 spaces, other fans maintain strict hierarchical functionality, neoliberal notions of capitalism, and regulation of fannish content.

One problem with linking fans to participatory culture is that it simplifies both fan activity and audience participation. As I have previously noted, there is an "over-emphasis on participatory fans in the academy."[21] In fact, there is a great variety of fan activity that runs the gamut from highly creative works to simply experiencing emotional satisfaction. Fan activity can be incredibly transformative, but it can also be highly replicative. And although this binary of transformative/replicative is handy (as I discuss later in this chapter), it is also reductive in terms of its analysis of actual fan activity, which is often a combination of both. For example, Hills describes "mimetic fandom" which "begins to deconstruct the binary of fan productions that either transform or imitate mainstream media content, just as textual/material productivities can also blur together, thereby complicating scholarly narratives seeking to clearly separate out these tendencies."[22] Mimetic fandom is the desire to replicate what is in the media text, but as Hills notes, such imitative processes also often lead to transformational details. To attempt to elaborate upon one particular type of fandom might mean shutting other fans out of the process. Fans are a group marked by emotional connection to a media text, but that connection can manifest in multiple ways.

Similarly, participation is a more complex proposition than just "doing things" with the media—as Amazon.com's 2013 drive to monetize fan fiction through Kindle Worlds illustrates. When Amazon announced that a range of popular media series, including *Gossip Girl* and *Vampire Diaries*, would become available for authorized fan fiction to be sold on the website, fan reaction was mixed.[23] On the one hand, fans could collect royalties on their stories. On the other hand, Kindle Worlds limited the authorized fan fiction to specific types ("no porn" … "doesn't violate laws or copyright …" "no crossovers," etc.), turning "participation" into a directly modulated and regulated activity.[24]

Relevant to paratextual board games in general, and the *Hunger Games* games in particular, this dichotomy between media fandom as participatory and media fandom as consumptive reveals different models of paratextuality. Paratextual board games link participatory culture and fandom in unique and culturally applicable ways. They allow individuals to feel as though they are an integral part of the textual world—even contributing to the development of narrative outcomes—all the while remaining tethered to the original text. For example, in the *E.T.: The Extra-Terrestrial* board game, released in 1982 by Parker Brothers, players take on the role of the eponymous alien as he attempts to build the pieces of his machine to "phone home." That the players of the game help him on this quest not only mirrors elements from the film, but also allows the players to play, however briefly, *as* E.T., to imaginatively inhabit the character through ludic manipulations. The same inhabitation occurs in *Star Trek: Expeditions* as players are encouraged to identify with the Star Fleet officer they play as.

This sort of identification is crucial to understanding why people play games at all: Sutton-Smith argues that "the most important identity for players is typically the role they are playing" in the game.[25] As I described in Chapter 3, James Paul Gee's notion of the projective identity in video games, "the interface between—the interactions between—the real-world person and the virtual character," is relevant to the affective relationship between character and text in board games.[26] For Gee, the more a player embodies a character, the more developed the projective identity can be. As players continue to play the game, to become invested in a particular character, the player's "real-world" identity imbricates the play with his or her persona. At the same time, the "virtual" identity of the character that is in the game manifests through the work of that player.[27] Although Gee is describing long-term characters in role-playing games, his work applies to how both *Hunger Games* games appropriate characteristics of participatory culture in order to develop their paratextual connections.

Playing *The Hunger Games*

Paratextual board games often develop scenes from the primary text that are underexplored using characters and narrative actions to build connections. As we have seen, *The Lord of the Rings: The Complete Trilogy* allows players to develop new narratives in Middle-earth, and *Star Trek: Fleet Captains* encompasses all *Star Trek* space and time to facilitate fan play within that franchise universe. Both *Hunger Games* paratextual board games ask the player to take on the role of a fan—to explore aspects of a media storyworld by cocreating stories and filling in gaps of a hyperdiegetic narrative. Character attributes in *Training Days* allow imaginative play with the novel; narrative development in *District 12* augments the player's understanding of the film. *District 12* offers snapshots of life within Katniss's District not shown in the film. But by giving players fewer choices, the game locks a particular reading of the narrative into place, closing off player interpretation. While it may expand the larger *Hunger Games* narrative through fan-like rereadings of the franchise text, *District 12* does not facilitate players' creation of their own rereading of the game's rereading. That is, players seem to be expected to experience the narrative *as given*, even though that narrative is already expanding a world of which the players are probably fans. One cannot "play" outside the authorized text, for instance, taking Katniss to a location not in the film.

While *District 12* fills in gaps without leaving openings for other fans to explore, *Training Days* provides multiple opportunities for players to cocreate a narrative within the gaps of the *Hunger Games* book by offering open-ended characterizations that players can populate with their own imaginative play. *Training Days* provides a set of character attributes that players may interpret as ancillary to those provided by the novel. That is, by providing a structured open-endedness, *Training Days* mirrors the experience of participatory fans by filling in the existing gaps as well as providing additional gaps. I will look first at the ways this recontextualization manifests in the two games through the lens of character attributes, and then at the way each game allows (or does not allow) players to make choices throughout the gaming experience.

With any type of media fandom, multiple ways to participate manifest in audience reception practices.[28] As I stated earlier, obsession_inc outlined two major themes to fan participation: affirmational fandom and transformational fandom (although, she notes both are more similar than different).[29] Some fans experience affirmational attachment through a close watching, reading, or rereading of their favored media text. Some fans may discuss it with others, in person or online.[30] Still others may attend conventions to meet stars and/or creators, listen or participate on panels, or socialize with other fans.[31] Some media fans may collect merchandise or DVDs of their favored text.[32] Transformational fans may be more involved in writing fan fiction, creating fan videos, or using social media to role-play.[33] Some may do many of these activities; others may find their fandom stemming from a more personal place that they rarely think about, but still feel nevertheless. Fandom can be expressed in multiple ways; it is as varied as the human experience.

As Henry Jenkins established early in the history of fan studies, one of the key characteristics of a fan culture is the way that fans "attempt to build their culture within the gaps and margins of commercially circulating texts." This "filling in the gaps" metaphor becomes one of the major fan strategies that Jenkins uses to understand the relationship between mainstream popular media and the acts of interpretation, appropriation, and reconstruction of fan-textual work (or "poaching").[34] There are many ways to fill in the gaps of a media text—Jenkins lists ten of them—and although not all fans participate in media fandom in this manner, it remains a central focus of the fan studies discipline.[35]

One of the reasons these sorts of gaps exist is the narrative hyperdiegesis. In the last chapter I cited Matt Hills' description of the hyperdiegetic narrative of cult media texts as the "creation of a vast and detailed narrative space, only a fraction of which is ever directly seen or encountered within the text." This hyperdiegetic space is never—and can never be—completely revealed in a cult text, as the "endlessly deferred narrative" provides "endless interpretation and speculation predicated upon a point of identity or closure."[36] *Star Trek's* hyperdiegesis, for instance, is infinite. Hills has gone on to develop this idea, writing that the hyperdiegesis can be satisfied through both fan-creative work and "official transmedia … brand extensions."[37] *The Hunger Games'* hyperdiegesis is overt: the world comprises 13 Districts and 1 Capitol, although as readers and viewers we spend time in only a few.[38] Opportunities for expansive detailing of the world exist throughout the texts. One particularly effective way of demonstrating hyperdiegetic narrative expansion is through what Hills has termed "affective play," or interactions with a media text that allow fans to experience and feel a reality within the text that applies to their own lives.[39] The hyperdiegetic text may "reward re-reading due to its richness and depth, but its role is … also one of stimulating creative speculation and providing a trusted environment for affective play."[40] By illustrating a large narrative that cannot be experienced all at once, a hyperdiegesis invites recontextualization of key moments in the plot.

In fact, this hyperdiegetic recontextualization is a key attribute in the way fans fill in these gaps, focusing particularly on the relationship between characters and audiences: "Much fan writing follows this same logic, drawing on moments of key emotional impact in the original texts … as points of entry into the character's larger emotional history; fans create scenes that precede or follow these moments."[41] Fan-made paratexts, just like professional paratexts, "often serve as a way for readers to access schema, critically understand themes, construct knowledge, and engage in multimodal content creation."[42] The fan-made card for *Battlestar Galactica* I mentioned in Chapter 4 is just one example of these fan-created paratexts. In this sense, the *Hunger Games* paratextual games approach hyperdiegetic narrative in two different ways—by leaving gaps and by filling in gaps—and the fan base has multiple opportunities to expand upon and recontextualize those gaps.

The two games reveal nuanced differences in terms of the style and content of the hyperdiegesis between the book and the film. As Mark Fisher explains in terms of style:

> The chief difference between novel and film is that the former has a first-person narrative. This leads to there being greater suspense in the film—the first-person

narration in the novel means that we expect Katniss to survive—but also a reduction in [the novel's] claustrophobia. Shifting to third person allows us a few glimpses into the world beyond the arena.[43]

In other words, in the novel *The Hunger Games* Katniss narrates all the events: we see the world through her eyes and experience her trials vicariously through her interpretation. M. Keith Booker argues that this makes Katniss "highly sympathetic" as the book "is very much centered on her personal feelings and experiences."[44] We learn her intimate thoughts and get to know her as a person. The film attempts to mirror this feeling by focusing most scenes around Katniss, but it also uses alternate points of view to show viewers scenes of other people talking without Katniss being present.

Similar differences between the two games lie in the avatar that players choose during the game play, and the decisions that players can make throughout the game. In *District 12*, the game based on the film, players play *as Katniss*—each player chooses a playing piece depicting Katniss with a different background color. There are no changing attributes; players simply move their pieces without making any decisions about the character. From a franchise point of view, this is a wise choice: the game presents Katniss's character *as writ*, with little variation in characteristics. This confirms the character as depicted in the film and solidifies her characteristics as given: without choice, there is stability. As Sara Gwenllian-Jones notes, fan activity surrounding cult texts hinges on character "latency, with [fans] reading through the surface semiotics of the diegesis and beyond into the implied interior and exterior realities of the characters and their world."[45] By making everyone Katniss, the game attempts to emulate the film's simulation of the novel's first-person perspective.

Everything in the game *District 12* is designed to mirror Katniss's point of view. These multiple Katnisses move around the board, visiting different locations from the film version of *District 12*. The game board is a single card with different areas of *District 12* labeled with images from the film (Figure 6.1).

The Bakery in the top right hand corner of the board has a picture of Peeta, the baker's son and Katniss's partner in the Hunger Games. The Everdeen house below the Bakery has images of Katniss's mother and sister. At each of these locations, players can draw resource cards. There are thirteen rounds (linking the game symbolically to the thirteen Districts of Panem) and in rounds, 4, 7, 10, and 13, game players have to discard some or all of these resource cards in order

Figure 6.1 *District 12* game board. *The Hunger Games: District 12 Strategy Game* ©WizKids 2012. Photo by Katie Booth.

to pay the Capitol. As I mentioned earlier, at the end of the game, one Katniss will be drawn from the Glass Ball to be the loser; the rest of the players count up the points in their hand and the one with the most points is the winner. In this respect, the game differs completely from the original film; although Katniss does go to the Hunger Games, it is because she volunteers when her sister's name is drawn. This act actually makes Katniss a hero to many, not a loser as the game indicates.

As we have seen with, for example, *The Walking Dead Board Game,* the choice of character is an important one in paratextual board games. In the two *Hunger Games* games, characters play a crucial role in the way that individual players achieve a sense of affective play, cohering the experience of playing the game with the immersion into the two games' narratives. Characters have been a central focus of many of the paratextual games analyzed so far in this book— from character attributes in *Arkham Horror* and *Battlestar Galactica* to character relationships in *The Walking Dead* and *The Lord of the Rings,* the explication of character development within paratextual board games reflects a cohesion between player, character, and game. The fact that the only character one can play in *District 12* is Katniss, limits the scope of the game's connection between player and character—while you may want to avoid the Glass Ball because you do not want to lose the game, you know that from a narrative point of view, Katniss *will* get reaped no matter what you do. Since everyone plays as the same character, there is no uncertainty in the outcome of the game's narrative.

By limiting everyone to Katniss's character, the game fills in the gaps of the larger *Hunger Games* film narrative, but in doing so it also closes off gaps for players to imbue with their own meaning. For example, the only time that Katniss travels to the Bakery in the film is in a flashback: she is starving and Peeta throws her some burned bread. By linking the Bakery with an image of Peeta to the playing piece standing in for Katniss, the game manages to fill in that gap in the narrative of *The Hunger Games*: "what if Katniss had visited Peeta at the Bakery?" the game seems to ask. But the question is never answered; or rather, the answer is the same as it is at every other location: Katniss draws a card (which might not even be food). At the same time, the game includes "special cards" that grant powers to the player that owns them, inherently changing the narrative. For instance, generally if a player lands in the woods, she can keep the food she finds there—narratively, this links to the film as Katniss is a hunter and would be able to keep what she poached from the woods. Drawing the "Gale" special card allows the holder to keep two kinds of resources, food and medicine, from the woods. Although this dramatically changes the game play, it does not fit within the basic structure of the character it is based upon: it is Katniss who knows about the medicinal properties of the forest, not Gale.

Because the narrative of the game is relatively basic—the world is limited to District 12 and there are only six places to visit—there is little opportunity for players to invest their own imaginative, affective play into the game. Each round features gameplay mechanics that generate uncertainty, like discarding or drawing cards, but there is little narrative structure guiding the action. Players can travel to any of the six locations, but there is nothing to do in that space other than drawing or discarding cards. Throughout the game, the different rounds ask players to sacrifice resources and to draw more resources, but players have little choice in or opportunity for decision-making throughout the game. One can discard cards of one's choice, but by the time of the reaping, it hardly matters which ones—only if you were able to fulfill the quota.

Although the game is billed as a "strategy" game, it relies more heavily on which cards are drawn rather than on which ones you discard. The final mechanic—drawing cards from the Reaping deck to see who loses—is simply a lesson in probability. It is entirely possible to lose even if you have played very well. While this ties in well with the dystopian future of the original film, it creates an uninteresting game. With little investment in the characters, there is little incentive to create more narrative, and little incentive to participate in the cocreation of meaning throughout the game. It is not that players *can't* do this, but rather that the game does not offer players easy opportunities to enact this type of participation. If, as Deborah Kaplan notes about fan fiction, "rewriting characters … is an interpretive act … in which the text offers one possible understanding of characterization," then *District 12* limits the participation of fans in rewriting Katniss's character: there simply isn't enough "character" present within the game to rewrite easily. Nor is there much incentive to do so. According to Kaplan, participating with the media through fan fiction—filling in the gaps—necessitates a deep understanding of the character. Regardless of what participation fan-players want to engage in, *District 12* does not reflect the type of "dynamic interpretive space in which a multitude of understandings of the source texts' characters can form, grow, and change."[46] To more fully participate in the construction of character and narrative in a paratextual board game, players need to feel like they can cocreate aspects of the narrative and of the characters within the game. Although the characters may be based on already extant media properties, for players to become invested in the *game* (as opposed to the franchise as a whole), the character needs to display flexibility and openness.

In contrast, the characters in *Training Days* present an enormous amount of flexibility to players to become invested in. As I discussed in reference to *The Walking Dead: The Board Game*, a deeper, more extensive past a character has, the more real the character seems. The unnamed characters in *Training Days* may thus seem less "real" than *District 12*'s Katniss because there is less character *given* in the narrative, but conversely this means that players can imagine them with characteristics from the original text or the player's own imagination.

To understand characters at all, we need to see past their semiotic construction and, simultaneously, see each as a mimetic being that "represents aspects of a 'real' person."[47] One way to examine the mimesis of characters, as Roberta Pearson reveals, is to identify the elements by which audiences make meaning of character. According to Pearson, there are six of these elements: psychological traits/habitual behaviors, physical characteristics/appearance, speech patterns, interactions with other characters, environment, and biography.[48] From combinations of these elements, multiple interpretations of characters can be realized. For instance, with *Star Trek: Expeditions*, we get a sense of the character of Kirk from his special attributes, the HeroClix miniature, text about him on the cards, the way his character interacts with others in the game, his rank on the ship, and his backstory from the film. In the book *The Hunger Games*, Katniss becomes a more fully mimetic, realized character because we know these psychological traits; they are told to us by Katniss, to herself.[49] As readers we are literally in her head. Because the film is told in a third-person style, viewers may feel as though they are not part of Katniss, but are merely observing her; she is less mimetic because she is external to viewers' minds. In the book, Katniss has a sense of what David Carr has called "temporal thickness," the sense of the presence of time within an object or character, the sense that this character has a past and a future.[50] The more strongly that sense is felt, the more thick the temporal structure. As Samuel Zakowski confirms, "adding (past and/or present) temporal thickness to characters or the fictional world contributes to the illusion of realism, which, in turn, leads to increased immersion" in the narrative.[51] The Katniss in *The Hunger Games* novel reveals more of her past (and dreams of her future) than does the Katniss in *The Hunger Games* film. Literary Katniss is more temporally thick than film Katniss, which translates to the paratextual board games.

According to Zakowski, writing here about video games, the more a character within a game has the appearance of an independent life, the more the player can become immersed within the storyworld of the game. He discusses the video game series *Mass Effect* as an exemplar of how the more backstory a character can manifest, the more closely a player can connect to it. Indeed, as he writes:

immersion is enhanced by providing characters and the world with a comprehensive temporal dimension—if the world extends beyond the story itself into the past, and if the characters seem to have their own mind, will, and emotions which affects their actions in the present, the illusion of realizing is that much more potent.[52]

His example of the *Mass Effect* video game series reveals the importance of character history for player immersion; such immersion may be difficult to achieve in a popular board game (do we feel connected to a green token in "Sorry!"), but in a paratextual board game, the characters come with built-in histories. The most relatable characters have histories but they are also open enough to allow fans to develop underexplored characteristics.

However, the characters in *Training Days* come with only the most basic history—they do not even have names. Jones notes how cult characters "are incomplete and incompletable. Lacking referents, they exist as liminal entities poised between tele-presence and absence."[53] The characters in *Training Days* are almost completely void of presence. In the game, players take on the roles of Tributes who have been chosen by lottery to participate in the Hunger Games. Think of *Training Days* as a sequel, of sorts, to *District 12*. It is not that one directly follows the other, but if one were to follow the exploits of the loser in *District 12* (the person picked out of the Glass Ball), one would necessarily then follow him or her to the training center. Training requires each of the Tributes to practice weaponry, tactics, and survival skills while being watched by the judges and the Game Maker—the person who put the Hunger Games arena together.

In the book, the Tributes are also keenly watched by the audiences of Panem—the entire Hunger Games is mandatory viewing for every member of every District. The ultimate reality television, the broadcast of the games, "is the Capitol's method of reminding the remaining Districts not to rebel."[54] After training, the Tributes are rated on a scale of 1 to 12, and the higher the rating, the more sponsors (rich benefactors who can send packages and supplies to the Tributes in the arena) will want to help the Tribute in the Games. The game *Training Days* follows the Tributes in their training as they participate in events to earn approval rating, use special events to earn additional abilities, and generate alliances with other characters to augment their skill set. Winning events is easier with an alliance, which can be formed by betting against other players. Alliances are not with other players, but with NPCs—nonplayer characters within the game. There is an immense level of satisfaction when an alliance pays off—when the two or more characters linked together achieve the goal.[55] The objective of the game is to have the highest approval rating at the end of three days of training (days are marked by random drawing of cards), but the best way to earn that rating is by aligning characters. Character alignment is thus one of the key mechanics of this game, as it is so crucial to the players' victory.

Rather than basing the characters on particular representations from the book series (e.g., Katniss and Peeta from District 12; Rue and Thresh from District 11), the game identifies the characters simply by their District number and sex, and each player picks the District and Tribute they would like to play as (e.g., I played as the female Tribute from District 7). The characters are also differentiated from each other by special abilities and varying skill sets, enumerated on the character card. Demarcated as strength, agility, cunning, and charm on a scale from 1 to 8, these skills are how the Tributes are measured against each other when they are competing for approval from the sponsors. Each character card links up with other character cards through the sides of the semicircle, which provide a clear indication of an alliance and also add to the character's skill set. In Figure 6.2, the person playing as the male Tribute from District 3 has allied himself with the female Tribute from District 3 (only one player may play a District). Meanwhile, the male Tribute from District 12 is waiting for an alliance. The player for District 8 has increased his strength by 3 points, as indicated by the completion of the two semicircles on the sides of the cards.

Each character in *Training Days* represents a Tribute from a District. In the original *Hunger Games* novel, each District sends two Tributes—a boy and a girl—to participate in the Hunger Games. The children are not trained for the games during their lives (although some from the more profitable Districts skirt around this), but they pick up skills from the work they do in each of their Districts. In *The Hunger Games,* each District has a particular industry. Katniss's home *District 12* specializes in coal mining. District 8 specializes in textiles; District 7 in lumber and paper. Interestingly, while some relation between the Tribute's particular skills is linked to the Districts, this is not always the case. District 4 is known for fishing and all the residents are superb swimmers; however, the two Tributes in the *Training Days* game have very low agility (the female Tribute's agility is a 4; the male's is a measly 2), which belies the attributes actual characters from District 4 might have had if they existed.

Throughout the game, then, players must continually imbue the characters with meaning, interpreting their various skill sets in order to ally advantageously with other Tributes. For instance, District 4's male Tribute will gain +3 from

Figure 6.2 Character cards and allies. *The Hunger Games: Training Days* ©WizKids 2010. Photo by Katie Booth.

whichever skill his ally brings. He might want to ally with someone who would increase his agility, like the female Tribute from District 7. Or, because he has such an enormous amount of charm (a full 8), he might want to dominate in those events that call for charm by allying himself with the male Tribute from District 10. The strategy of the game comes into play when deciding how to best win Event cards, and consequently earn approval points. Event cards list different talents needed to win in the Games—for instance, swordplay, archery, or sprinting. Players win cards by secretly betting 1, 3, and/or 6 points on a card. Each card is associated with a particular skill, and by combining the amount of the bet with the skill level of the player and adding to that the random roll of a die, the player may win the card and the points from the other players. If no one else bets on the card, the player wins the card automatically—as, if there was a real training day but only one person participated in that event, then that one person would earn all the approval points.

Training Days functions as a type of fan fiction. Although the original *Hunger Games* novel features scenes within the training center for the Hunger Games proper, because the story is told from Katniss's first-person point of view, readers of the novel rarely get to experience the training from the point of view of any of the other characters. (Even the film version closes off the training to mainly Katniss's point of view.) Readers experience the other participants in training through Katniss's interpretation, and do not learn as much about the Tributes as their varied personalities may offer. The presence of these textual and semiotic gaps in the narrative—gaps of characterization and gaps in narrative—are filled in through the game, but require the presence of the player to enact them.

In terms of filling in the gaps of characterization, *Training Days* also presents a type of participatory affinity space in which individual players help each other learn about the character development. The fact that the characters are constructed entirely by skill sets rather than personalities allows players to develop their own insights into the relationships between them. Furthermore, because the players have an active role in making decisions about the characters and how they will play the games, the development of the character may have more meaning for the player. But unlike *District 12*, in which the character of Katniss is relatively closed because it is already given to the players as written, the characters in *Training Days* present the opportunity for players to generate much more open-ended meaning in the characters.

By filling in the gaps of narrative, the game does not offer a clear-cut narrative trajectory that ties into the novel. Unlike *District 12*, which closes off the narrative by deliberately linking it to the narrative of the film version, any one of the Tributes could win the most approval points in *Training Days*. Because Katniss is not one of the characters, nor is the game closely aligned with a specific plot point in the novel, there is no diegetic rationale for a narrative, paratextual connection. It might not even be Katniss's Hunger Games. This means that the players of the game are given an open-ended opportunity to play in the large, cult world of *The Hunger Games* by creating their own trajectory through the story. As Jones notes of these hyperdiegetic worlds:

> The appeal of these vast, transmedia fictions lies precisely in their invitations to immersion and interactivity; they are constructed, marketed, and used by fans not as "texts" to be "read" but as cosmologies to be entered, experienced and imaginatively interacted with.[56]

Training Days does not force players to create a world, but merely gives players the opportunity to enter the world, to imaginatively interact with it. The openness of the game's narrative also allows the players to participate in the *Hunger Games* universe precisely as the characters in the novels do—as a game. As Holly Blackford states, *The Hunger Games* is first and foremost a series about *games*.[57] One of the allegorical discourses generated by Collins reflects "cultural anxieties about a generation of young people 'sucked into' games … [and who] will master the games and surpass adults with technological and strategic prowess." Throughout the book, Katniss is constantly having to play games—both formal games (as in the Hunger Games themselves) and more informal games, like having to "play" as Peeta's lover to gain sympathy and sponsors.[58] *Training Days* portrays just one minor game that all participants of the Hunger Games have to endure: the game of making oneself attractive to the sponsors. Through competition within *Training Days*, players vicariously (if not directly) experience what the characters in the novel might be experiencing. As a paratextual board game, *Training Days* reflects not only an aspect of the novel readers may want to explore in more detail, but also the thematics that underlie the story. *District 12* presents a portrait of living in Katniss's District, but does not focus on the larger narrative world at play in *The Hunger Games*.

"The odds are ever in your favor..."

The *Hunger Games* texts present the type of expansive cult world that creates a hyperdiegetic narrative space. The *Hunger Games* games populate that world with characters that reflect contemporary issues in fandom. As players of the games, we enter into aspects of *The Hunger Games* that are underexplored in both the novel and the film. The ways in which these games facilitate an interaction with players matches the multiple discourses that cult texts use to reach fan audiences. In this way, both games emulate the view of fans as active contributors to the media franchise. As mainstream media industries are becoming more aware of fandom and fan practices, they are finding ways to appropriate this fannish enthusiasm. In 2006 Henry Jenkins noted two different responses from the industries to participatory culture: the prohibitionists who "adopt … a scorched-earth policy toward their consumers" and attempt to criminalize fan participatory activity, and the collaborationists who "see fans as important collaborators in the production of content."[59] To this dichotomy, Suzanne Scott adds another method: the appropriationalists, who use fannish tactics to appeal to a particular fandom. According to Scott, such appropriationalists may cultivate "a parallel fan space alongside grassroots formations of fandom."[60] This parallel space may offer fans a type of affinity space for creating fan content, but they can also mold and shape that content in particular ways: the authority over this authorized space rests with the industry, not with the fans. Such "authorized resistance" uses fan enthusiasm for industrial purposes.

District 12 seems to embrace this appropriationalist mentality by offering a slice of narrative that is underexplored in the commercial text and generating an authorized affinity space for players to participate in co-constructing the narrative, but stops short of giving players the freedom to explore the world outside the bounds of the text itself. Players are Katniss and Katniss must enter the Games—there are no other options because that is the way the authorized narrative must go. This seems partially based on the externality of the point of view of Katniss in the films: because viewers will forever be external to Katniss, we must follow her exploits secondhand. Although fans can certainly play the game differently and create their own interpretations, the game itself funnels fandom in particular ways. In contrast, *Training Days* seems collaborationist. It too generates an affinity space that presents an underexplored aspect of Panem, but by focusing on the individual decision-making of the players as well as the open-ended nature of the narrative, it provides a space for active cocreation of the characters and story. Although players do not have to develop a narrative in *Training Days*, the opportunity to do so is clearer and more defined than in *District 12*.

As new media develop, online cultural participation will only increase. As critics like Sean Conners and Iris Shepard argue, young adult readers of *The Hunger Games* can be "encouraged to engage the books critically, reading them from the standpoint of theory and mining them for parallels that connect the dystopian vision Collins presents to contemporary life."[61] Collins' critiques of the dangers of absolute power, the brutality of totalitarian societies, and the brainwashing control of vacuous media can be played out not just in literature and film, but also in the various games based on them. Both *District 12* and *Training Days* help players feel more a part of Panem and Katniss's journey; that they do so in different ways does not diminish the paratextual connection to each requisite text. Winning either game comes about through a mixture of strategy and luck, whether the odds are in your favor or not.

Narratives and Databases in *Game of Thrones*

When you play the game of thrones, you win or you die. There is no middle ground.

Cersei Lannister, A Game of Thrones

The mighty families of Westeros are at war. Robert Baratheon, king and ruler over the seven kingdoms, has died. North of Moat Cailin, the Starks maintain their hold on the fortress at Winterfell with an eye toward the Iron Throne at King's Landing. But south of Riverrun, five major families also vie for control—the power-hungry and rich Lannisters, the bitter and sea-faring Greyjoys, the fierce and unforgiving Martell family, the ambitious yet chivalrous Tyrells, and the troubled and strong-willed Baratheon clan (the seventh family, House Targaryen, has been nearly decimated and its surviving members lie in exile off the board). An alliance develops between the Greyjoys and the Baratheons. The Lannisters, trying to make inroads into the center of Westeros, have spread their troops too thin. House Greyjoy and House Baratheon ponder: should they march? Should they defend? Should they attempt to gain power? The Martells and the Tyrells join forces. In a shocking turn of events, House Baratheon *betrays* House Greyjoy! Greyjoy attempts to piece together a defense, asking Martell to support their defenses. Martell refuses. House Baratheon destroys House Greyjoy, claiming Castle Crackclaw as their own and winning control over the kingdom of Westeros. The great families may ally with one another, but there can be only one king.

Meanwhile, on a smaller scale, the same war over the future of Westeros rages, as characters from House Stark and House Lannister attack and defend using cards depicting different House individuals. In play sit three Lannister cards: Maester Pycelle, whose scholarly, alchemical, and science training allow him a seat on the king's inner council. Next to him, the Lannister Men-at-arms, a series of indistinguishable, helmeted knights, provide military power. But the true hero of the Lannister deck is Ser Jamie Lannister, who not only has a strong military ability, but also provides a sense of intrigue. Across the table, three Stark family members are prepared to defend against the impending attack: Lady Catelyn Stark, whose intrigue and power scores outmatch Pycelle's; Hodor, who cannot attack but has amazing defensive strength; and Lord Robb Stark, who not only has strength, but also has a loyal dire wolf. Ser Jamie leads by attacking House Stark with his military might, but is countered by Hodor who repels the attack. Jamie continues to attack with intrigue, but is defended by Catelyn Stark. The Lannisters finally use Grand Maester Pycelle to power attack, which is successfully repelled by Robb Stark. But then, the Starks begin their attack....

Both of these games based on *Game of Thrones* revel in narrative and ludic complexity, but each performs paratextuality differently. *A Game of Thrones: The Board Game* focuses on the relationships between the families and Houses vying for power in the vast cult geography invented by George R. R. Martin for the seven-book series *A Song of Ice and Fire*, of which *Game of Thrones* is the first volume. Relying on alliances, House relationships, and geography, the game attempts to simulate the vast, interconnected networks of intrigue, power, and military might of the many kingdoms of Martin's Westeros through strategy and cooperation between players. The game relies on a database of information—armies, supplies, ports, other players' actions and alliances, and routes through the complex geography—that needs to be taken into account for strategic game play. Mirroring the database-like structure of new media, *The Board Game* provides a networked understanding of game play as players use an archive of information and their own social experiences to resolve the larger story of power within the game.

In contrast, HBO's *Game of Thrones: The Card Game*, the game based on the television series, relies less on geographic strategy and House networking and more on the order and procedure of playing cards based on individual characters from the television program. The HBO *Card Game* uses a serialized form of game play as the characters, supplies, and locations of Westeros are deployed in sequences that, as Kurt Lancaster describes of the *Babylon 5 Card Game*, "capture the flavor of the intrigues, diplomatic actions, and military strikes found in the series."[1] Rather than picturing the expansive geography of Westeros on a giant game board, this *Game of Thrones* game uses images from the television series on cards.[2] Through the regimented gameplay mechanics, which highlight game player order as well as turn phase order, the HBO *Card Game* reveals the serialization within paratextuality and highlights a more narratively focused interpretation of the series.

Although not technically a "board" game, as it does not use an actual game board, the HBO *Card Game* is a simplified version of a different game, Fantasy Flight Game's *Game of Thrones: The Card Game*, which does use a board, and, in turn, seems to straddle the vast geographic strategy of *The Board Game* and the individual character intrigue of the HBO *Card Game*. Based on Martin's novels, the Fantasy Flight *Card Game* is a "living card game," meaning that the base set comes with a number of cards, but expansion packs (which are released periodically) build onto this base set. These types of living card games, also called collectible card games, highlight the serialized nature of cult media products like television or fantasy book series.[3] The HBO game simplifies the living card game by reducing the number of players (from a maximum of four to a maximum of two), lessening some of the complexity of the original game, adjusting some card text, and streamlining the rules. In many respects, the complexity of the living card game is more akin to *The Board Game* than it is to the HBO *Card Game*; with both being based on the more complex book series rather than the simplified (but still complex) television show, this makes some sense.

In this chapter, I expand on my discussion of participation in paratextual board games to look at the importance of not just an individual's activity in regard to gaming, but also how gaming fits within a larger structure of an interconnected culture.[4] *Game of Thrones*, the first in George R. R. Martin's *A Song of Ice and Fire* series (which, at the time of writing, is still unfinished), is a vast fantasy epic that details the struggles between seven kingdoms in a fictional medieval world. With hundreds of characters and thousands of relationships embedded within the 5,000 page series (with two more 1,000+ page books on the horizon), there is much lineage complexity in the book series. While simplifying the novel in some ways, HBO's *Game of Thrones* still retains one of the largest casts on television as well as the complex backstory for many of the characters. The television story is told from multiple locations and follows many of the main characters throughout their adventures in and around Westeros.

In *The Board Game*, players take on the role of one of these Houses, controlling the progression of House armies and attempting to take over the continent. Like *Arkham Horror,* which uses multiple elements to tell the story, *The Board Game* emphasizes a database of possible narratives. Families are more important than any one person, as it is the complex *nonlinear* interactions between the Houses—the networked relationships of individual elements—that help develop the paratextual game play. In contrast, in the HBO *Card Game*, players control individual characters and play out more intimate combat scenarios. The HBO

Card Game is played in a serialized fashion, just like *Lord of the Rings: The Complete Trilogy,* creating a narrative out of the turn order.[5] It focuses on serialization and developing a *linear* understanding of game play, using the individual to stand in for the Westeros family. In other words, in *The Board Game,* each player plays as a network of relationships while in the HBO *Card Game,* each player sits in the center of his or her own network of individual characters. These differences between the types of games highlight the thirteenth principle of paratextual board games:

Principle 13: Paratextual board games expose the database and the serial at the heart of licensed gaming, revealing connections between players, texts, and actions through the mechanisms of play, algorithmic procedure, narrative, and player interaction.

Furthermore, different emphases of thematic content within the *Game of Thrones* paratextual games reflect a similar tension between the narrative and the database in contemporary digital media. The games' twinned emphases on these concepts lead to a fourteenth principle of paratextual board gaming:

Principle 14: Paratextuality can be achieved in multiple ways through differing emphases on simulating thematic content.

It is not that one version of *Game of Thrones* necessarily exemplifies one element over another, but that the *games* augment one particular facet of the text at the expense of others. Both paratextual games use database-like elements and serialized elements; however, the differing emphases of each create different styles of game play. I explore these elements by first discussing the way database and narrative styles of game play unfold in each game, and then focusing on the impact of socialization as a key mechanic in each game. Finally, I conclude the chapter by looking at win conditions and how ending the games helps shape player interpretation of the narrative.

Networking and serialization

The thematic and playable differences between *The Board Game,* the HBO *Card Game,* and the Fantasy Flight *Card Game* speak to the larger structures of the database and narrative in the contemporary media environment. Imagine a collection of photographs held in a folder on your computer's desktop. These photographs form a database that can be accessed and ordered by any number of tagged elements: size of the photo, type of camera used, date taken, etc. According to media theorist Lev Manovich, databases do not tell stories: "in fact, they do not have any development, thematically, formally, or otherwise that would organize their elements into a sequence." Instead, he argues that narrative only exists at the level of the user interface, where retrieving information relies on searching and organization. A narrative is the linear and structured retelling of that data in a particular order. Once you sort the images in that folder into any particular order, you have artificially created a serialized retelling of those photos. The database makes use of networked connections to add versatility and robust searchability in digital documents. The narrative highlights serialized elements within a correlated structure to develop an underlying logic. Indeed, Manovich holds the database and narrative organizational structures as "natural enemies" that compete "for the same territory of human culture, each claim[ing] an exclusive right to make meaning out of the world."[6]

Games make use of this same structure/serial tension, and Manovich even uses the video game as an example of a text that uses both a database structure to organize data and a narrative structure to access that data. Although some might claim that video games are narratively driven, Manovich asserts that "if the user simply accesses different elements, one after another ... there is no reason to assume these elements will form a narrative at all."[7] Even though a player can access elements of a game in one particular order, the game itself is still structured as a database of information, an archive of text, image, audio, and video that gets deployed at algorithmically controlled times.

Although Manovich might be correct in addressing the database-like qualities of the video game, paratextual board games offer a more open-ended exploration of this database/narrative structure. Board games are also constructed from a database of elements (as any player who has spent hours of time punching out miniatures and tokens can attest), but player-generated content creates an organized structure onto that inherently unordered collection. From *Arkham Horror*'s unstructure, developed from the over 700 pieces of the game, to *Star Trek: Fleet Captains*'s mutability, developed from the many randomized elements, paratextual board games become a flexible platform for player interaction. For example, while playing *A Game of Thrones: The Board Game*, my board game group used the 404 separate playing pieces and tokens as the game prescribed: we fit the tokens and troops within a database of uses, in ways that, while never codified by us, were still algorithmically planned into the game. But at the same time, like with *The Lord of the Rings: The Complete Trilogy*, we generated content that Christian Petersen, the creator of *The Board Game*, might never have anticipated; we made the game more narratively driven, including developing the alliance between House Martell and House Baratheon and role-playing the characteristics of the cold, lonely House Stark.

As I have previously described, the new media environment is rife with instances of database/narrative structural mergers, as fans can use a "narractive" approach to generative content in online archives like wikis. Instead of *either* accessing data on vast stores of online archives, *or* representing a plot through a specific order, fans can do both, using wikis and the "inherent hypertextuality of the web to create connections between narrative elements." Through the creation of a "narrative database," fans structure a "narrative through communal interaction. It is not the same as taking units from a random archive, but rather of reassembling units in a new order."[8] Fans' work to construct narrative databases like *A Wiki of Ice and Fire* hinges on the interactive potential of both serialized and networked elements.[9] At the same time, there is an additional element of narrative serialization within the database in other fan work online, as fans can rewrite and reproduce cult media texts through social media sites like Tumblr. For instance, fan-made GIFs and GIFfics of *A Game of Thrones* tell amateur stories using the database of elements available to fans in the digital age.[10]

Beyond fandom, social media harnesses this database/narrative bridge to create other types of new texts. For example, José van Dijck describes the transition in social network from "databases of personal information" to "tools for (personal) storytelling and narrative self-presentation." Facebook's 2011 introduction of its Timeline feature demonstrates this shift. When Facebook was first developed, it acted more like a database of elements: it collated information about a user's life and displayed it to the user's friends. There was an attempt to demonstrate each particular identity as "a database *of* users and *for* users."[11] Facebook's Timeline "actively rearranged users' profiles so that events were listed chronologically, on a seemingly endless timeline of a user's life. Everyone's timeline starts on the day of his or her birth and, depending on his or her overall usage of Facebook, continues to add information throughout the user's own personal timeline."[12] This narrative rearrangement of information brings a serialized structure to the database—a structure that I have previously described as a "narrative paradox"—and "requires not only adding new data to already existing content, it also triggers a new awareness of *how* you want your life story be told, *to whom* and *for what purpose*."[13] In other words, Timeline creates a serial life out of a database of possibilities, turning individual events from periodic and chronological "updates" to an ever-growing (digital) corpus.

Playing the seven kingdoms

Although *Game of Thrones* as multiple franchises makes use of both database-like and narrative-like structures, each paratextual game relies on one or the other for its core game mechanic. The complexity at the heart of George R. R. Martin's *Game of Thrones* reveals the presence and power of *connections*, both familial and regal.[14] At the same time, the serialized nature of the book and film series reveals the importance of narrative structure and seriality within the *telling* of these connections. For both games, this complexity does not just occur through the rules that players must understand in order to play, or the complicated mechanics by which play occurs, but also through the interrelated connections between the players, their social interaction, and the game system itself. As Stewart Woods points out, "cross-pollination between different game media may foster innovative interpersonal mechanics"; that is, different styles of player interaction within a game can highlight the specific database-like or serialized characteristics that make a game unique within a larger ludic structure.[15]

Database game play

A Game of Thrones: The Board Game finds two to six players playing as different Houses in Westeros. Each House is attempting to become the ruler of the seven kingdoms of the country. To do this, each House must travel across the country but must also balance their own stockpile of resources with those needed to fight. Additionally, players can ally with other players, sharing in the spoils—but also the losses—of war.

The Board Game mirrors its literary counterpart's complexity through its simulation of the books' construction of the backstory and history of Westeros. In her narratological examination of Martin's *Game of Thrones*, Ida Adi discusses the complex storytelling within the series. She points out that the chapters are seemingly unconnected, with unrelated plotlines, nonlinear storytelling, and subjective point-of-view narration. Each chapter is told from the personal standpoint of one particular character, influencing the reader's available information.[16] Since the character may not (and probably does not) have access to knowledge elsewhere within the series, the reader is often left to connect multiple viewpoints into a coherent picture, synthesizing a database of possible realities, a network of viewpoints, into one cohesive plotline. Each chapter adds to a deepening database of information.

This synthesis between the book and the game occurs in the game as players role-play as the great Houses. In *The Board Game*, each element is based on its *relationship to other elements*, making the game a uniquely social experience that relies on what Woods studies as the "game mechanics and the social interactions which emerge from them."[17] These social interactions become emblematic of and constituent to the construction of a networked understanding of the mechanics and aesthetics of paratextual board games, and also reflective of the nature of socialization online. The relationship between sociality within paratextual board games and the larger, macro-relationship between the paratext and the text itself reflects a type of networked collectivism that defines contemporary online discourse. Nancy Baym, working initially with fans in the Swedish music scene, has defined "networked collectivism" as "groups of people networking throughout the internet and related mobile media, creating a shared but distributed group identity."[18] Networked collectivism looks at how different groups overlap in the digital environment and is usually applied to online discourse that reflects a dispersed but cohesive group of people. Understanding the network at the heart of this collectivism reveals an underlying database structure to (digital) human connectivity; that is, the networked collective highlights an unordered but structured collection of individuals. This networked collectivism appears in, for instance, the development of wikis, using collective intelligence, or the collective authorship of some forms of fan fiction. Networked collectivism reveals a structure connecting multiple individuals; this structure is revealed particularly through *The Board Game*'s gameplay mechanics as the character interactions, dependent on the players' socialization, determines the game play.

A Game of Thrones: The Board Game illustrates a networked collectivism as a singular database. Unlike the novel's close look at individual characters, *The Board Game* focuses on larger familial concerns. These familial histories of the Great Houses—the larger interconnected relationships between families—has an effect on the way the game progresses, as it plays a part in the availability of resources, power, and order within the game. This does not mean that knowledge of these characters' interpersonal relationships had no effect on the game itself: my game group experienced much mirth at my expense when I played as House Lannister, as they found plenty of opportunities to invoke the Lannister's various acts of incest into their game play, taunting and trash-talking. But at the macro-level, the game does not revolve around individual characters. In a sense, the loosely grouped individuals allied with a particular House form a collection of networked individuals who share allegiances; in the game these networked relationships become subsumed under one moniker, the name of the Great House.

A typical game round in *The Board Game* follows a pattern. First, the top card from each of the three Westeros card decks is drawn, which determines game and round procedures—whether players will muster new units, adjust their supplies, bid for new positions of power, or face a Wildling attack, among others. This random initial draw helps to keep the game fresh as the constant reshuffling of power, supplies, and armies requires constant access to information from the players' mental database.

The second turn of the round is the "planning" turn, in which players choose which orders they will give to their armies. There are five types of orders: Raid, March, Defense, Support, and Consolidate Power. Importantly, the number of orders played (and, often, the type) depends on the number of troops a player has marshaled. The number of armies depends, in turn, on the amount of supplies that each player has earned. Supplies are earned by the number of areas controlled, and some areas provide more supplies than others, as represented by barrels. Areas become controlled through marching, supporting, and defending, actions dependent on supplies. For instance, wealthy Lannisport contains two supplies, strategic Riverrun contains just one supply, and barren Stoney Sept has none (Figure 7.1). To earn additional

Figure 7.1 Supplies in Westeros are earned via representations of barrels. Game board from *A Game of Thrones: The Board Game* © 2011 Fantasy Flight Publishing, Inc.

locations, players must play their March orders—which also depend on the supplies in each location. Indeed, much of the game play within *A Game of Thrones: The Board Game* relies on players negotiating their limited resources into armies.

Thus, there is a cyclical nature to the turn, as each individual facet of game play depends on the others: armies need supplies, which are earned by marching, which takes armies. Ultimately, the database of places within Martin's literary world of Westeros plays an important role in the way the game mechanics function, and, as I mentioned above, reflects new media concerns. For example, digital technology allows multiple ways of accessing information about, say, cult media texts like *A Game of Thrones*. Partly because of its database-like qualities, *A Song of Ice and Fire* has spawned scores of fan-written wikis online like *A Wiki of Ice and Fire*. These databases of narrative information hold blocks of data about the series in much the same way as individual players must negotiate and navigate their own understandings of the elements of their Houses compared with other Houses. The pleasure of successfully planning a strategic move two turns in advance depends on a database-like understanding of not only what your own House is doing but also on the deductions gleaned from the orders given to the other Great Houses.

Battles are also won through the comparison of a number of interdependent items, including the support of armies surrounding the attacked location, the strength of the defense in comparison with the strength of the attacker, and the House cards. Each player is in control of seven cards that can augment an attack or a defense. The cards depict characters that belong to each House and can offer strength and/or abilities. For instance, as House Lannister, I could play as Ser Gregor Clegane, who not only can add a strength of three to my combat but also can kill three armies if I win the battle. Cards also feature text, as on the Tywin Lannister card, which aids the larger game play for the Lannisters (Figure 7.2).

House cards change the focus of the battle from a mere mathematical comparison (I have four armies and you have three, therefore I win) to a more strategic play. One must be able to not only understand the larger war strategy of the game but also "out think" one's opponent by playing a card that combats the particular strategy one's opponent is using. This mechanic of algorithmic strategy combined with interpersonal thematics suggests player agency within the game. As Woods notes, the most successful games depend not just on understanding the game play but also on understanding the game *players*: "the player continues

Figure 7.2 House cards for "Tywin Lannister," "Ser Gregor Clegane," and "The Hound" from *A Game of Thrones: The Board Game* © 2011 Fantasy Flight Publishing, Inc.

to have agency in the game world."[19] Only through understanding a combination of both the players and the play does one win the "game of thrones."

Beyond the mechanics of the game, the actual play experience of *The Board Game* ultimately hinges on players' social interactions as well.[20] As Pulsipher notes, multiple players in games can lead to exponentially more complex social interactions.[21] Even though players are disparately involved in various aspects of the game, there is a "sociality pattern" that highlights the interrelated connectivity of the players.[22] While some players can be more active, other players can "turtle," or try to avoid conflict, while others can ally or betray enemy Houses.[23] In this way, the game seems to mirror how the characters in the novels are constantly adjusting their allegiances and their connections to other Great Houses. Players of *The Board Game* do not retain control over any one particular *character*, but rather negotiate between *families* as alliances are made and broken. These alliances can be formed informally throughout the game, and it is a significant mechanic in the game that alliances *should* be broken. In his description of how alliances work in the rules, Peterson notes:

> players are always free … to make promises and seek alliances with other Houses. Promises and alliances, however, are never binding and can be broken for **any** reason. Even the staunchest ally cannot be 100% sure of the good intentions of his partners.[24]

By mirroring the multiple alliances within the world of *A Game of Thrones: The Board Game* highlights these multiple social connections between players.

In these connections, one aspect of the novel that is referenced throughout the game is the significance of the geography and land of Westeros. As Amelia Barikin notes, geography plays a major role in Martin's *A Song of Ice and Fire* series, not just as a plan of action, or as a metaphor for the networked interaction between character and families, but also as a way for fans to grasp the narrative:

> The serial deployment of a world across disparate formats and contexts makes it amenable to inhabitation because it leaves something open for readers or participants to hook onto and adapt. In order to remain durable, a world needs to be shared, and it needs to be built upon. It needs, in other words, to be paradoxically complete but fragmentary. It needs to have a modular frame.[25]

Sara Gwenllian-Jones also notes how the creation of vast cult geographies allows viewers to imaginatively place themselves within that world, something Lancaster terms "immersion in an imaginary entertainment environment."[26] According to Lancaster, fans can use games not just to experience the narrative of a favored series, but also to "immerse themselves more deeply in the … universe … by touching, playing, and performing with the cultural objects" of that universe.[27] As such, player alliances in the *Game of Thrones* games rely on an unspoken but shared connection between players. This added social level of game play reflects what Woods argues is a key component of complex board games, that of the art of negotiation.[28] This state of constant insecurity about alliances within the game adds interest, because it necessarily rests on the level of discourse that exists within the board game group itself. For instance, by the time my group of friends met to play *Game of Thrones*, we had been playing paratextual board games together for almost six months: we had begun to learn each other's habits, personalities, and gameplay personas. When one of my allies needed help defending an area against the onslaught of the Greyjoy/Baratheon alliance, not a word was spoken, because I knew where she was likely to play. But this sense of knowing your friends, which Woods calls "a pivotal part of gameplay," can turn social capital into a game mechanic, and as one by one your friends may betray you, this "social metagame … is as much a part of gameplay as the simple map upon which the outcome of these negotiations unfold."[29] Success in *A Game of Thrones: The Board Game* is thus determined by forging alliances and also by knowing when to break them, which mirrors the alliance strategies in the books. Strategy hinges on social negotiation.

Serialized game play

If the player is an individual controlling an entire group in *The Board Game*, the player instead becomes a central figure in his or her own network in the HBO *Card Game*. *Game of Thrones: The Card Game* is a two-player game involving battles between characters from the television series. Each character has certain attributes—character abilities that let him or her attack and defend in certain ways. In addition, characters can use up to three types of attacks—military, power, or intrigue. Players take turns using their characters to battle in one or more of these types of attacks. If these battles are won, players can earn power tokens, with fifteen power tokens winning the game. Everything in the HBO *Card Game* is revealed through specific serialized gameplay mechanics that rely on the individual actions of both the players and the characters. The HBO *Card Game* relies on a highly structured turn-taking system, comprising seven sequences: Plot, Draw, Marshall, Challenge, Dominance, Stand, Taxation. Turn-taking in this ritualized manner highlights the serialized nature of *Game of Thrones* itself. This order parallels the television program's focus on narrative serialization in the progression of the episodes as well as the chronological exposition of the show: as a serialized drama, each episode of the show develops the larger narrative, rather than simply beginning and ending one episodic narrative.[30]

Additionally, as previously mentioned, the HBO *Card Game* is actually based on a more complex card game, the Fantasy Flight *Card Game*, which allows four people to play and features multiple card expansion packs that feed a continuing commercial enterprise. These expansion packs also generate interest in individual players who might want to mirror the anticipation of the release of a new volume in the novel series or television show. The HBO *Card Game* is not expandable—or, at least, expansions have not been created for it as of this writing—meaning that the economic structure of the game does not precisely mirror the serialization of the television show, even if the game play does. This is strange as most card games of this sort are specifically designed to be "living" card games—to be ever-expandable.

Each player of the HBO *Card Game* controls one of two of the Great Houses of Westeros—House Stark or House Lannister—and thus "sits at the center of his or her own personal community."[31] While part of a House, the player controls each character individually. The HBO *Card Game* concentrates more on the serialized nature of the characters' growth and development, what Baym identifies as a "networked individualism" in which individuals form the central node of his or her own personal community.[32] Networked individualism highlights a more personalized understanding of social networks: we see ourselves as the center of our own social networks. Networked individualism shifts the focus from group collectivity to the person: "people connect, communicate, and exchange information ... at the autonomous center" of their networks, seeing themselves as key figures.[33] Zizi Papacharissi calls this the "networked self," the conception of the individual through "polysemic pertinence," or the way that multiple online communities reveal different aspects of the individual.[34] Ultimately, the HBO *Card Game* focusing on this networked individualism illustrates the close ties between the serialization of the game and the creation of narrative within our digital lives, as we attempt to apply a coherent structure to the multiple communities of which we are a part. As they manifest and reflect a networked understanding of the digital media environment, the *Games of Thrones* games demonstrate player effort, networked sociality, and narrativized game play, just as the original book and television show engender similar attributes.

In contrast to *The Board Game*, HBO's *Game of Thrones: The Card Game* presents a highly serialized narrative structure throughout the game play, mirroring the larger serialized narrative structure of the television series upon which it is based. Like *A Game of Thrones: The Board Game*, the HBO card game is also based on a number of turns; however, in the HBO *Card Game* the turns are much more ritualized and highly focused on particular actions at particular times. There are more turns, but fewer things to do in one of them, highlighting the serialization *of* the turns rather than the action *within* them. When playing the game, my opponent and I found ourselves intoning which turn we were on at any particular instance, fulfilling what Wagner describes as the "complex … relationship between rituals and games."[35]

Each player has a deck of cards with various abilities on them. By drawing cards in random order, but from a limited deck, players can attempt to out-deal their opponents. Kurt Lancaster describes this type of card play as games of "dominance," as players can use "different cards to support or oppose an attack or to lead a fleet of ships into battle, play … certain cards to enhance others, and so forth."[36] Cards all have certain abilities, but are separated into different types. Character cards are used as attackers or defenders in three types of attacks: military, intrigue, and power. Location cards provide players with benefits, such as additional gold reserves with which to buy cards. Attachments are cards that are played with a particular character and can modify his or her abilities: for example, playing a Bodyguard attachment on a Regal character can save that character from death. Event cards change the flow of the game by affecting characters and locations. Players keep a deck constructed of these types of cards; playing the cards may suggest a story, although that story is necessarily filtered through an understanding of the unfolding of events in the first season of the HBO series upon which the game is based.

This serialization at the game level, however, can best be seen through the use of plot cards. The first turn of each round begins with each player secretly selecting one of seven plots. Plots provide players with income, determine the play order for the round, and establish unique abilities that shape the overall structure of the round. In this way, plot cards shape the game structure through narrative intervention.

Plot cards are directly tied into narrative moments from the HBO series. For example, the "Dark Wings, Dark Worlds" plot reads "When revealed, cancel the effects of your opponent's plot, then your opponent must choose and reveal a new plot." As indicated by the image of the messenger raven, this plot attribute references moments in the show when the transfer of information can force different sides to change their plans, and the phrase "Dark Wings, Dark Worlds" is used to describe the ominous tidings they often herald. Another plot card, "Marched to the Wall," references moments when characters are killed or die as a result of being taken to the giant wall of ice guarding Westeros from the Northern Lands. A third plot card, "The Kings Tourney," describes a specific moment in the first season when King Robert Baratheon declared a tournament to be held to celebrate his appointment of Eddard Stark as Hand of the King. During this "Tourney of the Hand," the weaker Ser Loras Tyrell won the joust against a much stronger opponent, Ser Gregor Clegane.

The original Fantasy Flight *Card Game* allows up to four players, each one exponentially multiplying the complexity of the plots. Four plots playing at once creates a networked understanding of key elements of the narrative; plots can intersect in a variety of ways. By reducing the game to two players, the HBO *Card Game* elides much of the networking potential of the game and reveals the serialized narrative at its heart.

Serialization emerges from more than just how the game is played; HBO's *Game of Thrones Card Game* highlights individual player action as a constituent of meaning, as "the players end up 'telling' a 'story' by juxtaposing the different cards within play."[37] In the HBO *Card Game*, players use the different card types in a specific order, in order to defeat the other player. Lancaster calls this a narrative juxtaposition, as "the rules themselves help determine the meaning of the cards' juxtaposition with each other."[38] The order of attack matters to the outcome, and the individual cards played in a particular order constitute "mnemonic juxtapositions, [as] players create their own game narrative" through their personal connection to the choice of cards they play.[39] Players lay down as many cards as they can afford—each card comes with a cost, and the amount of money a player has is determined by the plot card he or she played at the start of the round. The strategy of the game arrives through the order in which those three attacks are commenced.

For example, an initial hand of four cards might change the outcome of the round. Cards can be characters, which allow players to engage in combat; attachments, which can augment character cards; and locations, which can earn players gold, reduce cost, or increase power. Some of these cards indicate fidelity to the narrative. For instance, playing the Winterfell Keep card symbolizes access to the wealth of Winterfell, and thus on each turn the player can add +1 gold to his or her store. Playing the general Winterfell location references the connection to the family's home in the show, and thus adds strength to every Stark character in play. Fidelity can occur with character play as well. For instance, in the game, Hodor cannot attack; he can only defend. In the show, Hodor is a gentle giant— he protects weaker characters like Bran but rarely goes on the offensive.

However, some cards allow a deviance from the larger narrative. The Iron Throne card symbolizes the power to rule in Westeros. Both players have a copy of this card, and thus both can vie for dominance. If only one player plays this card, though, that player receives dominance for the round, even if the *characters* are not in control of the kingdom. Or, when playing an attachment like Needle, the sword of Arya Stark, the player must place it on a particular character, regardless of whether that character is Arya or not. This deviation from the original narrative allows greater fluidity in the players' interpretation of the story. Lancaster offers a similar example in the *Babylon 5 Card Game,* when the "declare war" card depicts a particular alien species but that species does not have to match the actual event in the game.[40] Such player-created agency to shift narrative is dependent on the cards that are drawn, but present within the possibilities of the card set. Through player action, a form of narrative is achieved.

Once each player has laid down his or her hand of cards, the "marshaling forces" round of play, the "challenge round," begins and, like the previous round, it is also based in serialized action. Much as in the "conflict phase" of the *Babylon 5 Card Game,* in which "players … initiate a military, diplomatic, or intrigue action," in the HBO *Card Game,* players choose attacks "in an attempt to gain the upper hand."[41] Once both players have played their cards, the first player can initiate an attack against the other player. Players have the choice of which type of challenge they will start with.

Characters face off against each other, each fighting with his or her particular skills until no fights are left for the round. Following a game through its seven rounds in this fashion, players begin to form a particular and peculiar narrative of the *Game of Thrones* story that may or may not follow precisely what happens on the show, but will invoke moments or elements within the original text. In this, the designers of the game have attempted to translate the show's story into a linear chronology and "to build character development in the structure of the game." As Lancaster notes, by encouraging players to participate in the game, and linking specific characters to specific actions, the designers "have attempted to make the game a nexus between the story ... and the actors' performance of this story through a structure that allows game players to recuperate both of these elements within an amateur performance."[42] Success in the game is measured by the serialized order in which a player organizes their challenges, with the "story" being constructed out of the combination of player action and character ability. From a database of possibilities, only one narrative can be constructed that reflects the game ending.

"There is no middle ground..."

Winning the "game of thrones" in the novel and in the television series takes military might, economic power, intrigue abilities, and an understanding of interpersonal and social relationships and geography. Winning *A Game of Thrones: The Board Game* or HBO's *Game of Thrones: The Card Game* hinges on similar characteristics. For Woods the win condition of any game "acts as a motivation to engage with the game mechanics and is a vital facet of the circumscribed nature of contested play."[43]

Yet winning can be achieved in multiple ways, and perhaps the difference between these two games' win conditions can be attributable to their connection to an original text. To win *A Game of Thrones: The Board Game*, one must occupy seven castles and/or strongholds. There are multiple ways to achieve this single win condition. On the game board, there are twenty different castles and strongholds, which means there is a veritable database of possibilities for winning—so many combinations of occupation that the possibilities seem endless. This mechanic of multiple paths to victory is what Fay argues is a key characteristic of good game play.[44] In contrast, the HBO *Card Game* game marks victory through scoring "power" tokens, a condition dependent on a narrativized sense of game play. Although one can earn power in four different ways—by besting an opponent in a power challenge, by winning a challenge unopposed, by winning "dominance" (more players standing at the end of a round), and by winning a battle with a regal character—there is only one way to victory, and that is through playing the proper narrative within the game: "each move becomes a strategy, bringing the player closer to winning."[45] One can only win if one completes the narratives as they are enacted by the cards.

Each of these win conditions—as with the mechanics at the game level and at the play level, as described above—hinges on a relationship to the original text as either a *network of information in a database structure* or as a *serialized connection organized in a narrative framework*. It is not that the novel series and the television series reflect one of these aspects over the other; rather, both of these texts can be examined using either organizational principle. There are database-like characteristics within the novel and within the show. Similarly, there are serialized characteristics within both.

Understanding *The Board Game* as a database highlights a larger understanding of the *Game of Thrones* stories, and the digital context in which they sit. This, in turn, allows players to reexamine their understanding of the novels. Paratextual board games allow us to reread the original text through a new lens. Seen through the structure of the database, Martin's *A Song of Ice and Fire* becomes akin to what Gwenllian-Jones calls "deterritorialized fiction." Comparing the encyclopedic form of cult narratives to a virtual world constructed in readers' minds, Gwenllian-Jones describes how a database of information about a cult world becomes "explicit data and implicit potential of the text *and* the readers' internalized encyclopedia of the real world *and* the reader's imagination."[46] Interpreting the novel *Game of Thrones* in this manner allows readers and players alike to imaginatively enter this hyperdiegetic text. Martin's world of Westeros, as with other fantasy worlds like Tolkien's Middle-earth or Roddenberry's Federation of Planets, is larger than the works that contain them. Interpreted as a database of information—highlighting the network of connections between elements (e.g., this battle took place *here* with *these* people who are related through *this* ancestor)—the novel becomes an archive of information to be accessed as the player/reader desires.

Because the HBO *Card Game* focuses more on a narrative serialization for its game play, it allows the players to experience the television series as a narrative of events, mirroring the digital experience of serialization as well. This understanding highlights the way individual elements can have particular effects on others; the cause-effect structure becomes more obvious and stronger when viewed through a narrative lens. Instead of viewing the show as an encyclopedia of events, places, people, and battles, when interpreted through the forced serialization of the game, the show reveals the progression of events as dependent on individual action—much like the game itself. In *Game of Thrones*, one person *can* make a difference: Tyrion Lannister can change the course of a battle in the novel; Arya Stark can influence a leader like Tywin in the show. The same is true of the HBO *Card Game*. One player can lead his or her family, made identifiable through the images on the cards, to victory. Conversely, *A Game of Thrones: The Board Game* does not offer that same sense of individualized victory. A specific character does not win; a family does. A specific player does not win alone, but must ally with others in order to do so.

Ultimately, both games reveal the effect of examining a particular media text through a particular structural lens. Although Manovich notes that the database and the narrative are two competing structures within new media technologies and texts, the renewed presence and popularity of paratextual board games indicates that these structural lenses exist for multiple forms of media, old and new, ludic or otherwise.

Ludic Interaction in *Doctor Who*

This song is ending, but the story never ends.

Ood Sigma, *Doctor Who*

As I have shown, the paratextual potential of board games must always be tempered with an awareness of the particular mechanics of the game as they apply to the media franchise. That is, different games for different franchises must fit into the narrative imaginings of that storyworld/universe, but at the same time must create unique gameplay situations to support and augment player understandings of that universe. This final chapter, then, will draw lines of connection between these two concepts with the hope of broadening board game media scholarship. In this conclusion, I explore how paratextual board games facilitate ludic interaction with the original media text. A ludic interaction demonstrates not the copying of a narrative from one medium to another, but rather the transference of a particular identification across a ludic landscape.

To investigate ludic interaction, I examine *Doctor Who: The Interactive Electronic Board Game* and *Doctor Who: The Time Travelling Action Game*, both based on new series of the eponymous British science fiction television show. Both games use game-controlled "interactivity" as a selling point. *The Interactive Electronic Board Game* uses a randomized, talking TARDIS, the Doctor's blue Police Box time machine, to manifest ludic interaction—an interactive process of identification with the original media product through the generation of paratextual meaning. In comparison, *The Time Travelling Action Game* uses an automatic, spinning game board to match specific alien characters from the show. In this way, it uses interactivity as a type of "media ritual" that formalizes gameplay affect in the users. For Nick Couldry, media rituals are "any actions organized around key media-related categories and boundaries ... [that] act out, indeed naturalize, the myth of the media's social centrality."[1] He uses the examples of live media events, media pilgrimages, and reality television to develop an understanding of how the media reinforce their own importance in our lives. Applying his work to games leads to the fifteenth principle of paratextual board games:

Principle 15: When seen as strict adaptations, paratextual board games close off interpretation of the media text; when seen as ludic interaction, they open up player dialogue with the media text.

While our media environment has become more convergent across multiple corporations and multiple outlets, and as the numerous methods for viewing books, films, and television converge, the paratextual board game sits at the nexus of multiple production spaces at once. As game designer Raph Koster notes, "the more rigidly constructed your game is, the more limited it will be."[2] Ultimately, this chapter sets the stage for the next board game researcher by hypothesizing about what "the future" of paratextual games might bring. Future research will, of course, be necessary to judge the place of board games within a media environment that itself changes over time. Paratextual board games are analog but hinge on digital changes; they are game based but rely on narratological principles. Through a discussion of interactive play and ludic interaction, I describe in this chapter how paratextual board games reveal the diversity within the media sphere, and highlight the ranges of meanings constructed by audiences and creators alike.

Interactive play in paratextual board games

Throughout this book I have examined particular manifestations of paratextual board games for their different play mechanics, their diverse narrative focuses, and, importantly, their larger connection to digital media culture. Although many paratextual board games can develop strong inter- or intratextual connections to the original text, this relationship can also be problematic. Contemporary media products retain a strong sense of narrative development and character development, two things that board games have difficulty augmenting with the same referent or intensity as the original text. At the same time, contemporary cult media franchises thrive on the intense worldbuilding of fantasy, sci-fi, and/ or dystopian storyworlds. The most successful media franchises, those that tend to generate paratextual board games, have fully realized worlds where multiple variants on narrative and character development can thrive. As Andrea Phillips describes, along with the creation of narrative backstories, developing fully realized characters and detailed worlds are important elements of building any transmedia franchise.[3] In this case, paratextual board games not only help generate complex worlds, but also engender audience engagement with those worlds. With the right positioning within the narrative framework, matching ideologically but differing in practice, paratextual board games can not only strengthen and cohere these cult worlds, but *can actually make the storyworlds more real.* Paratextual board games make the abstract tangible; there is physical interaction within a fictional diegesis. Board games replace visualization with imagination, spectacle with player investment.

The imaginative play of paratextual board games represents a new way of approaching the relationship between board games and their representative text. *Doctor Who: The Interactive Electronic Board Game* and *Doctor Who: The Time Travelling Action Game* represent salient aspects of ludic interaction, a way of interacting with the medium that is more than experiential.[4] Both games provide a scaffold upon which to build the game elements while allowing the freedom to imagine new scenarios. Both games make use of "interactive" elements to generate randomness within the play and to create a more satisfying game experience. The interactive elements use battery power and electronics to automatically move the board or create random elements without player involvement. At the same time, these interactive elements function as rituals that attempt to cohere the player to the original *Doctor Who* text. By seemingly increasing the randomness of the game, the interactive mechanisms mirror the "uncertainty" of a cult narrative, but like a narrative once watched, this interactivity eventually becomes rote.

Released in 2005, the same year that the first new series of *Doctor Who* premiered in the UK, *The Interactive Electronic Board Game* features a model of the TARDIS that randomly offers one of twelve different scenarios whenever a player lands on a particular space on the board. These scenarios include "A Black Hole is pulling us in!" which instructs the player to lose two turns, or "Looks like the Daleks are leaving," which gives the player two extra turns. In contrast, *The Time Travelling Action Game*, which was released two years after David Tennant took the role of the titular Time Lord, features an electronically controlled game board that rotates at random moments in the game, rearranging the spaces on the board. Where one's playing piece may be two spaces away from the end, the rotating board can move it further or closer to its goal.

The inclusion of automated randomness in the two *Doctor Who* board games follows a number of "interactive" board games, many of which use DVDs or VHS tapes to create a multimedia game experience. These games, like *Star Trek:*

The Interactive VCR Board Game or *Indiana Jones: DVD Adventure Game*, use another form of media to occasionally interrupt the flow of the play experience and instruct players on what they must do. The unexpected interruption usually occurs when one is first playing the game; playing through multiple times leads to a certain memorization of the interactive elements in these VHS/DVD games. In general, paratextual board games—like all board games—engender interactivity as players can manipulate pieces (e.g., *Star Trek: Fleet Captains* and *Star Trek: Expeditions*), move the game board (e.g., *LOTR* and *The Lord of the Rings: The Complete Trilogy*), adjust their characters' stats (e.g., *Arkham Horror* and *Training Days*), and even make decisions that change the outcome of the game (e.g., *Battlestar Galactica: The Board Game* and *A Game of Thrones: The Board Game*). And players of interactive paratextual games may be encouraged to participate with the game pieces, the game board, and the in-game media text to develop cohesion between players and narratives.

For many players of paratextual board games, including the *Doctor Who* games, the game has "done its job" if it has facilitated a meaningful and playful interaction with an already experienced text. At the same time, this interruption becomes a type of "media ritual," reaffirming the player's connection to the original text. The two *Doctor Who* paratextual board games structurally reinforce the experience of *watching Doctor Who* and thus become dependent upon *Doctor Who* for their ultimate meaning. Paratextuality portends the idealized experience of the original media text.

Paratextual board games have something meaningful to contribute to the larger context of the media franchise, contextualizing the original text by adding meaning through interpretive framing. Paratextual board games can reveal more than just a way of playing games; they can also reveal a chance to play with the media environment.

The act of play simulates lived experiences and paratextual board games allow us to play in a world we expressly inhabit during viewership. That is, while reading or watching our favorite cult media franchises, we can "visit" the worlds by participating in what Roger Aden has called a symbolic pilgrimage. Media viewers can interpret the world of the narrative as a geography to visit, creating a transcendental relationship with the text.[5] Paratextual board games allow us to become recognized tourists on this symbolic pilgrimage: we can collect souvenirs (pieces of the narrative represented as cards, dice, HeroClix, or figurines), we can follow the journeys of our protagonists (either on the board or through narrative developments), and we can participate in the narrative.

The miniature images of David Tennant as the Doctor in the *Time Travelling Action Game* become totems of memory—linked both to the show itself (or the character/actor), and to the experience of playing the game. Interaction with a text, especially fan interaction, has tended to fall under three types of activities, as defined by John Fiske: semiotic productivity (making meaning from watching), enunciative productivity (making conversation with others), or textual productivity (creating fan work).[6] In a digital environment, as Hills suggests, these three merge, highlighting a "fluidity of semiotic, enunciative, and textual productivity" across audiences in the digital environment.[7] In contrast, paratextual board games engender a different type of activity that I term "ludic productivity." In this form of paratextual activity, the boundaries of the text and the paratext become conjoined through the interactive potentiality espoused by the game itself. That is, players must negotiate their own activity within the larger boundaries encompassing the game and the original text.[8] This form of productivity hinges on the sense of paratextuality at the heart of the franchise, and the connectivity permeating the two.

Ludic interaction and imaginative transformation in *Doctor Who*

In some crucial ways, paratextual games do not merely extend the world of the original text, but rather, as H. Porter Abbott might suggest, adapt that world for a new medium.[9] Such discussion requires a revisitation of contemporary paratextual theories. The concept of ludic interaction creates a sense of grounded, but new, meanings within the paratextual board game, rather than seeing it as a shadow of the original text.[10]

Whereas the concept of "adaptation" is a linear model of media interaction, developed out of literary theory, ludic interaction references play with the original text, the back-and-forth construction of meaning between paratextual game and original text. For Dudley Andrews, adaptation can take many forms, but the most common is a type of transformation that assumes a particular fidelity to the original.[11] Andrews calls this a "tiresome" mode, as it implicitly creates a hierarchy between media texts. Removed from the context of *filmic adaptations* (the subject of his book), the idea of *ludic interaction* as a transformative act becomes relevant to games. For Andrews, all media are adaptations of already extant ideological and cultural meanings, and all adaptation is "the appropriation of meaning" itself from larger ideological structures.[12] Linda Hutcheon complicates these structures, calling adaptation both a *product* that has specific ties to an original text and a *process* that "permits us to think about how adaptations allow people to tell, show, or interact with stories."[13] Processes of adaptation reveal a more complex version of linearized, narratively based meanings, and further complicate our understanding of storytelling

I have previously written about the need for new theoretical models to explain the multifaceted and nonlinear interpretation of culture from contemporary vantage points.[14] Board games, although an ancient form of play, illustrate the need for new models, specifically in their connection with contemporary media. When narrativized, linear media become the default. Consequently, scholars and players ignore the important contributions that ludism brings to contemporary cultural studies. Adaptation by itself is out-moded and functionally misunderstood in the context of board games. Quite simply, adaptation does not describe what paratextual board games *do*. While video games have been analyzed as one way of reexamining adaptation, board games have not. Bogost uses the term "procedural adaptation" to describe the various ways that video games "do more than just replicate the licensed property's characters, scenes, or logos"—they intermix "playable scenes ... with rendered cinematics that fill in the scenes left unplayable."[15] Through the innovative use of cut scenes, animated characters, and gameplay mechanics, video games provide a useful way of examining ludic *adaptation*. But board games cannot replicate those same affordances within the scope of an analog system—they require a player's ludic *interaction*.

This interpretation of ludic interaction combines aspects of what Andrews has called "transforming" adaptation, the "reproduction ... of something essential about an original text"[16] with a rhetorical model of ludism described by Sutton-Smith as a rhetoric of "play as the imaginary."[17] Indeed, I would argue, what is transformative about board game adaptations is not just "fidelity to the spirit, to the original's tone, values, imagery, and rhythm," but also a specific transformation of the meaning behind the consumption of the media text.[18] It is telling that media scholars tend to use the word "read" to describe books, films, and television series but rarely do we talk about "reading" a game—instead, we play it. The type of play engendered by fictional texts, at least according to Sutton-Smith, could be considered "playful improvisation ... idealiz[ing] the imagination flexibility, and creativity of the ... human play worlds."[19] For Sutton-Smith, this type of play is not imaginary because it is frivolous, but rather because it deliberately manifests characteristics of both creativity and imagination—composers who "play" the piano and children who "play" at imaginative games are both equally participating in a rhetoric of play as imaginary.

In terms of imaginative ludic interaction, the *Doctor Who* games offer referents to the television series while forming completely new mechanics and mechanisms that, even while echoing *Doctor Who*, do not mirror it. *The Interactive Electronic Board Game* is themed around the first series of the new *Doctor Who*, featuring six different locations on the board, each of which matches various places encountered by the Ninth Doctor: present day London; 200,000 years in the future on Satellite 5; 5 billion years in the future on Platform 1; Victorian Cardiff; 2012 in Utah; and London during the Blitz. At each location, the player can imaginatively reexperience the Doctor's adventures. The game, however, does not *prescribe* such readings. While in the Victorian London area, for example, the game board displays an image of a horse-drawn carriage that evokes moments from that episode; the image of Satellite 5 that accompanies those spaces on the board similarly reminds players of the show. But the game itself does not require, nor even reward, player knowledge of *Doctor Who*. Although some versions of the game were produced that featured images of the Ninth Doctor (Christopher Eccleston) on the playing pieces, the version I received depicted the Doctor in shadow—although the general outline of the Ninth Doctor appears on the playing piece, there are few identifying marks and it could be anyone (Figure 8.1).[20] Other fans have created their own version of playing pieces that feature images of other Doctors as well.[21] The voice that emanates from the Interactive TARDIS does not sound like that of any actor

Figure 8.1 Components of *Doctor Who: The Interactive Electronic Board Game* ©Toy Brokers Ltd., 2005. Photo by the author.

that has played the role. Indeed, of all the components that attempt fidelity to *Doctor Who,* only the Daleks are authentic. The model Daleks match reasonably well their television counterparts, and the voice on the model TARDIS when the Daleks scream "YOU WILL OBEY" is quite reminiscent of the original.

The actual game play involves unique game-specific moments that have little to do with any specific iteration of the show, but do mirror the particular components that one might point to as being *Doctor Who*-esque. As Matt Hills points out, this "image of 'ideal' *Who,* a kind of Platonic essence of the series ... may never have been realized fully in any one story" but can be shaped by multiple components.[22] At the same time, *The Interactive Electronic Board Game* represents an adaptive formula for portraying *Doctor Who* in board game form. The "plot" of the game is that the TARDIS needs to stop at each of six locations, but throughout its journey, the ship is being chased by the Daleks. During their turns, players move both their piece and the Dalek pieces to try to ambush the other players. In this sense, players are competing against each other, but two can also work together to use the Daleks as foils against a third. Additionally, the interaction of the electronic talking TARDIS generates more randomness within the game. Although the twelve possible instructions that can emerge from the TARDIS could have been simulated with a 12-sided die (as has been pointed out in the discussion thread about this game on boardgamegeek),[23] the fact that an interactive TARDIS generates instructions lends credibility to the nature of the game (however, whether it is a mistake throughout all the game sets or just in the one that I own, the fact that the TARDIS light is green, not the traditional white, counters this somewhat).

Winning the game means not just avoiding the Daleks, but also traveling to each of the locations to retrieve a card from that particular spot. Players can trade cards, can fight Daleks using cards, and can travel through time portals to other parts of the board. Because the game does not mirror a particular episode of *Doctor Who,* players can engage in the game play in whatever imaginative modalities they wish. For Sutton-Smith, this form of imaginative play resides in the mind as a "rhetoric of the imaginary."[24] This ludic interaction of *The Interactive Electronic Board Game* occurs because it seems to capture the "spirit" of *Doctor Who.* While the pieces may not look like the Doctor and the TARDIS's light may not be the correct color, the generative experience of playing the game seems to adapt not specific moments from the text, but the general feeling of the text. It captures both the experience of being a fan of *Doctor Who* and the feeling of being a part of the series.

One can be interactive in a game without communicating with others, but this does not mean that interactivity is a simple concept in the sphere of paratextual board games. By definition, paratextual board games have to fit within an already-extant story universe—one cannot play *Battlestar Galactica* and expect to find the Starship *Enterprise* flying around piloted by Hobbits, and fighting Cthulhu with blasters (although this a great idea for a crossover). Similarly, a game that invokes specific characters or situations from a film, television show, or book should not depict those characters working differently from how they might act in their more familiar roles. The characters in *Star Trek: Expeditions* are not given abilities outside standard moral and ethical boundaries. Players would not expect their character to turn to another character and shoot him with a phaser in the middle of the game. Although focusing mainly on video games, Alexander Galloway describes game play not as images or stories but as specific *actions* within the sphere of media objects. To describe games as actions implies that they develop codes through which specific changes can be enacted. Games must also have a certain flexibility to enable user control over interactive elements. Galloway argues that flexibility is both a core principle of Internet design and a core protocol of game design: "All elements of the game are put in quantitative, dynamic relationships with each other."[25] To be flexible means to support interactive elements within the game play in a way that generates meaning in and for game players. But by dint of the relationship between the game and the original media text, the flexibility of the game is necessarily limited.

This lack of flexibility is revealed when playing *The Time Travelling Action Game*. Although the semantics of the game mirror those from the show, the syntactics of what those elements *mean* is so different that it seems almost unrelated. The game has relatively simple mechanics. Just as with Katniss in *The Hunger Games: District 12*, each player of *The Time Travelling Action Game* plays as the Doctor using different colored pieces. As such, multiple instances of the same character make narrative development difficult. However, each of these Doctors draws four different alien cards from a pack of 24. These aliens are also featured on spaces on the rotating game board, twelve of which randomly change as the board rotates. Players must land on the spaces for which they have a card and pay a number of "energy tokens" equal to the number printed on the alien card plus the roll of a spinner. If they are able to pay that many energy tokens, they have "defeated" the alien. If not, they continue to roam the board looking for more aliens. The only other options available on the board are energy spaces,

Figure 8.2 Interactive game board. *Doctor Who: The Time Travelling Action Game* ©Toy Brokers Ltd., 2007. Photo by the author.

where tokens can be won or lost, and "time portals," which allow the player to bypass the normal movement route (Figure 8.2).

All the elements of the game match *Doctor Who* precisely—the images on the cards are from the series, the playing pieces feature a lovely image of David Tennant, and the TARDIS is accurate in terms of sound and shape. However, the game simply does not feel like *Doctor Who* when one is playing it. For example, the Doctor rarely travels around the universe looking for fights. Rather, he attempts to solve his problems peacefully instead of combating aliens. The distribution of alien power is also somewhat random. Both the Slitheen, a race of farting green alien scavengers, and the Reaper, a giant creature that lives outside time and space and can destroy a planet, are defeated using three energy tokens. In the diegesis of *Doctor Who*, a Slitheen would be powerless compared to a Reaper. Similarly, both a Cyberman drone, a member of a cyborgian race, and The Beast, a humongous manifestation of the Devil itself, are defeated with six energy tokens. Even at their most powerful, the Cybermen would never be on equal footing with the Devil itself.

Rather than esoteric semantics about *Doctor Who*, these are crucial details for fans. They simply ring false for the series, and alienate the player of the paratextual game from the *Doctor Who* universe. Although this *looks* like the Doctor, he does not *act* like the Doctor. *The Time Travelling Action Game* is not a ludic interaction with the series—semantic elements are carried over but the syntactics that create meaning with those elements are not. At the same time, the rules of the game offer a note that hints toward a more active player interaction with the game. Unusually for a paratextual board game, the *Time Travelling Action Game* rules end on a celebratory note for players: "Good luck and remember that if you fail to understand any of these rules, do not despair, it is only a game and as long as everyone is in agreement, the rules can be flexible!!"[26] By not only facilitating, but also encouraging, the players' freedom to experiment with the official rules and develop their own rules, the game subtly focuses on player creativity rather than slavish obedience. This focus on original rules facilitates the "cocreation" of game play as I described in Chapter 2. Players become part of the *Doctor Who* universe not through the actual game play, but through the mechanics by which the game encourages interactive creativity.

The imaginary space that *The Interactive Electronic Board Game* embodies is an adaptation not of *Doctor Who* itself, but rather of the *Doctor Who* experience—of being a part of the series without affecting the series. *Doctor Who* as a television series is many things: an adventure story, a science fiction spectacular, a romance, a fantasy. Following the Doctor through time and space is not just about being a part of an alternate world; it is also about allowing oneself as a viewer to be positioned in multiple ways at different times. Just as the genre changes, just as the narrative changes, so too does the show change. *Doctor Who* is, in fact, and always has been, about change and renewal.[27] At the core of *Doctor Who* is change itself, personified by the Doctor who can regenerate himself.[28] Players do not so much embody the Doctor as they embody the idea of playing as the Doctor. They do not so much recall the specific locations, but rather play at recalling those locations. *The Interactive Electronic Board Game* represents a simulation of *Doctor Who* from a strategy of ludic interaction—a strategy that encourages not just more consumption of *Doctor Who*, but also the experience of being a part of a group for whom *Doctor Who* itself is meaningful. Imaginative transformation is a form of ludic interaction of an experience, not a text—a feeling, not a narrative. Imaginative transformation identifies the core meaning of a text—the heart of what makes that text uniquely *that* text—and ascribes onto it gameplay mechanics. Imaginative ludic interaction offers new ways to perform and play contemporary games.

"This song is ending, but the story never ends..."

We live in a digital age, and our media is becoming more and more digitized. As I write this, three major video game consoles have been released that rely on streaming services for game play. The Nintendo Wii U, the Xbox One, and the

Playstation 4 are some of the most advanced gaming systems on the market, with state-of-the-art graphics, game engines, and CPUs. With the capacity to download thousands of games, to connect people via the Internet through online game play, and to provide more complex types of game texts, these systems are truly revolutionizing the video game market.

But just as video games are making more money than Hollywood, a quieter, subtler shift is happening in the board game world. Complex, detailed, and engrossing board games are becoming more popular. As I was researching this book, two events happened to me that revealed this popularity. At an academic conference in Seattle, I was chatting with a local resident who was on his way to attend his weekly board game group at a local bar. It was 11 p.m. and I was returning from dinner; his night, he said, was just starting and he would be playing games until 4 a.m. A few weeks later, I walked into a board game store in a local mall and found scores of people playing a board game tournament—the owners of the store had organized an official competition. The place was crowded with players, each hovering over his or her own side of the many game boards on the tables.

Video games may have become more serious business, but board games reflect a focus on more intimate, social experiences. Board games are inherently a social medium, and the very act of playing a game generates interaction with other people. Although board games are played (generally) in private spaces, they are done so with other people, and in close proximity. The game board itself becomes a force for social coherence. The necessity for intimate closeness with a board game engenders this sense of community. Board games' inherently social aspects make them active, and although one can attempt to passively play a game, the very act of playing a game is generative of performance. And even though many video games are social, today we often play them over networks rather than in person, online rather than next to each other on the couch.

Throughout this book, I have investigated this paratextual potential in order to explore two attributes of paratextual board games: (1) that they perform particular versions of their original text; and (2) that they manifest characteristics of the new media environment. Just as board games have facilitated great socialization around more complex narratives, they are also indicative of a shift in the contemporary media landscape. Our media is synthesizing, as transmedia connections create texts larger than any one medium can hold. Paratextual board games, those based on extant media products, reflect this environment not just because they can become part of media franchises, but also because they perform this synthesis themselves. They are at the same time part of the media franchise but also apart from the narrative. Because paratextual board games cannot build narrative within the franchise, they reveal that non-narrative components of contemporary media are equally, if not more, important than plot. This *unstructure* complicates and problematizes our traditional notions of mediation, game narrative, and play. They are text and paratext, classic and innovative, adaptation and extension. Board games are representative of a new way of performing the media.

Paratextual board games allow us to see the media environment as constructed not by absolute delineations between one text and other, but as a series of shifting signifiers, each of which performs different interpretations of textual moments. The paratextual board game is a mediated performance, a connection between player, audience member, and text that can only be generated in the moment of play. This moment is cocreated by audience, game designer, and original media text, and is never concretized. Each game session is unique, each play individual.

If anything, *Game Play* has shown how serious game playing can be. Far from mere "pasted on themes," paratextual board games reveal a complex relationship with the contemporary media environment. But hopefully *Game Play* has also revealed how much fun game playing can be. We play games because they are entertaining and because they bring us together as friends and family. In *Game Play* I have hopefully started a conversation about the importance of paratextuality in board gaming, but I hope the discussion continues. There is so much left to play.

Glossary

Throughout *Game Play* I have tried to use terminology that will be easily understood by different communities. However, some complex or site-specific terminology is unavoidable, especially given complex topics like media scholarship and game play. In providing this glossary of terms from the book, I don't mean to suggest that alternate meanings of these terms don't exist, but rather to focus on how I've used these terms in this book.

Adaptation: The process of recasting a text into a new format.

Affect: How emotions are generated through a text.

Affective play: Matt Hills's terms for interactions with a media text that allow fans to experience and feel a reality within the text as it applies to their own lives.

Affinity space: James Paul Gee's term for a space where individuals can interact and learn using common activities. Affinity spaces engender community through mutual interest.

Affirmational fan: Noted fan obsession_inc's term for a fan who interprets the source text as canonized and embraces producer-centric ways of reading the text.

Affordance: As defined by J. J. Gibson, the actionable properties between the world and an actor; the interaction an object facilitates in its users (e.g., buttons are to be pushed, knobs are to be turned).

Algorithm: A step-by-step procedure for calculations in mathematics based on rules.

Ally: A term for a character in a game that is either partnered with or helps the player's character.

Alternate reality game: A game that takes place in the "real world" by using everyday media as elements to follow; a sort of large-scale puzzle-solving scavenger hunt.

Ameritrash games: A term by Greg Costikyan that refers to modern American complex board games, often with complex themes and heroic game play.

Appropriationalist: A term used by Suzanne Scott for media producers who use fannish tactics to appeal to a particular fandom.

Autoethnography: A research methodology that asks the researcher to examine his or her own place within the media environment; as Matt Hills defines it, an autoethnographic methodology examines not just the tastes, values, attachments, and investments of the community under study, but also asks the person undertaking it to question their own place within the values of their culture.

Automated: A characteristic of a text that works without human intervention.

Boardgamegeek: A popular website and community that houses conversation, critique, and analysis of board games.

Branching path narrative: A narrative form where different story paths lead from single points; like a *Choose Your Own Adventure* novel, different paths can contradict others (also, *Forking-path narrative*).

Canonical: Part of an authorized, official narrative.

Character: The people and elements that populate the cult world; characters can have semiotic (artificial) and mimetic (life-like) qualities; Roberta Pearson notes six ways of identifying characters: psychological traits/habitual behaviors, physical characteristics/appearance, speech patterns, interactions with other characters, environment, and biography.

Classical games: Stewart Woods's term for games with no readily attributable authorship, and which no company can claim as their own; e.g., Chess or Go.

Collaborationists: Henry Jenkins's term for media producers who see fans as important collaborators in the production of content.

Collaborative: A style of game play wherein all players work together as a team, sharing the rewards and punishments; everyone wins and loses together.

Competitive: A style of game play wherein each player works against the others and only one person can win.

Components: The parts of the game (e.g., cards, dice, figures, board).

Conceits: Thematic elements of a game that might affect the game play.

Constituent elements: Components that are essential to the game play.

Constitutive rules: The mathematical logics that guide the allowable permutations of a game.

Convergence: Henry Jenkins's term for the spread of media content between both producers and audiences.

Cooperation: A style of game play wherein each player works with the others but the play does not guarantee a balanced outcome; according to Jonas Linderoth there are two types of cooperation—"pure cooperation" wherein everyone works together equally and the "tragedy of the commons" style of cooperation, where the system falls apart if players are too individualistic.

Crossover: A type of text where one text includes constituent elements of another text.

Cult media: A type of media text defined by Matt Hills as something different from mainstream media; cult media tend to garner overt fan cultures and have "geek" followings.

Culture: Katie Salen and Eric Zimmerman's third schema for understanding games; a way of understanding the larger context in which the games sit, a surrounding milieu.

Database: An organizational structure wherein elements are networked to others through multiple connections.

Diegetic: Part of the world of the text.

Digital cosplay: A style of fan interaction with a media text where the fan uses social media to depict stylish outfits for media characters.

Dynamic elements: Parts of a media text that can change when adapted to a different medium.

Empathy: That which allows players to feel within a fictional world and for fictional characters.

Enunciative productivity: John Fiske's term for the meaning created when fans have conversations with others.

Eurogames: For Stewart Woods, a modern complex board game popularized in Europe that is strategic, doesn't take too long to play, has high-quality components, and emphasizes different styles of game play.

Eustress: Positive or healthy stress.

Expansion packs: Additional components of a game that can be purchased to augment the game play.

Fan: A media viewer/reader/player who has an emotional connection to a media text.

Fan fiction: A type of fan productivity in which fans write original stories based on media characters, often referred to as "filling in the gaps" of the media narrative.

Fan videos: Re-edited videos created by fans that can emphasize the original narrative, highlight emotional moments, or create new narratives.

Fantasy Flight Games: A game production house that specializes in paratextual board games.

Feelies: Material artifacts that are packaged with video games.

Forking path narrative: Create different narratives as different stories developed from the same points (also, *Branching path narrative*).

Franchising: The replication of multiple media products under one brand; an industrial process by which a media text may be replicated across multiple cultural contexts.

Game FAQs: Online paratexts where game players can ask and answer questions about different board games.

Game mechanics: Constructs within the game intended to produce a particular result; players can sometimes directly manipulate, understand, and experience these constructs themselves.

Game play: The experience of playing a particular game in one particular session.

GIF: The Graphics Interchange Format is a type of image that supports short animations.

GIFfic: A story told with multiple animated GIFs.

Hobby games: Stewart Woods's term for contemporary complex board games that have clear authors, but are not mass-market games.

Homo Ludens: A classic book on play by Johan Huizinga; the term means "playful (hu) man."

Hyperdiegesis: Matt Hills's term for a cult media's vast narrative space, "only a fraction of which is ever directly seen or encountered within the text, but which nevertheless appears to operate according to principles of internal logic and extension."

Imaginative play: The capacity of the player/reader/viewer of media to imagine different directions for the narrative.

Implicit rules: The social and cultural contracts that we subscribe to when we agree to play with each other.

Interactive board games: Games that use interactivity as marketing to illustrate artificially generated interactive elements like additional media (VHS/DVD) or electronic components.

Interactive narrative: A narrative that adjusts to cues from players/readers/viewers.

Interactivity: The ability to manipulate a game, either through physical manipulation of parts or implicit manipulation of the game play or narrative.

Intertextuality: Elements of one text that appear in or influence a different text.

Licensed board game: A mass-market game based on a media text.

Linear: Taking place in a particular order.

Living card game: A card game with a base set and periodically released expansion packs that build onto this base.

Ludic: Having to do with play; playful.

Ludic interaction: The mechanism by which paratextual board games reflect not the content but the *feeling* of the original text.

Ludic productivity: The meaning generated by fans playing games and exceeding the boundaries of the text and the paratext.

Ludology: The study of games as inherently play based.

Magic circle: Johan Huizinga's term for the playspace of the game world.

Manipulation: The characteristic of new media objects to be subject to change.

Mass-market games: Commercial titles that are produced and sold in large numbers year after year, and which constitute the common perception of commercial board games (e.g., *Monopoly*).

Materiality: The specific tactile interaction players can have with individual pieces of a game; the tactile and sensual aspects of a board game.

Media rituals: Nick Couldry's term for aspects of the media system that reinforce the media's social centrality.

Mimetic fandom: The desire to replicate what's in the media text.

Modular: Constructed of interchangeable parts.

Mutability: The quality of a game to be different each time it is played.

Narrative: A term indicating the way fan communities can create narrative through interaction.

Narrative database: The creation of a structure that tells a story through the unordered accumulation of details.

Narratology: The study of games as inherently based in stories.

Neoliberal: An economic and social philosophy highlighting individualism, commercialism, and laissez-faire trade.

Networked collectivism: Nancy Baym's term for groups of people networking using media, creating a shared but distributed group identity.

Networked individualism: Nancy Baym's term for individuals who form the central node of his or her own personal community.

Networking: Making connections between elements.

New media: Media forms that make use of digital elements to generate user participation.

Nondiegetic: Outside the world of the text (e.g., the credits of a film are part of the film but not part of the diegesis).

Nonlinear: Not following a particular order.

Nonplayer Character (NPC): A character in a game that is controlled by the game system.

Operational rules: Guidelines that players must follow in order to play; the rules written in a rulebook.

Paratextual: A text that is separated from a related text but informs our understanding of that text; material that surrounds the text.

Paratextual board games: Contemporary original board games based on media texts.

Participatory culture: A type of community that encourages interaction with and original creation of media texts.

Pathos: The emotional appeal a text can make.

Performance: The acting out ("play") of a particular identity in a particular context.

Philosophy of playfulness: A phrase that describes the fun-filled, playful, and exuberant media landscape.

Play: Katie Salen and Eric Zimmerman's second schema for understanding games; the experience of the game as it is occurring.

Procedural rhetoric: Ian Bogost's term for the practice of using game mechanics persuasively.

Produsage: Axel Bruns's term for the intersection of production and usage within a digital environment.

Prohibitionists: Henry Jenkins's term for media producers who attempt to criminalize fan participatory activity.

Projective identity: James Paul Gee's term for the hypothetical identity that exists between the game player and the game character.

Randomness: Elements of a game that are controlled by chance.

Replay value: Affective capital generated by a game's ability to be entertaining despite having already been played.

Role-play: The act of pretending to be another person or character, usually in the context of a game.

Rounds: The length of time in a game during which all players have taken a turn.

Rules: Katie Salen and Eric Zimmerman's first schema for understanding games; the underlying structure that guides how players play a game; rules govern the game and help define the game for what it is and also what it is not.

Sandbagging: Players pretending to be in a worse-off position than they are during a game.

Semiotic productivity: John Fiske's term for the meaning created when fans watch or read media texts.

Serial: A particular ordered experience of a media text.

Skills/character attributes: Mutable elements of a game character that affect the abilities of that character.

Snowball storytelling: A type of transmedia franchise that consists of a core narrative that becomes so popular that it inspires multiple products to be created after its release.

Spatial-temporal environment: The elements of the cult world.

Spimatic cycle: The particular and unique interactions each player will have with a media franchise.

Spime: Bruce Sterling's term for a digital and physical trace of an object through both time and space; physical objects that begin and end as data.

Static elements: Parts of a media text that remain the same when adapted to a different medium.

Storyworld: The complete environmental and temporal understanding of a cult world.

Symbolic pilgrimage: Roger Aden's term for how media viewers interpret the world of the narrative as a geography to visit.

Synchronic: Highly engaged with time.

System storytelling: A type of transmedia franchise that has been deliberately designed to use more than one medium to tell one story.

Systemic analysis: An analysis of a game that examines the unique characteristics of the game that help make the game what it is.

Temporal thickness: A term for the presence of time within an object or character; the feeling that a character has a past and a future.

Text: Any media product that can be interpreted; this includes books, movies, television programs, graphic novels, games, fashion, or any other "readable" medium.

Textual analysis: A methodology used to discover the most likely interpretations that might be made of that text.

Textual productivity: John Fiske's term for the meaning generated when fans create their own texts.

Traitor mechanic: A game mechanic wherein one player works against the group unbeknownst to the others.

Transcoding: Lev Manovich's term for the influence the computer has over our understanding of traditional media and culture.

Transformational fan: Noted fan obsession_inc's term for a fan who alters and transforms the text, manipulating it to their own desires.

Transgressive play: Espen Aarseth's term for moments of rebellion when players act against the game system.

Transmedia: The expansion of a narrative across multiple media products.

Transmedia extensions: Elements of a story that fans collect to increase their encyclopedic knowledge of the narrative.

Transmedia pathos: The close connection between the player and the character that translates between elements in a transmedia franchise.

Turn: The full actions of one player during a round.

Turtling: A style of game play wherein one player avoids conflict while other players fight a debilitating war.

Uncanny valley: The experience of something being so close to human that it appears creepy or otherwise eerie.

Uncertainty: Not knowing the outcome or the specific unfolding of a game.

Unknowability: Knowing that knowledge exists without comprehending what that knowledge is.

Unstructure: The inability to define or recognize the underlying basis for a structure within a system; deliberately unknowable to make elements appear random for an effect.

Variable: Something that can be adjusted to suit the context.

"What If" transmedia: Jason Mittell's term for a transmedia franchise that poses hypothetical possibilities rather than canonical certainties.

"What Is" transmedia: Jason Mittell's term for a transmedia franchise that focuses on expanding the storyworld through augmentation.

Win conditions: The specific circumstances that lead to a player or team winning the game.

Notes

Introduction

1 Todd Martens, "Board Games Return to Popularity," *Los Angeles Times*, November 12, 2012 (accessed June 01, 2014), http://www.jsonline.com/business/board-games-return-to-popularity-sd7lkjk-180549421.html.

2 Nick Wingfield, "High-Tech Push Has Board Games Rolling Again," *New York Times*, May 05, 2014 (accessed May 05, 2014), http://www.nytimes.com/2014/05/06/technology/high-tech-push-has-board-games-rolling-again.html.

3 "Annual Sales Data," *Toy Industry Association, Inc.*, 2013 (accessed July 08, 2014), http://www.toyassociation.org/TIA/Industry_Facts/salesdata/IndustryFacts/Sales_Data/Sales_Data.aspx#.UzGI_a1dUTY.

4 Stewart Woods, *Eurogames: The Design, Culture, and Play of Modern European Board Games* (Jefferson City, NC: McFarland, 2012).

5 Cherri Lawson, "No Batteries Required: Board Game Sales Soar," *NPR*, December 24, 2009 (accessed June 01, 2014), http://www.npr.org/templates/story/story.php?storyId=121841016.

6 Wingfield, "High-Tech Push."

7 Michael G. Robinson, "I Outwit Your Outwit: HeroClix, Superhero Fans, and Collectible Miniature Games," in *Super/Heroes: From Hercules to Superman*, eds. Wendy Haslem, Angela Ndalianis, and Chris Mackie (Washington, DC: New Academia Publishing, 2007), 335.

8 Woods, *Eurogames*, 121, citing Arthur Armstrong and John Hagel III, "The Real Value of On-Line Communities," *Harvard Business Review* 74, no. 3 (1996).

9 Woods, *Eurogames*; Alexa.com.

10 Mark Deuze, *Media Life* (Cambridge, MA: Polity Press, 2012).

11 "The Game of *Alice in Wonderland*," Boardgamegeek, 2014 (accessed July 08, 2014), http://www.boardgamegeek.com/boardgame/130692/the-game-of-alice-in-wonderland.

12 Linda Hutcheon, *A Theory of Adaptation*, 2nd ed. (London: Routledge, 2012); Henry Jenkins, *Convergence Culture: Where Old and New Media Collide* (New York: New York University Press, 2006); Derek Johnson, *Media Franchising* (New York: New York University Press, 2013).

13 See Clara Fernández-Vara, *Introduction to Game Analysis* (New York: Routledge, 2015).

14 Raph Koster, *A Theory of Fun for Game Designers*, 2nd ed. (Sebastopol, CA: O'Reilly Media, 2014), 14, 52.

15 Mary Flanagan, *Critical Play: Radical Game Design* (Cambridge, MA: MIT Press, 2009), 67.

16 Matt Hills, "Media Fandom, Neoreligiosity, and Cult(ural) Studies," *Velvet Light Trap* 46 (2000): 73.

17 Matt Hills, "Mainstream Cult," in *The Cult TV Book*, ed. Stacey Abbott (London: IB Tauris, 2010), 67. Although he does add that it is "tricky, if not impossible," to fully define the term.

18 Woods, *Eurogames,* 20.

19 Gérard Genette, *Paratexts: Thresholds of Interpretation*, trans. Jane Lewin (Cambridge: Cambridge University Press, 1997), 2.

20 Jonathan Gray, *Show Sold Separately: Promos, Spoilers, and Other Media Paratexts* (New York: New York University Press, 2010), 23.

21 Gray, *Show Sold Separately,* 188.

22 Mia Consalvo, *Cheating* (Cambridge, MA: MIT Press, 2007), 8.

23 Ian Peters, "Peril-Sensitive Sunglasses, Superheroes in Miniature, and Pink Polka-Dot Boxers: Artifact and Collectible Video Game Feelies, Play, and the Paratextual Gaming Experience," *Transformative Works and Cultures* 16 (2014), http://dx.doi.org/10.3983/twc.2014.0509, ¶1.3

24 Bethan Jones, "Unusual Geography: Discworld Board Games and Paratextual L-Space," *Intensities: The Journal of Cult Media* 7 (2014), https://intensitiescultmedia.files.wordpress.com/2014/08/6-jones-unusual-geography-pp-55-73.pdf.

25 Lincoln Geraghty, "Aging Toys and Players: Fan Identity and Cultural Capital," in *Finding the Force of the Star Wars Franchise: Fans, Merchandise, and Critics*, eds. Matthew Wilhelm Kapell and John Shelton Lawrence (New York: Peter Lang, 2006), 209; see also Lincoln Geraghty, *Cult Collectors* (London: Routledge, 2014), 93.

26 See Britta Stöckmann and Jens Jahnke, "Playing by the Book: Literature and Board Games at the Beginning of 21st Century," *Homo Communcativus* 5 (2008), http://www.hc.amu.edu.pl/numery/5/stockjahnke.pdf, for an exception, although they look specifically at board games based on novels.

27 David Parlett, *Oxford History of Board Games* (Oxford: Oxford University Press, 1999), 7.

28 David Parlett, "Conquest," in *Tabletop: Analog Game Design*, eds. Greg Costikyan and Drew Davidson (US: ETC Press, 2011), 103.

29 Jack Botermans, Tony Burrett, Pieter van Delft, and Carla van Splunteren, *The World of Games: Their Origins and History, How to Play Them, and How to Make Them* (New York: Facts on File, 1987), 180.

30 John Sharp, "Pandemic," in *Tabletop: Analog Game Design*, eds. Greg Costikyan and Drew Davidson (US: ETC Press, 2011), 130–31.

31 Greg Costikyan, "Boardgame Aesthetics," in *Tabletop: Analog Game Design*, eds. Greg Costikyan and Drew Davidson (US: ETC Press, 2011), 179–80, 183.

32 Johnson, *Media Franchising*.

33 Nick Bentley, "Board Game Publishers Are Doing It Wrong," September 30, 2013 (accessed July 08, 2014), http://nickbentleygames.wordpress.com/2013/09/30/board-game-publishers-are-doing-it-wrong/.

34 Paul Booth, *Digital Fandom: New Media Studies* (New York: Peter Lang, 2010).

35 Kurt Lancaster, *Interacting with Babylon 5* (Austin, TX: University of Texas Press, 2001), 67.

36 Woods, *Eurogames*, 16, 19, 79

37 Woods, *Eurogames*, 17–18.

38 George Elias, Richard Garfield, and K. Robert Gutschera, *Characteristics of Games* (Cambridge, MA: MIT Press, 2012), 214.

39 Geraghty, *Cult Collectors*, 30.

40 Kevin Wilson, "One Story, Many Media," in *Second Person: Role-Playing and Story in Games and Playable Media*, eds. Pat Harrigan and Noah Wardrip-Fruin (Cambridge, MA: MIT Press, 2007), 91.

41 Stewart Woods, "Last Man Standing: Risk and Elimination in Social Game Play," *Leonardo Electronic Almanac* 16, no. 2–3 (2008), http://leoalmanac.org/journal/vol_16/lea_v16_n2-3/JChatelain.asp.

42 Elias, Garfield, and Gutschera, *Characteristics of Games*, 71.

43 Alan McKee, *Textual Analysis: A Beginner's Guide* (London: Sage, 2003), 1.

44 Matt Hills, *Fan Cultures* (London: Routledge, 2002), 72–76.

45 Booth, *Digital Fandom*, 2.

46 Johan Huizinga, *Homo Ludens: A Study of the Play Element in Culture* (Boston: Beacon Press, 1950).

47 Katie Salen and Eric Zimmerman, *Rules of Play: Game Design Fundamentals* (Cambridge, MA: MIT Press, 2004).

48 Lev Manovich, *The Language of New Media* (Cambridge, MA: MIT Press, 2001).

49 Jenkins, *Convergence Culture*; Salen and Zimmerman, *Rules of Play*.

50 Henry Jenkins, "Transmedia Storytelling," January 15, 2003 (accessed June 12, 2013), http://www.technologyreview.com/news/401760/transmedia-storytelling/.

51 Axel Bruns, *Blogs, Wikipedia, Second Life, and Beyond* (New York: Peter Lang, 2008).

Chapter 1

1 Ira Fay, "Filtering Feedback," in *Tabletop: Analog Game Design*, eds. Greg Costikyan and Drew Davidson (US: ETC Press, 2011), 62.

2 Salen and Zimmerman, *Rules of Play*, 117.

3 Elias, Garfield, and Gutschera, *Characteristics of Games*.

4 Rachel Wagner, *Godwired: Religion, Ritual and Virtual Reality* (New York: Routledge, 2012), 64.

5 Huizinga, *Homo Ludens*, 13.

6 Roger Caillois, *Man, Play, and Games* (Chicago: University of Illinois Press, 1961), 7, 10.

7 Tom Dowd, Michael Niederman, Michael Fry, and Joe Steiff, *Storytelling Across Worlds: Transmedia for Creatives and Producers* (New York: Focal Press, 2013); Sara Gwenllian Jones, "The Sex Lives of Cult Television Characters," *Screen* 43, no. 1 (2002); Andrea Phillips, *A Creator's Guide to Transmedia Storytelling: How to Captivate and Engage Audiences Across Multiple Platforms* (Columbus, OH: McGraw-Hills, 2012).

8 Arthur C. Clarke, *Profiles of the Future* (London: Gollancz, 1962), 21.

9 Diamond Book Distributors, 2011 (accessed July 08, 2014), http://www.diamondbookdistributors.com/downloads/DBDProse2011.pdf.

10 Wilson, "One Story."

11 Robert M. Price, "With Strange Aeons: H. P. Lovecraft's Cthulhu Mythos as One Vast Narrative," in *Third Person: Authoring and Exploring Vast Narratives*, eds. Pat Harrigan and Noah Wardrip-Fruin (Cambridge, MA: MIT Press, 2009), 225.

12 Robert M. Price, "Lovecraft's 'Artificial Mythology'," in *An Epicure in the Terrible: A Centennial Anthology of Essays in Honor of H. P. Lovecraft*, eds. David E. Schultz and S. T. Joshi (Cranbury, NJ: Associated University Presses, 1991), 247.

13 Gavia Baker-Whitelaw, "'Star Wars' Just Nuked Its Entire Expanded Universe," *Daily Dot*, April 26, 2014 (accessed April 26, 2014), http://www.dailydot.com/geek/star-wars-expanded-universe-not-canon/.

14 Price, "With Strange Aeons," 231; David E. Schultz, "From Microcosm to Macrocosm: The Growth of Lovecraft's Cosmic Vision," in *An Epicure in the Terrible: A Centennial Anthology of Essays in Honor of H. P. Lovecraft*, eds. David E. Schultz and S. T. Joshi (Cranbury, NJ: Associated University Presses, 1991), 199.

15 Salen and Zimmerman, *Rules of Play*, 120–30.

16 Flanagan, *Critical Play*, 8.

17 Matthew Berland, "Understanding Strategic Boardgames as Computational-Thinking Training Machines," in *Tabletop: Analog Game Design*, eds. Greg Costikyan and Drew Davidson (US: ETC Press, 2011), 171.

18 Greg Costikyan, *Uncertainty in Games* (Cambridge, MA: MIT Press, 2013), 10.

19 Mark Deuze, "Participation, Remediation, Bricolage: Considering Principal Components of a Digital Culture," *The Information Society* 22, no. 2 (2006): 63.

20 Manovich, *Language of New Media,* 27, 46–47.

21 Marie-Laure Ryan, *Narrative as Virtual Reality: Immersion and Interactivity in Literature and Electronic Media* (Baltimore, MD: John Hopkins University Press, 2001).

22 Steven J. Mariconda, "Lovecraft's Cosmic Imagery," in *An Epicure in the Terrible: A Centennial Anthology of Essays in Honor of H. P. Lovecraft*, eds. David E. Schultz and S. T. Joshi (Cranbury, NJ: Associated University Presses, 1991), 188.

23 John Kaufeld, "Randomness, Player Choice, and Player Experience," in *Tabletop: Analog Game Design*, eds. Greg Costikyan and Drew Davidson (US: ETC Press, 2011), 35–36.

24 Chris Klug, "Dice as Dramaturge," in *Tabletop: Analog Game Design*, eds. Greg Costikyan and Drew Davidson (US: ETC Press, 2011), 42.

25 Klug, "Dice as Dramaturge," 46.

26 Consalvo, *Cheating.*

27 H. P. Lovecraft, "The Dream-Quest of Unknown Kadath," in *H.P. Lovecraft: The Complete Fiction* (New York: Barnes and Noble, 2011), 410.

28 H. P. Lovecraft, "Nyarlathotep," in *H.P. Lovecraft: The Complete Fiction* (New York: Barnes and Noble, 2011), 121.

29 Burleson identifies the first of these themes as *denied primacy*, or a sense that humans are completely insignificant in the universe. A second theme, of *forbidden knowledge*, reveals that there are some forms of knowledge "only by the avoidance or suppression of which can humankind maintain a semblance of well-being." Another theme, *illusory surface appearances*, means that things in the world are not as they seem. Burleson identifies *unwholesome survival* as a fourth theme of Lovecraft, where some things outlive their rightful existence. Finally, the theme of *oneiric objectivism*, where "there is at best an ambiguous distinction between dreaming and reality," is a predominant aspect of Lovecraft's work. See, Donald R. Burleson, "On Lovecraft's Themes: Touching the Glass," in *An Epicure in the Terrible: A Centennial Anthology of Essays in Honor of H. P. Lovecraft*, eds. David E. Schultz and S. T. Joshi (Cranbury, NJ: Associated University Presses, 1991), 136.

30 Price, "With Strange Aeons," 226, 228–29, 236.

31 Donald R. Burleson, "Lovecraft's The Color Out of Space," *Explicator* 52, no. 1 (1993): 48–49.

32 Jacques Derrida, *On Grammatology*, trans. Gayatri Chakravorty Spivak (Baltimore, MD: Johns Hopkins University Press, 1967), 145; Price, "With Strange Aeons," 232.

33 Lin Carter, *Lovecraft: A Look Behind the "Cthulhu Mythos"* (USA: Ballantine Books, 1972), 26–27.

34 Price, "With Strange Aeons," 232.

35 Ian Bogost, "The Rhetoric of Video Games," in *The Ecology of Games: Connecting Youth, Games, and Learning*, ed. Katie Salen (Cambridge, MA: MIT Press, 2008), 125.

36 Flanagan, *Critical Play*, 84.

37 Wagner, *Godwired*, 58.

38 Ian Bogost, "Videogame Adaptation and Translation," *Ian Bogost*, 2006 (accessed June 01, 2014), http://www.bogost.com/teaching/videogame_adaptation_and_trans.shtml.

39 Wilson, "One Story," 93.

40 Flanagan, *Critical Play*, 11.

41 Jonas Linderoth, "Exploring Anonymity in Cooperative Board Games," *Proceedings of DiGRA 2011 Conference: Think Design Play*, 2011 (accessed June 01, 2014), http://www.digra.org/wp-content/uploads/digital-library/11312.15167.pdf.

42 *Arkham Horror*, 13.

43 Price, "With Strange Aeons," 231.

44 *Arkham Horror*, 5.

45 Wilson, "One Story," 92.

46 Wilson, "One Story," 92.

47 Barton Levy St. Armand, "Synchronistic Worlds: Lovecraft and Borges," in *An Epicure in the Terrible: A Centennial Anthology of Essays in Honor of H. P. Lovecraft*, eds. David E. Schultz and S. T. Joshi (Cranbury, NJ: Associated University Presses, 1991), 298.

48 Costikyan, *Uncertainty in Games*, 95.

49 Greg Costikyan, "Games, Storytelling, and Breaking the String," in *Second Person: Role-Playing and Story in Games and Playable Media*, eds. Pat Harrigan and Noah Wardrip-Fruin (Cambridge, MA: MIT Press, 2007), 6, 12.

50 St Armand, "Synchronistic Worlds," 319.

51 Price, "With Strange Aeons," 241.

52 Kenneth Hite, "Narrative Structure and Creative Tension in Call of Cthulhu," in *Second Person: Role-Playing and Story in Games and Playable Media*, eds. Pat Harrigan and Noah Wardrip-Fruin (Cambridge, MA: MIT Press, 2007), 32, 37.

53 Price, "With Strange Aeons," 239–40.

54 Peter Lunenfeld, "Unfinished Business," in *The Digital Dialectic*, ed. Peter Lunenfeld (Cambridge, MA: MIT Press, 1999).

Chapter 2

1 Celia Pearce, *Communities of Play: Emergent Cultures in Multiplayer Games and Virtual Worlds* (Cambridge, MA: MIT Press, 2009).

2 "*Lord of the Rings* (board game)," 2014 (accessed July 09, 2014), http://en.wikipedia.org/wiki/Lord_of_the_Rings_(board_game).

3 Juan José Fernández, "Board Game Sales Stats (Now with Sources)," September 12, 2009 (accessed July 09, 2014), http://www.boardgamegeek.com/geeklist/22976/board-game-sales-stats-now-with-sources/page/6?.

4 Kevin Yore, "Dice and Digital—Rehabilitating the Board Game Geek," *BBC News,* March 01, 2013 (accessed June 01, 2014), http://www.bbc.com/news/business-21615083, ¶16.

5 José P. Zagal, Jochen Rick, and Idris Hsi, "Collaborative Games: Lessons Learned from Board Games," *Simulation and Gaming* 37, no. 1 (2006): 28.

6 Reiner Knizia, "The Design and Testing of the Board Game—*Lord of the Rings*," in *Rules of Play: Game Design Fundamentals*, eds. Katie Salen and Eric Zimmerman (Cambridge, MA: MIT Press, 2004), 22.

7 "How Big Is It?" 2004 (accessed July 09, 2014), https://web.archive.org/web/20071013162924/http://spielboy.com/printrun.php.

8 Parlett, *Oxford,* 7.

9 Salen and Zimmerman, *Rules of Play*, 6.

10 Brian Sutton-Smith, *The Ambiguity of Play* (Boston: Harvard University Press, 1997), 1.

11 Salen and Zimmerman, *Rules of Play*, 304.

12 Booth, *Digital Fandom.*

13 Huizinga, *Homo Ludens.*

14 Jon Dovey and Helen W. Kennedy, *Game Cultures: Computer Games as New Media* (Maidenhead, UK: McGraw-Hill, 2006), 102.

15 Jenkins, *Convergence Culture*, 18; Henry Jenkins, Sam Ford, and Joshua Green, *Spreadable Media: Creating Value and Meaning in a Networked Culture* (New York: New York University Press, 2013).

16 Salen and Zimmerman, *Rules of Play*, 104.

17 Wagner, *Godwired*, 63.

18 Roger Silverstone, *Why Study the Media?* (London: Sage, 1999), 64, cited in Hills, *Fan Cultures*, 90.

19 Shanley Dixon and Sandra Weber, "Playspaces, Childhood, and Video Games," in *Growing Up Online: Young People and Digital Technologies*, eds. Sandra Weber and Shanley Dixon (New York: Palgrave, 2007), 15; see Mimi Ito, *Hanging Out, Messing Around, and Geeking Out: Kids Living and Learning with New Media* (Cambridge, MA: MIT Press, 2010).

20   Booth, *Digital Fandom*, 2.

21   Koster, *Theory of Fun*.

22   Caillois, *Man, Play, and Games*, 6.

23   Costikyan, *Uncertainty in Games*, 13.

24   Umberto Eco, "Casablanca: Cult Movies and Intertextual Collage," in *Travels in Hyper Reality: Essays* (New York: Harcourt Brace, 1986), 198.

25   Sara Gwenllian-Jones, "Starring Lucy Lawless?" *Continuum: Journal of Media & Cultural Studies* 14, no. 1 (2000): 12–13.

26   Woods, *Eurogames*, 76.

27   Kevin Jacklin, "Simply Knizia," in *Tabletop: Analog Game Design*, eds. Greg Costikyan and Drew Davidson (US: ETC Press, 2011), 56.

28   Zagal, Rick, and Hsi, "Collaborative Games," 30.

29   Knizia, "The Design and Testing of the Board Game," 22–23.

30   Jane Chance, *The Lord of the Rings: The Mythology of Power*, rev. ed. (Lexington, KY: The University Press of Kentucky, 2001), 45, 96.

31   David Harvey, *A Brief History of Neoliberalism* (Oxford: Oxford University Press, 2005).

32   Sutton-Smith, *Ambiguity of Play*, 103–6.

33   Elias, Garfield, and Gutschera, *Characteristics of Games*, 64n2, 22–23.

34   Mark Deuze, "Convergence Culture in the Creative Industries," *International Journal of Cultural Studies* 10, no. 2 (2007); Henry Jenkins, "The Cultural Logic of Media Convergence," *International Journal of Cultural Studies* 7, no. 1 (2004); Jenkins, *Convergence Culture*.

35   Jenkins, *Convergence Culture*, 2.

36   Deuze, "Convergence," 259.

37   Gray, *Show Sold Separately*, 6.

38   Knizia, "The Design and Testing of the Board Game," 23.

39   All images, this chapter: The copyrightable portions of *The Lord of the Rings: The Board Game* and its expansions are ©2001–2010 Sophisticated Games, Ltd. *Lord of the Rings* and the characters, events, items and places therein, are trademarks of The Saul Zaentz Company d/b/a Middle-Earth Enterprises and are used under license by Sophisticated Games, Ltd. and their respective licensees. Fantasy Flight Supply is a trademark of Fantasy Flight Publishing, Inc.

40   Gray, *Show Sold Separately*, 178, citing Ellen Seiter, *Sold Separately: Children and Parents in Consumer Culture* (New Brunswick, NJ: Rutgers University Press, 1995), 191.

41   Graham Meikle and Sherman Young, *Media Convergence: Networked Digital Media in Everyday Life* (Houndsmill, UK: Palgrave Macmillan, 2012), 9.

42   Knizia, "The Design and Testing of the Board Game," 24–26.

43 Elana Shefrin, "*Lord of the Rings, Star Wars*, and Participatory Fandom: Mapping New Congruencies between the Internet and Media Entertainment Culture," *Critical Studies in Media Communication* 21, no. 3 (2004): 263.

44 Ernest Mathijs, "Popular Culture in Global Context: *The Lord of the Rings* Phenomenon," in *The Lord of the Rings: Popular Culture in Global Context*, ed. Ernest Mathijs (London: Wallflower Press, 2006), 1–2.

45 J. R. R. Tolkien, *The Lord of the Rings: The Fellowship of the Ring*, 2nd ed. (London: HarperCollins, 1966), xvii, cited in Mathijs, "Popular Culture in Global Context," 2.

46 Mathijs, ed., *The Lord of the Rings*; Jim Smith and J. Clive Matthews, *The Lord of the Rings: The Films, the Books, the Radio Series* (London: Virgin Books, 2004).

47 Chance, *The Lord of the Rings*, 1.

48 Zagal, Rick, and Hsi, "Collaborative Games," 32.

49 Zagal, Rick, and Hsi, "Collaborative Games," 33.

50 Knizia, "The Design and Testing of the Board Game," 22.

51 *Lord of the Rings*, 12.

52 Zagal, Rick, and Hsi, "Collaborative Games," 30.

53 Lancaster, *Interacting with Babylon*, 5.

54 Pat Harrigan and Noah Wardrip-Fruin, Introduction to *Third Person: Authoring and Exploring Vast Narratives*, eds. Pat Harrigan and Noah Wardrip-Fruin (Cambridge, MA: MIT Press, 2009), 2–3.

55 Smith and Matthews, *The Lord of the Rings*.

56 Clint Hocking, "Ludonarrative Dissonance in *BioShock*," *Clicknothing: Design from a Long Time Ago*, October 07, 2007 (accessed May 13, 2013), http://clicknothing. typepad.com/click_nothing/2007/10/ludonarrative-d.html; Noah Wardrip-Fruin and Pat Harrigan, eds, *First Person: New Media as Story, Performance, and Game* (Cambridge, MA: MIT Press, 2004).

57 Stöckmann and Jahnke, "Playing by the Book," 129, 142.

58 Jane McGonigal, *Reality is Broken: Why Games Make Us Better and How They Can Change the World* (New York: Penguin, 2011), 32.

59 Smith and Matthews, *Lord of the Rings*.

60 Stöckmann and Jahnke, "Playing by the Book," 143.

61 Gary Alan Fine, *Shared Fantasy: Role Playing Games as Social Worlds* (Chicago, IL: University of Chicago Press, 2002), 165.

62 See, regarding video games, Matt Garite, "The Ideology of Interactivity or, Video Games and the Taylorization of Leisure," *Level Up, Digital Games Research Association Conference DiGRA*, Utrecht, 2003 (accessed May 14, 2013), http://www.digra.org/wp-content/uploads/digital-library/05150.15436.pdf.

63 Chance, *The Lord of the Rings*.

64 Shefrin, "*Lord of the Rings, Star Wars*, and Participatory Fandom," 262, citing Jenkins, "Transmedia Storytelling."

65 Kenneth Hite, "Another Form of Story Telling," presentation at *Capricon 34*, Wheeling, IL, 2014.

66 Salen and Zimmerman, *Rules of Play*, 462, my emphasis.

Chapter 3

1 Adam Brown and Deb Waterhouse-Watson, "Reconfiguring Narrative in Contemporary Board Games: Story-Making Across the Competitive-Cooperative Spectrum," *Intensities: The Journal of Cult Media* 7 (2014), https://intensitiescultmedia.files.wordpress.com/2014/08/2-brown-and-waterhouse-watson-reconfiguring-narrative-pp-5-19.pdf.

2 Marie-Laure Ryan, "Transmedial Storytelling and Transfictionality," *Poetics Today* 34, no. 3 (2013), http://users.frii.com/mlryan/transmedia.html.

3 Chrisy Dena, "Current State of Cross Media Storytelling: Preliminary Observations for Future Design," *European Information Systems Technologies Event*, 2004 (accessed June 06, 2013), http://www.christydena.com/Docs/DENA_CrossMediaObservations.pdf.

4 Jason Mittell, "Transmedia Storytelling," *Complex TV: The Poetics of Contemporary Television Storytelling*, pre-publication edition, MediaCommons Press, 2012 (accessed May 13, 2013), http://mediacommons.futureofthebook.org/mcpress/complextelevision/transmedia-storytelling/, ¶48–56.

5 Kevin Veale, "Capital, Dialogue, and Community Engagement—*My Little Pony: Friendship Is Magic* Understood as an Alternate Reality Game," *Transformative Works and Cultures* 14 (2013), http://dx.doi.org/10.3983/twc.2013.0510, ¶1.8.

6 Salen and Zimmerman, *Rules of Play*, 6.

7 Salen and Zimmerman, *Rules of Play*, 503.

8 Booth, *Digital Fandom*; M. J. Clarke, *Transmedia Television: New Trends in Network Serial Production* (New York: Bloomsbury, 2013); Elizabeth Evans, *Transmedia Television: Audiences, New Media, and Daily Life* (New York: Routledge, 2011); Jenkins, *Convergence Culture*; Jenkins, Ford, and Green, *Spreadable Media*.

9 Ryan, "Transmedial Storytelling"; Price, "With Strange Aeons."

10 Jenkins, "Transmedia Storytelling," ¶3.

11 Jenkins, *Convergence Culture*, 95–96.

12 Edward Branigan, *Narrative Comprehension and Film* (New York: Routledge, 1992), 17–20.

13 Samuel Zakowski, "Time and Temporality in the *Mass Effect* Series: A Narratological Approach," *Games and Culture* 9, no. 1 (2014).

14 Ryan, "Transmedial Storytelling," ¶3–4.

15 Tom Abba, "Hybrid Stories: Examining the Future of Transmedia Narrative," *Science Fiction Film and Television* 2, no. 1 (2009); Jenkins, *Convergence Culture*.

16 Mélanie Bourdaa, "'Following the Pattern': The Creation of an Encyclopaedic Universe with Transmedia Storytelling," *Adaptation* (2013): 202–14.

17 Dena, "Current State of Cross Media Storytelling," 10.

18 Craig Fischer, "Meaninglessness," in *Triumph of The Walking Dead*, ed. James Lowder (Dallas, TX: Benbella Books, 2011).

19 Henry Jenkins, "*The Walking Dead*: Adapting Comics," in *How to Watch Television*, eds. Ethan Thompson and Jason Mittell (New York: New York University Press, 2013).

20 Hutcheon, *A Theory of Adaptation*, 2, 6.

21 Dudley Andrews, *Concepts in Film Theory* (Oxford: Oxford University Press, 1984), 96.

22 Deborah Cartmell, *Screen Adaptations: Jane Austen's Pride and Prejudice: The Relationship between Text and Film* (York, UK: Methuen Drama, 2010), 20.

23 Hutcheon, *A Theory of Adaptation,* 4.

24 Carlos Alberto Scolari, "Transmedia Storytelling: Implicit Consumers, Narrative Worlds, and Branding in Contemporary Media Production," *International Journal of Communication* 3 (2009): 587.

25 Robert A. Brookey, *Hollywood Gamers: Digital Convergence in the Film and Video Game Industries* (Bloomington, IN: Indiana University Press, 2010).

26 Gray, *Show Sold Separately*; Jenkins, *Convergence Culture*; Johnson, *Media Franchising*.

27 Geraghty, *Cult Collectors*, 175; Sara Gwenllian-Jones, "Virtual Reality and Cult Television," in *Cult Television*, eds. Sara Gwenllian-Jones and Roberta Pearson (Minneapolis, MN: University of Minnesota Press, 2004).

28 Henry Jenkins, "Game Design as Narrative Architecture," in *First Person: New Media as Story, Performance and Game*, eds. Noah Wardrip-Fruin and Pat Harrigan (Cambridge, MA: MIT Press, 2004), 122.

29 Hills, *Fan Cultures*; Gwenllian-Jones, "Virtual Reality."

30 Markus Montola, "Social Constructionism and Ludology: Implications for the Study of Games," *Simulation and Gaming*, 43, no. 3 (2012): 314, citing Pearce, *Communities of Play*.

31 Zagal, Rick, and Hsi, "Collaborative Games," 26, 28.

32 Wilson, "One Story," 91–92.

33 Jenkins, "Game Design," 124.

34 Ryan, "Transmedial Storytelling," ¶6.

35 Ryan, "Transmedial Storytelling," ¶3.

36 Espen Aarseth, *Cybertext: Perspectives on Ergodic Literature* (Baltimore, MD: The John Hopkins University Press, 1997); Gonzolo Frasca, "Ludology Meets Narratology: Similitude and Differences Between (Video) Games And Narrative," *Parnasso* 3 (1999), http://www.ludology.org/articles/ludology.htm; Jenkins, "Game Design"; Celia Pearce, "Theory Wars: An Argument Against Arguments in the So-Called Ludology/Narratology Debate." *DiGRA Conference: Changing Views—Worlds in Play*, 1–6, 2005 (accessed June 07, 2013), http://lmc.gatech.edu/~cpearce3/PearcePubs/PearceDiGRA05.pdf.

37 Costikyan, "Games, Storytelling, and Breaking the String," 5.

38 Eric Zimmerman, "Narrative, Interactivity, Play, and Games: Four Naughty Concepts in Need of Discipline," in *First Person: New Media as Story, Performance and Game*, eds. Noah Wardrip-Fruin and Pat Harrigan (Cambridge, MA: MIT Press, 2004).

39 Ryan, "Transmedial Storytelling," ¶25.

40 Hocking, "Ludonarrative Dissonance."

41 Montola, "Social Constructionism," 313.

42 Kyle W. Bishop, "The Pathos of *The Walking Dead*," in *Triumph of The Walking Dead*, ed. James Lowder (Dallas, TX: Benbella Books, 2011), 10.

43 Jay Bonansinga, "A Novelist and a Zombie Walk into a Bar," in *Triumph of The Walking Dead*, ed. James Lowder (Dallas, TX: Benbella Books, 2011), 55.

44 Salen and Zimmerman, *Rules of Play*.

45 Pearce, "Theory Wars."

46 Klug, "Dice as Dramaturge," 41.

47 Elias, Garfield, and Gutschera, *Characteristics of Games*, 167.

48 Fischer, "Meaninglessness."

49 Bishop, "The Pathos of *The Walking Dead*"; Emma Vossen, "Where's the Sex?" *First Person Scholar*, June 05, 2013 (accessed June 05, 2013), http://www.firstpersonscholar.com/wheres-the-sex/; Kay Steiger, "No Clean Slate," in *Triumph of The Walking Dead*, ed. James Lowder (Dallas, TX: Benbella Books, 2011).

50 Bonansinga, "A Novelist and a Zombie," 60.

51 Scott McCloud, *Understanding Comics: The Invisible Art* (New York: Kitchen Sink Press, 1993), 63–69.

52 Matt Morgan, "ZMan Games Set to Debut *The Walking Dead* at SDCC," *MTV Geek,* July 07, 2011 (accessed June 01, 2014), http://geek-news.mtv.com/2011/07/07/z-man-games-set-to-debut-the-walking-dead-at-sdcc, ¶5, ¶7.

53 Matt Morgan, "Cryptozoic's Cory Jones Unearths *The Walking Dead* Board Game," *MTV Geek*, June 14, 2011 (accessed June 01, 2014), http://geek-news.mtv.

com/2011/06/15/interview-cryptozoics-cory-jones-unearths-the-walking-dead-board-game, ¶10.

54 James Paul Gee, *What Video Games Have to Teach Us about Learning and Literacy*, rev. ed. (New York: Palgrave Macmillan, 2007), 55.

55 Ryan, "Transmedial Storytelling."

56 Steven E. Jones, "Dickens on *Lost*: Text, Paratext, Fan-Based Media," *The Wordsworth Circle* 38, no. 2 (2007): 74.

57 Morgan, "Cryptozoic's," ¶18.

58 Brookey, *Hollywood Gamers*; Johnson, *Media Franchising*.

59 Morgan, "Cryptozoic's," ¶17.

60 Hamish Thompson, "'She's Not Your Mother Anymore, She's a Zombie!' Zombies, Value, and Personal Identity," in *The Undead and Philosophy*, eds. Richard Green and K. Silem Mohammad (La Salle, IL: Open Court Publishing Company, 2006), 27.

61 Brendan Riley, "Zombie People," in *Triumph of The Walking Dead*, ed. James Lowder (Dallas, TX: Benbella Books, 2011), 81–82.

62 T. J. Dietsch, "Exclusive: Adlard Covers 'The Walking Dead*: The Board Game," *Comic Book Resources*, 2011 (accessed June 01, 2014), http://www.comicbookresources.com/?page=article&id=33349.

63 Morgan, "ZMan Games," 3.

64 Jenkins, *Walking Dead*.

65 Morgan, "ZMan Games."

66 Meredith Woerner, "First Full Cast Picture from AMC's *The Walking Dead*," *io9*, July 15, 2010 (accessed June 01, 2014), http://io9.com/5587483/first-full-castpicture-from-amcs-the-walking-dead.

67 Johnson, *Media Franchising*.

68 Flanagan, *Critical Play*, 65.

69 Knizia, "The Design and Testing of the Board Game," 22.

70 Jenkins, Ford, and Green, *Spreadable Media*, 133.

71 Johnson, *Media Franchising*, 45.

72 Jenkins, Ford, and Green, *Spreadable Media*, 140.

73 Jennifer G. Cover, *The Creation of Narrative in Tabletop Role-Playing Games* (Jefferson, NC: McFarland, 2010), 71.

Chapter 4

1 Booth, *Digital Fandom*.

2 Lancaster, *Interacting with Babylon 5*, 25–34.

3 Bruce Sterling, *Shaping Things* (Cambridge, MA: MIT Press, 2005), 11.

4 Lewis Call, "Death, Sex and the Cylon: Living Authentically on *Battlestar Galactica*," *Science Fiction Film and Television* 5, no. 1 (2012).

5 David J. Gunkel, *Hacking Cyberspace* (Boulder, CO: Westview Press, 2001); David J. Gunkel, *The Machine Question* (Cambridge, MA: MIT Press, 2012).

6 Huizinga, *Homo Ludens*.

7 Ray Mazza, "The Greatest Gift," in *Tabletop: Analog Game Design*, eds. Greg Costikyan and Drew Davidson (US: ETC Press, 2011), 112.

8 Karl Bergström, Staffan Björk, and Sus Lundgren, "Exploring Aesthetical Gameplay Design Patterns—Camaraderie in Four Games," *MindTrek*, October 06, 2010 (accessed June 01, 2014), http://dl.acm.org/citation.cfm?id=1930493, 5.

9 Lincoln Geraghty, *American Science Fiction Film and Television* (Oxford: Berg, 2009), 118.

10 C. W. Marshall and Tiffany Porter, "'I See the Patterns': *Battlestar Galactica* and the Things That Matter," in *Cylons in America*, eds. Tiffany Porter and C. W. Marshall (New York: Continuum, 2008), 4.

11 Geraghty, *American Science Fiction*, 62.

12 Jane Banks and Jonathan David Tankel, "Science as Fiction: Technology in Prime Time Television," *Critical Studies in Mass Communication* 7 (1990); Ryan Britt, "Why the 1978 *Battlestar Galactica* Doesn't Suck," *Tor.com*, March 20, 2013 (accessed June 01, 2014), http://www.tor.com/blogs/2013/03/why-the-1978-battlestar-galactica-doesnt-suck; Geraghty, *American Science Fiction*; Jennifer Stoy, "Of Great Zeitgeist and Bad Faith: An Introduction to *Battlestar Galactica*," in *Battlestar Galactica: Investigating Flesh, Spirit and Steel*, eds. Roz Kaverney and Jennifer Stoy (London: IB Tauris, 2010), 2.

13 Geraghty, *American Science Fiction*, 118.

14 Vivian Sobchack, *Screening Space: The American Science Fiction Film*, 2nd ed. (New Brunswick, NJ: Rutgers University Press, 1997), 255.

15 Paul Booth, *Time on TV: Temporal Displacement and Mashup Television* (New York: Peter Lang, 2012), 4

16 Glen Creeber, *Serial Television: Big Drama on the Small Screen* (London: BFI Publishing, 2004), 12.

17 Geraghty, *American Science Fiction*, 120.

18 Robert W. Moore, "'To Be a Person': Sharon Agathon and the Social Expression of Individuality," in *Cylons in America*, eds. Tiffany Porter and C. W. Marshall (New York: Continuum, 2008), 106.

19 Bergström, Björk, and Lundgren, "Exploring Aesthetical Gameplay Design," 2, emphasis in original.

20 Lewis Pulsipher, "The Three Player Problem," in *Tabletop: Analog Game Design*, eds. Greg Costikyan and Drew Davidson (US: ETC Press, 2011), 23–24.

21 *Battlestar Galactica: A Parker Brothers Game*, 1.
22 Sterling, *Shaping Things*, 77.
23 Linderoth, "Exploring Anonymity," 7.
24 Paul Booth, "Frak-tured Postmodern Lives, Or, How I Found Out I Was a Cylon," in *Battlestar Galactica and Philosophy*, eds. Josef Steiff and Tristan D. Tamplin (Chicago, IL: Open Court Press, 2008).
25 For example, Stefania Garassini, "Internet of Things," *Domus* 917 (2008); P. McFedries, "The Age of Spimes," *IEEE Spectrum* 25 (2010).
26 James Allen-Robertson and David Beer, "Mobile Ideas: Tracking a Concept Through Time and Space," *Mobilities* 5, no. 4 (2010): 530, 542.
27 Daren C. Brabham, "Crowdsourcing: A Model for Leveraging Online Communities," in *The Participatory Cultures Handbook*, eds. Aaron Delwiche and Jennifer Jacobs Henderson (New York: Routledge, 2013), 120–29.
28 Sterling, *Shaping Things*, 53.
29 Call, "Death, Sex and the Cylon," 85.
30 Geraghty, *American Science Fiction*, 76.
31 Sue Thomas, "The End of Cyberspace and Other Surprises," *Convergence: The International Journal of Research into New Media Technologies* 12, no. 4 (2006): 388.
32 Berland, "Understanding Strategic Boardgames," 174.
33 Moore, "'To Be a Person.'"
34 *Battlestar Galactica: A Parker Brothers Game*, 1.
35 Sharp, "Pandemic," 129.
36 David J. Gunkel, "Do Machines Have Rights? Ethics in the Age of Artificial Intelligence," Interview with Paul Kellogg, *Aurora Online*, 2014 (accessed June 01, 2014), http://aurora.icaap.org/index.php/aurora/article/view/92/114.
37 Stone Librande, "15 Games in 15 Years," in *Tabletop: Analog Game Design*, eds. Greg Costikyan and Drew Davidson (US: ETC Press, 2011).
38 Flanagan, *Critical Play*, 77.
39 Lane Roth, "'Vraisemblance' and the Western Setting in Contemporary Science Fiction Film," *Literature/Film Quarterly* 13, no. 3 (1985); James E. Ford, "*Battlestar Galactica* and Mormon Theology," *Journal of Popular Culture* 17, no. 2 (1983).
40 Geraghty, *American Science Fiction*, 65.
41 Marshall and Potter, "'I See Patterns,'" 7.
42 Suzanne Scott, "Authorized Resistance: Is Fan Production Frakked?" in *Cylons in America*, eds. Tiffany Potter and C. W. Marshall (New York: Continuum, 2008), 210; Suzanne Scott, "*Battlestar Galactica*: Fans and Ancillary Content," in *How to Watch Television*, eds. Ethan Thompson and Jason Mittell (New York: New York University Press, 2013), 320.

43 Matthew Gumpert, "Hybridity's End," in *Cylons in America*, eds. Tiffany Porter and C. W. Marshall (New York: Continuum, 2008), 143.

44 Bogost, "The Rhetoric of Video Games."

45 Lancaster, *Interacting with Babylon 5*, 38.

46 Geraghty, *American Science Fiction*, 117.

47 Lancaster, *Interacting with Babylon 5*, 39.

48 Consalvo, *Cheating*, 178.

49 "Effect of 'Keep in Play' on 'Thirty-Three' Crisis Card?" *Board & Card Games*, November 24, 2010 (accessed July 10, 2014), http://boardgames.stackexchange.com/questions/1509/effect-of-keep-in-play-on-thirty-three-crisis-card.

50 Lancaster, *Interacting with Babylon 5*, 37.

51 Sterling, *Shaping Things*, 12.

52 Lancaster, *Interacting with Babylon 5*, 59.

Chapter 5

1 "Die with honor!"

2 Gray, *Show Sold Separately*, 11, here talking about *The Simpsons*, but his description is applicable to *Star Trek* as well.

3 Robinson, "I Outwit Your Outwit," 335.

4 Geraghty, *Cult Collectors*, 5.

5 Peters, "Peril-Sensitive Sunglasses," ¶1.2.

6 Geraghty, *Cult Collectors*, 14.

7 Bruns, *Blogs, Wikipedia, Second Life*.

8 Paul Booth, *Playing Fans: Negotiating Fandom and Media in the Digital Age* (Iowa City, IA: University of Iowa Press, 2015); Lincoln Geraghty, *Living with Star Trek: American Culture and the Star Trek Universe* (London: IB Tauris, 2007).

9 Geraghty, *Living with Star Trek*, 6.

10 Koster, *A Theory of Fun*, 164.

11 Robinson, "I Outwit Your Outwit," 340–41.

12 Robinson, "I Outwit Your Outwit," 336.

13 Gray, *Show Sold Separately*, 187.

14 Espen Aarseth, "I Fought the Law: Transgressive Play and the Implied Player," Situated Play Proceedings of DiGRA, 2007 (accessed June 01, 2014), http://lmc.gatech.edu/~cpearce3/DiGRA07/Proceedings/017.pdf, 132.

15 Erving Goffman, *Encounters: Two Studies in the Sociology of Interaction* (New York: Penguin, 1972), 19, cited in Jesper Juul, *Half-Real: Video Games Between Real Rules and Fictional Worlds* (Cambridge, MA: MIT Press, 2005).

16 Juul, *Half-Real*, 15.

17 Peters, "Peril-Sensitive Sunglasses," ¶1.2.

18 Robinson, "I Outwit Your Outwit," 341.

19 Greg Costikyan, "I Have No Words & I Must Design," in *The Game Design Reader*, eds. Katie Salen and Eric Zimmerman (Cambridge, MA: MIT Press, 2006), 206.

20 Matt Hills, "The Cultural Lives of *Doctor Who*: What's Special About Multiple Multi-Doctor Specials?" *Antenna*, 2013 (accessed October 15, 2013), http://blog.commarts.wisc.edu/2013/10/15/the-cultural-lives-of-doctor-who-whats-special-about-multiple-multi-doctor-specials/; see also Matt Hills, "From Dalek Half Balls to Daft Punk Helmets: Mimetic Fandom and the Crafting of Replicas," *Transformative Works and Cultures* 16 (2014), http://dx.doi.org/10.3983/twc.2014.0531.

21 J. J. Gibson, "The Theory of Affordances," in *Perceiving, Acting, and Knowing*, eds. Robert Shaw and John Bransford (Hillsdale, NJ: Lawrence Erlbaum Associates, 1977); J. J. Gibson, *The Ecological Approach to Visual Perception* (Boston: Houghton Mifflin, 1979), cited in Donald Norman, "Affordance, Conventions, and Design," *Interactions* 6, no. 3 (1999).

22 Donald Norman, *The Design of Everyday Things* (New York, NY: Doubleday, 1990).

23 Robinson, "I Outwit Your Outwit," 339.

24 Jon Peterson, *Playing at the World* (US: Unreason Press, 2012), 15, 251, 532, see Sarah Bowman, *The Functions of Role-Playing Games* (Jefferson City, NC: McFarland, 2010).

25 Geraghty, *Cult Collectors*, 48, 122.

26 Gray, *Show Sold Separately*, 186.

27 Geraghty, *Cult Collectors*, 174.

28 Costikyan, "I Have No Words," 205.

29 Costikyan, "I Have No Words," 205.

30 Alain d'Astous and Karine Gagnon, "An Inquiry into the Factors That Impact on Consumer Appreciation of a Board Game," *Journal of Consumer Marketing* 24, no. 2 (2007): 88.

31 Bruns, *Blogs, Wikipedia, Second Life*, 21, 27.

32 Johnson, *Media Franchising*, 109, 113.

33 Suzanne Scott, "Who's Steering the Mothership? The Role of the Fanboy Auteur in Transmedia Storytelling," in *The Participatory Cultures Handbook*, eds. Aaron Delwiche and Jennifer Jacobs Henderson (New York: Routledge, 2013), 43.

34 Johnson, *Media Franchising*, 151.

35 Koster, *A Theory of Fun*, 54.

36 Librande, "15 Games in 15 Years," 74.

37 Sharp, "Pandemic," 132.

38   Geraghty, *Living with Star Trek*, 141.

39   Costikyan, "I Have No Words," 148, 205.

40   Ryan, *Narrative as Virtual Reality.*

41   Allan Cameron, *Modular Narratives in Contemporary Cinema* (New York: Palgrave Macmillan, 2008), 10.

42   Hills, *Fan Cultures*, 137.

43   Salen and Zimmerman, *Rules of Play.*

44   See Peters, "Peril-Sensitive Sunglasses"; also, Ian Bogost, *A Slow Year* (Louisville, KY: Open Texture, 2010).

45   Bruns, *Blogs, Wikipedia, Second Life*, 2.

46   Johnson, *Media Franchising*, 115.

Chapter 6

1   Nicola Balkind, *Fan Phenomena: The Hunger Games* (Bristol, UK: Intellect Press, 2014).

2   Hills, *Fan Cultures*; Henry Jenkins, *Textual Poachers: Television Fans and Participatory Culture*, 2nd ed. (New York: Routledge, 2012); Jones, "Sex Lives."

3   Mittell, "Transmedia Storytelling."

4   Ito, *Hanging Out*; Jenkins, *Convergence Culture*; Henry Jenkins, with Ravi Purushotma, Margaret Weigel, Katie Clinton, and Alice J. Robison, *Confronting the Challenges of Participatory Culture: Media Education for the 21st Century* (Cambridge, MA: MIT Press, 2009), http://mitpress.mit.edu/sites/default/files/titles/free_download/9780262513623_Confronting_the_Challenges.pdf.

5   Paul Booth, "Augmenting Fan/Academic Dialogue: New Directions in Fan Research," *Journal of Fandom Studies* 1, no. 2 (2013); Booth, *Playing Fans.*

6   See obsession_inc, "Affirmational Fandom vs. Transformational Fandom," June 01, 2009 (accessed August 21, 2013), http://obsession-inc.dreamwidth.org/82589.html; also, Scott, "*Battlestar Galactica*"; Scott, "Who's Steering the Mothership?"; Louisa E. Stein and Kristina Busse, "Introduction: The Literary, Televisual and Digital Adventures of the Beloved Detective," in *Sherlock and Transmedia Fandom*, eds. Louisa Ellen Stein and Kristina Busse (Jefferson, NC: McFarland, 2012), 5.

7   Stein and Busse, "Introduction," 15.

8   V. Arrow, *The Panem Companion: An Unofficial Guide to Suzanne Collins' Hunger Games, From Mellark Bakery to Mockingjays* (Dallas, TX: Benbella Books, 2012); Balkind, *Fan Phenomena.*

9   Jen Scott Curwood, "*The Hunger Games*: Literature, Literacy, and Online Affinity Spaces," *Language Arts* 90, no. 6 (2013): 417.

10 James Paul Gee, *Situated Language and Learning: A Critique of Traditional Schooling* (New York: Routledge, 2004).

11 Curwood, *The Hunger Games,* 420; Jayne C. Lammers, Jen Scott Curwood, and Alecia Marie Magnifico, "Toward an Affinity Space Methodology: Considerations for Literacy Research," *English Teaching: Practice and Critique* 11, no. 2 (2012); Dean Schneider, "Katniss, Harry, and Percy: *The Hunger Games* by Suzanne Collins and the Lure of Fantasy Series," *Book Links* (2011), http://www. booklistonline.com/Books-and-Authors-Katniss-Harry-and-Percy-The-Hunger-Games-by-Suzanne-Collins-and-the-Lure-of-Fantasy-Series-Dean-Schneider/ pid=4770980.

12 Curwood, *The Hunger Games,* 417, 422.

13 Melissa Anelli, *Harry, a History* (New York: Pocket Books, 2008).

14 Booth, *Playing Fans.*

15 Roberta Pearson, "Fandom in the Digital Era," *Journal of Popular Communication* 8 (2010): 88, 92; see Scott, "Authorized Resistance."

16 Mark Andrejevic, "Watching Television Without Pity: The Productivity of Online Fans," *Television and New Media* 9, no. 1 (2008).

17 Booth, *Playing Fans*; Teresa Forde, "'You Anorak': The *Doctor Who* Experience and Experiencing *Doctor Who*," in *Fan Phenomena: Doctor Who*, ed. Paul Booth (Bristol, UK: Intellect Press, 2013).

18 Paul Booth, "Rereading Fandom: MySpace Character Personas and Narrative Identification," *Critical Studies in Media Communication* 25, no. 5 (2008).

19 Jenkins, *Convergence Culture*; Jenkins, *Walking Dead*; Scott, "Who's Steering the Mothership?"

20 Leora Hadas, "The Web Planet: How the Changing Internet Divided *Doctor Who* Fan Fiction Writers," *Transformative Works and Cultures* 3 (2009), http://dx.doi. org/10.3983/twc.2009.0129, ¶1.2.

21 Booth, "Augmenting Fan/Academic Dialogue"; Rhiannon Bury, Ruth Deller, Adam Greenwood, and Bethan Jones, "From Usenet to Tumblr: The Changing Role of Social Media," *Participations* 10, no. 1 (2013), http://www.participations. org/Volume 10/Issue 1/14 Bury et al 10.1.pdf, 316.

22 Hills, "From Dalek Half Balls," ¶1.2, see also Matt Hills, "As Seen on Screen? Mimetic SF Fandom & the Crafting of Replica(nt)s," *Media Res,* September 10, 2010 (accessed June 01, 2013), http://mediacommons.futureofthebook.org/ imr/2010/09/10/seen-screen-mimetic-sf-fandom-crafting-replicants.

23 Amazon Publishing, "Press Release: Amazon Publishing Introduces 'Kindle Worlds,' a New Publishing Model for Authors Inspired To Write Fan Fiction—Launching with an Initial License of Popular Titles from Warner Bros. Television Group's Alloy Entertainment," *Amazon.com,* 2013 (accessed

May 23, 2013), http://phx.corporate-ir.net/phoenix.zhtml?c=176060&p=irol-newsArticle&ID=1823219&highlight=.

24   Gavia Baker-Whitelaw, "The Problem with Amazon's New Fanfiction Platform, Kindle Worlds," *Daily Dot*, May 22, 2013 (accessed May 28, 2013), http://www.dailydot.com/business/kindle-words-amazon-fanfiction-problems/; Adi Robertson, "How Amazon's Commercial Fan Fiction Misses the Point," *The Verge*, June 04, 2013 (accessed June 01, 2013), http://www.theverge.com/2013/6/4/4392572/does-amazon-kindle-worlds-miss-the-point-of-fanfiction.

25   Sutton-Smith, *Ambiguity of Play*, 106.

26   Gee, "Video Games," 50.

27   Amber Davisson and Paul Booth, "Reconceptualizing Communication and Agency in Fan Activity: A Proposal for a Projected Interactivity Model for Fan Studies," *Texas Speech Communication Journal* 32, no. 1 (2007).

28   Mark Duffett, *Understanding Fandom: An Introduction to the Study of Media Fan Culture* (London: Bloomsbury, 2013); Janet Staiger, *Media Reception Studies* (New York: New York University Press, 2005).

29   obsession_inc, "Affirmational Fandom vs. Transformational Fandom."

30   Nancy Baym, *Tune in, Log On: Soaps, Fandom, and Online Community* (Thousand Oaks, CA: Sage Press, 2000); John Fiske, "The Cultural Economy of Fandom," in *The Adoring Audience*, ed. Lisa A. Lewis (London: Routledge, 1992); Jenkins, *Textual Poachers*.

31   Booth, "Augmenting Fan/Academic Dialogue"; Lynn Zubernis and Katherine Larsen, *Fandom at the Crossroads: Celebration, Shame and Fan/Producer Relationships* (Newcastle, UK: Cambridge Scholars Press, 2012).

32   Geraghty, *Cult Collectors*; Gray, *Show Sold Separately*.

33   Rebecca Black, *Adolescents and Online Fan Fiction* (New York: Peter Lang, 2008); Booth, "Rereading Fandom"; Booth, *Digital Fandom*; Paul Booth, "Mashup as Temporal Amalgam: Time, Taste, and Temporality," *Transformative Works and Cultures* 9 (2012), http://dx.doi:10.3983/twc.2012.0297; Inger-Lise Kalviknes Bore and Jonathan Hickman, "Continuing *The West Wing* in 140 Characters or Less: Improvised Simulation on Twitter," *Journal of Fandom Studies* 1, no. 2 (2013); Kristina Busse and Karen Hellekson, "Introduction: Work in Progress," in *Fan Fiction and Fan Communities in the Age of the Internet*, eds. Karen Hellekson and Kristina Busse (Jefferson, NC: McFarland, 2006), 6; Francesca Coppa, "Women, *Star Trek*, and the Early Development of Fannish Vidding," *Transformative Works and Cultures* 1 (2007), http://journal.transformativeworks.org/index.php/twc/article/view/44/64; Ann McClellan, "A Case of Identity: Role Playing, Social Media, and BBC *Sherlock*," *Journal of Fandom Studies* 1, no. 2 (2013); Megan M. Wood and Linda Baughman, "*Glee* Fandom and Twitter: Something New, or More of the Same Old Thing?" *Communication Studies* 63, no. 3 (2012).

34 Jenkins, *Textual Poachers*, 35, 165.

35 See Booth, "Augmenting Fan/Academic Dialogue"; Booth, *Playing Fans*; Hills, *Fan Cultures*; Matt Hills, "'*Twilight*' Fans Represented in Commercial Paratexts and Inter-Fandoms: Resisting and Repurposing Negative Fan Stereotypes," in *Genre, Reception, and Adaptation in the Twilight Series*, ed. Anne More (Farnham, UK: Ashgate, 2012).

36 Hills, *Fan Cultures*, 104, 108.

37 Matt Hills, "*Torchwood*'s Trans-Transmedia: Media Tie-Ins and Brand 'Fanagement,'" *Participations: The Journal of Audience and Reception Studies* 9, no. 2 (2012), http://www.participations.org/Volume%209/Issue%202/23%20Hills.pdf, 415.

38 Mark Fisher, "Precarious Dystopias: *The Hunger Games*, *Time*, and *Never Let Me Go*," *Film Quarterly* 65, no. 4 (2012): 27.

39 Hills, *Fan Cultures*; see Angela Thomas, "Fan Fiction Online," *Australian Journal of Language and Literacy* 29, no. 3 (2006).

40 Hills, *Fan Cultures*, 104.

41 Jenkins, *Textual Poachers*, 166.

42 Curwood, *The Hunger Games*, 423.

43 Fisher, "Precarious Dystopias," 28.

44 M. Keith Booker, "On Contemporary Speculative Fiction," in *Critical Insights: Contemporary Speculative Fiction*, ed. M. Keith Booker (Amenia, NY: Grey House Publishing, Inc, 2013), xxv.

45 Jones, "Sex Lives," 86.

46 Deborah Kaplan, "Construction of Character through Narrative," in *Fan Fiction and Fan Communities in the Age of the Internet*, eds. Karen Hellekson and Kristina Busse (Jefferson, NC: McFarland, 2006), 136–37.

47 Booth, *Time on TV*, 80; citing James Phelan, *Reading People, Reading Plots: Character, Progression, and the Interpretation of Narrative* (Chicago, IL: University of Chicago Press, 1989).

48 Roberta Pearson, "Anatomising Gilbert Grissom: The Structure and Function of the Televisual Character," in *Reading CSI: Television under the Microscope*, ed. Michael Allen (London: IB Tauris, 2007).

49 Booker, "On Contemporary Speculative Fiction"; Fisher, "Precarious Dystopias."

50 David Carr, *Time, Narrative, and History* (Bloomington, IN: Indiana University Press, 1986).

51 Zakowski, "Time and Temporality," 71.

52 Zakowski, "Time and Temporality," 64–65.

53 Jones, "Sex Lives," 86.

54 *Training Days*, 1.

55 Flanagan, *Critical Play*, 88.

56   Jones, "Sex Lives," 84.

57   Holly Blackford, "The Games People Play: Speculative Childhood and Virtual Culture from *Enter* to *Hunger*" in *Critical Insights: Contemporary Speculative Fiction*, ed. M. Keith Booker (Amenia, NY: Grey House Publishing, 2013).

58   Blackford, "The Games People Play," 34–35, 39.

59   Jenkins, *Convergence Culture,* 134.

60   Suzanne Scott, "Repackaging Fan Culture: The Regifting Economy of Ancillary Content Models," *Transformative Works and Cultures* 3 (2009), http://dx.doi:10.3983/twc.2009.0150, ¶1.6.

61   Sean P. Conners and Iris Shepard, "Who's Betting on *The Hunger Games*? A Case for Young-Adult Literature," in *Critical Insights: Contemporary Speculative Fiction*, ed. M. Keith Booker (Amenia, NY: Grey House Publishing, 2013), 132.

Chapter 7

1   Lancaster, *Interacting with Babylon 5,* 93.

2   Flanagan, *Critical Play,* 65.

3   Eric Lang with Pat Harrigan, "Design Decisions and Concepts in Licensed Collectible Card Games," in *Second Person: Role-Playing and Story in Games and Playable Media*, eds. Pat Harrigan and Noah Wardrip-Fruin (Cambridge, MA: MIT Press, 2007); Jason Mittell, "Narrative Complexity in Contemporary American Television," *The Velvet Light Trap* 58 (2006); Jack Zipes, "The Age of Commodified Fantasticism: Reflections of Children's Literature and the Fantastic," *Children's Literature Association Quarterly* 9, no. 4 (1984–5).

4   Manuel Castells, *The Rise of the Network Society: The Information Age* (Malden, MA: Wiley-Blackwell, 2009).

5   Wagner, *Godwired.*

6   Manovich, *Language of New Media,* 218–19, 225, 322–23.

7   Manovich, *Language of New Media,* 228.

8   Booth, *Digital Fandom,* 82, 88.

9   Jason Mittell, "Sites of Participation: Wiki Fandom and the Case of Lostpedia," *Transformative Works & Cultures* 3 (2009), http://dx.doi.org/10.3983/twc.2009.0118.

10   Booth, *Playing Fans.*

11   José Van Dijck, "'You Have One Identity': Performing the Self on Facebook and LinkedIn," *Media, Culture and Society* 35, no. 2 (2013): 200, 203, 206.

12   Paul Booth, "Quest of the Magi: Playful Ideology and Demediation in MagiQuest," in *Produsing Theory: The Intersection of Audiences and Production in a Digital World*, ed. Rebecca Ann Lind (New York: Peter Lang, 2012), 134.

13 Booth, "Quest of the Magi," 134; van Dijck, "'You Have One Identity,'" 205.

14 Henry Jacoby, ed., *Game of Thrones and Philosophy* (Hoboken, NJ: John Wiley and Sons, 2012); James Lowder (ed.), *Beyond the Wall: Exploring George R.R. Martin's A Song of Ice and Fire, from* A Game of Thrones *to* A Dance with Dragons (Dallas, TX: Benbella Books, 2012).

15 Woods, "Last Man," 1.

16 Ida Rochani Adi, "Popularizing Epic Narrative in George R.R. Martin's *A Game of Thrones*," *Humaniora* 24 (2012).

17 Adi, "Popularizing Epic Narrative," 2.

18 Nancy Baym, *Personal Connections in the Digital Age* (Cambridge, MA: Polity Press, 2010), 91.

19 Woods, "Last Man," 4.

20 Peterson, *Playing at the World*; Woods, "Last Man."

21 Pulsipher, "The Three Player Problem."

22 Giovanna Mascheroni, "Citizenship Online: Identity, Subactivism and Participation," *Observatorio Journal* 7, no. 3 (2013): 95.

23 Pulsipher, "The Three Player Problem," 23.

24 Peterson, *Playing at the World,* 24.

25 Amelia Barikin, "Making Worlds in Art And Science Fiction," in *Proceedings of the 19th International Symposium of Electronic Art, ISEA2013*, Sydney, eds. Kathy Cleland, Laura Fisher, and Ross Harley, 2013 (accessed June 01, 2014), http://ses.library.usyd.edu.au/handle/2123/9475, 2.

26 Gwenllian-Jones, "Virtual Reality"; Lancaster, *Interacting with Babylon 5,* 30.

27 Lancaster, *Interacting with Babylon 5,* 30.

28 Woods, "Last Man," 2.

29 Woods, "Last Man," 7.

30 Mittell, "Narrative Complexity."

31 Baym, *Personal Connections*, 90.

32 Baym, *Personal Connections*, 91–92.

33 Lee Rainie and Barry Wellman, *Networked: The New Social Operating System* (Cambridge, MA: MIT Press, 2012), 7.

34 Zizi Papacharissi, "A Networked Self: Identity Performance and Sociability on Social Network Sites," in *Frontiers in New Media Research*, eds. Francis L. F. Lee, Louis Leung, Jack Linchuan Qiu, and Donna S. C. Chu (New York: Routledge, 2013), 210.

35 Wagner, *Godwired*, 54.

36 Lancaster, *Interacting with Babylon 5,* 93.

37 Lancaster, *Interacting with Babylon 5*, 98.

38 Lancaster, *Interacting with Babylon 5*, 98.

39 Lancaster, *Interacting with Babylon 5*, 98.

40   Lancaster, *Interacting with Babylon 5*, 98.

41   Lancaster, *Interacting with Babylon 5*, 93.

42   Lancaster, *Interacting with Babylon 5*, 95, 99–100.

43   Woods, "Last Man," 3.

44   Fay, "Filtering Feedback," 63.

45   Lancaster, *Interacting with Babylon 5,* 100.

46   Gwenllinan-Jones, "Virtual Reality," 91–92.

Chapter 8

1   Nick Couldry, *Media Rituals: A Critical Approach* (London: Routledge, 2003), 2.

2   Koster, *A Theory of Fun,* 38.

3   Phillips, *A Creator's Guide,* 41–54.

4   Koster, *A Theory of Fun,* 144.

5   Roger C. Aden, *Popular Stories and Promised Lands: Fan Cultures and Symbolic Pilgrimages* (Tuscaloosa, AL: Alabama University Press, 1999).

6   Fiske, "The Cultural Economy of Fandom."

7   Matt Hills, "Fiske's 'Textual Productivity' and Digital Fandom: Web 2.0 Democratization Versus Fan Distinction?" *Participations: The Journal of Audience and Reception Studies* 10, no. 1 (2013), http://www.participations.org/ Volume%2010/Issue%201/9%20Hills%2010.1.pdf, 130.

8   Paul Booth, "Board, Game, and Media: Interactive Board Games as Multimedia Convergence," *Convergence* (2015), ArticleFirst. doi:10.1177/1354856514561828.

9   H. Porter Abbott, *The Cambridge Introduction to Narrative*, 2nd ed. (Cambridge: Cambridge University Press, 2008), 112.

10   Megan Condis, "Adaptation and Space: Thematic and Atmospheric Considerations for Board Game Environment Construction," *Intensities: The Journal of Cult Media* 7 (2014), https://intensitiescultmedia.files.wordpress.com/2014/08/8-condis-adaptation-and-space-pp-84-90.pdf, 84.

11   Andrews, *Concepts in Film Theory*; John Desmond and Peter Hawkes, *Adaptation: Studying Film and Literature* (New York: McGaw, 2005), 44.

12   Andrews, *Concepts in Film Theory*, 97.

13   Hutcheon, *A Theory of Adaptation,* 22.

14   Booth, *Time on TV.*

15   Ian Bogost, *Persuasive Games* (Cambridge, MA: MIT Press, 2010), 175–76.

16   Andrews, *Concepts in Film Theory*, 100.

17   Sutton-Smith, *Ambiguity of Play,* 10.

18   Andrews, *Concepts in Film Theory*, 100.

19 Sutton-Smith, *Ambiguity of Play*, 11.

20 Compare the Ninth Doctor images here http://www.boardgamegeek.com/thread/139140/component-review, with the generic images here http://www.boardgamegeek.com/image/416335/doctor-who-interactive-electronic-board-game.

21 See http://www.boardgamegeek.com/image/441137/doctor-who-interactive-electronic-board-game.

22 Matt Hills, *Triumph of a Time Lord: Regenerating Doctor Who in the Twenty-First Century* (London: IB Tauris, 2010), 5.

23 "*Doctor Who: The Interactive Electronic Board Game*," n.d. (accessed July 10, 2013), http://www.boardgamegeek.com/collection/items/boardgame/19378?rated=1.

24 Sutton-Smith, *Ambiguity of Play*, 149.

25 Alexander Galloway, *Gaming: Essays on Algorithmic Culture* (Minneapolis, MN: University of Minnesota Press, 2006), 37, 100.

26 *Doctor Who: Time Travelling Action Game*, 6.

27 David Butler, Introduction to *Time and Relative Dissertations in Space*, ed. David Butler (Manchester, UK: Manchester University Press, 2007), 7.

28 Paul Booth and Jef Burnham, "Who Are We? Re-Envisioning the Doctor in the 21st Century," in *Remake Television: Reboot, Re-use, Recycle*, ed. Carlen Lavigne (Lanham, MD: Lexington Books, 2014); Hills, *Triumph of a Time Lord*.

Bibliography

List of references

Aarseth, Espen. *Cybertext: Perspectives on Ergodic Literature.* Baltimore, MD: The John Hopkins University Press, 1997.

—. "I Fought the Law: Transgressive Play and the Implied Player." *Situated Play. Proceedings of DiGRA* (2007): 24–28. Accessed June 01, 2014. http://lmc.gatech. edu/~cpearce3/DiGRA07/Proceedings/017.pdf.

Abba, Tom. "Hybrid Stories: Examining the Future of Transmedia Narrative." *Science Fiction Film and Television* 2, no. 1 (2009): 59–76.

Abbott, H. Porter. *The Cambridge Introduction to Narrative,* 2nd ed. Cambridge: Cambridge University Press, 2008.

Aden, Roger C. *Popular Stories and Promised Lands: Fan Cultures and Symbolic Pilgrimages.* Tuscaloosa, AL: Alabama University Press, 1999.

Adi, Ida Rochani. "Popularizing Epic Narrative in George R.R. Martin's *A Game of Thrones.*" *Humaniora* 24 (2012): 303–14.

Allen-Robertson, James, and David Beer. "Mobile Ideas: Tracking a Concept Through Time and Space." *Mobilities* 5, no. 4 (2010): 529–45.

Amazon Publishing. "Press Release: Amazon Publishing Introduces 'Kindle Worlds,' a New Publishing Model for Authors Inspired to Write Fan Fiction—Launching with an Initial License of Popular Titles from Warner Bros. Television Group's Alloy Entertainment." *Amazon.com.* 2013. Accessed May 23, 2014. http://phx.corporate-ir. net/phoenix.zhtml?c=176060&p=irol-newsArticle&ID=1823219&highlight=.

Andrejevic, Mark. "Watching Television Without Pity: The Productivity of Online Fans." *Television and New Media* 9, no. 1 (2008): 24–46.

Andrews, Dudley. *Concepts in Film Theory.* Oxford: Oxford University Press, 1984.

Anelli, Melissa. *Harry, a History.* New York: Pocket Books, 2008.

"Annual Sales Data." *Toy Industry Association, Inc.* 2013. Accessed July 08, 2014. http:// www.toyassociation.org/TIA/Industry_Facts/salesdata/IndustryFacts/Sales_Data/ Sales_Data.aspx#.UzGI_a1dUTY.

Armstrong, Arthur, and John Hagel III. "The Real Value of On-Line Communities." *Harvard Business Review* 74, no. 3 (1996): 134–41.

Arrow, V. *The Panem Companion: An Unofficial Guide to Suzanne Collins' Hunger Games, From Mellark Bakery to Mockingjays.* Dallas, TX: Benbella Books, 2012.

Baker-Whitelaw, Gavia. "The Problem with Amazon's New Fanfiction Platform, Kindle Worlds." *Daily Dot.* May 22, 2013. Accessed May 28, 2013. http://www.dailydot.com/ business/kindle-words-amazon-fanfiction-problems/.

—. "'Star Wars' Just Nuked Its Entire Expanded Universe." *Daily Dot*. April 26, 2014. Accessed April 26, 2014. http://www.dailydot.com/geek/star-wars-expanded-universe-not-canon/.

Balkind, Nicola. *Fan Phenomena: The Hunger Games*. Bristol, UK: Intellect Press, 2014.

Banks, Jane, and Jonathan David Tankel. "Science as Fiction: Technology in Prime Time Television." *Critical Studies in Mass Communication* 7 (1990): 24–36.

Barikin, Amelia. "Making Worlds in Art and Science Fiction." In *Proceedings of the 19th International Symposium of Electronic Art*, edited by Kathy Cleland, Laura Fisher and Ross Harley. 2013. Accessed June 01, 2014. http://ses.library.usyd.edu.au/handle/2123/9475.

Baym, Nancy. *Personal Connections in the Digital Age*. Cambridge, MA: Polity Press, 2010.

—. *Tune in, Log On: Soaps, Fandom, and Online Community*. Thousand Oaks, CA: Sage Press, 2000.

Bentley, Nick. "Board Game Publishers Are Doing It Wrong." September 30, 2013. Accessed July 08, 2014. http://nickbentleygames.wordpress.com/2013/09/30/board-game-publishers-are-doing-it-wrong/.

Bergström, Karl, Staffan Björk, and Sus Lundgren. "Exploring Aesthetical Gameplay Design Patterns—Camaraderie in Four Games." *MindTrek*. October 06, 2010. Accessed June 01, 2014. http://dl.acm.org/citation.cfm?id=1930493.

Berland, Matthew. "Understanding Strategic Boardgames as Computational-Thinking Training Machines." In *Tabletop: Analog Game Design*, edited by Greg Costikyan and Drew Davidson, 171–78. US: ETC Press, 2011.

Bishop, Kyle W. "The Pathos of *The Walking Dead*." In *Triumph of The Walking Dead*, edited by James Lowder, 1–14. Dallas, TX: Benbella Books, 2011.

Black, Rebecca. *Adolescents and Online Fan Fiction*. New York: Peter Lang, 2008.

Blackford, Holly. "The Games People Play: Speculative Childhood and Virtual Culture from *Enter* to *Hunger*." In *Critical Insights: Contemporary Speculative Fiction*, edited by M. Keith Booker, 31–50. Amenia, NY: Grey House Publishing, 2013.

Bogost, Ian. *Persuasive Games*. Cambridge, MA: MIT Press, 2010.

—. "The Rhetoric of Video Games." In *The Ecology of Games: Connecting Youth, Games, and Learning*, edited by Katie Salen, 117–40. Cambridge, MA: MIT Press, 2008.

—. *A Slow Year*. Louisville, KY: Open Texture, 2010.

—. "Videogame Adaptation and Translation." *Ian Bogost*. 2006. Accessed June 01, 2014. http://www.bogost.com/teaching/videogame_adaptation_and_trans.shtml.

Bonansinga, Jay. "A Novelist and a Zombie Walk into a Bar." In *Triumph of The Walking Dead*, edited by James Lowder, 53–66. Dallas, TX: Benbella Books, 2011.

Booker, M. Keith. "On Contemporary Speculative Fiction." In *Critical Insights: Contemporary Speculative Fiction*, edited by M. Keith Booker, xiv–xxvii. Amenia, NY: Grey House Publishing, Inc, 2013.

Booth, Paul. "Augmenting Fan/Academic Dialogue: New Directions in Fan Research," *Journal of Fandom Studies* 1, no. 2 (2013): 119–37.

—."Board, Game, and Media: Interactive Board Games as Multimedia Convergence." *Convergence* (2015). ArticleFirst. doi: 10.1177/1354856514561828.

—. *Digital Fandom: New Media Studies*. New York: Peter Lang, 2010.

—. "Frak-tured Postmodern Lives, Or, How I Found Out I Was a Cylon." In *Battlestar Galactica and Philosophy*, edited by Josef Steiff and Tristan D. Tamplin, 17–27. Chicago, IL: Open Court Press, 2008.

—. "Mashup as Temporal Amalgam: Time, Taste, and Temporality." *Transformative Works and Cultures* 9 (2012), doi:10.3983/twc.2012.0297.

—. *Playing Fans: Negotiating Fandom and Media in the Digital Age*. Iowa City, IA: University of Iowa Press, 2015.

—. "Quest of the Magi: Playful Ideology and Demediation in MagiQuest." In *Produsing Theory: The Intersection of Audiences and Production in a Digital World*, edited by Rebecca Ann Lind, 69–85. New York: Peter Lang, 2012.

—. "Rereading Fandom: MySpace Character Personas and Narrative Identification." *Critical Studies in Media Communication* 25, no. 5 (2008): 514–36.

—. *Time on TV: Temporal Displacement and Mashup Television*. New York: Peter Lang, 2012.

Booth, Paul, and Jef Burnham. "Who Are We? Re-Envisioning the Doctor in the 21st Century." In *Remake Television: Reboot, Re-use, Recycle*, edited by Carlen Lavigne, 203–20. Lanham, MD: Lexington Books, 2014.

Bore, Inger-Lise Kalviknes, and Jonathan Hickman. "Continuing *The West Wing* in 140 Characters or Less: Improvised Simulation on Twitter." *Journal of Fandom Studies* 1, no. 2 (2013): 219–38.

Botermans, Jack, Tony Burrett, Pieter van Delft, and Carla van Splunteren. *The World of Games: Their Origins and History, How to Play Them, and How to Make Them*. New York: Facts on File, 1987.

Bourdaa, Mélanie. "'Following the Pattern': The Creation of an Encyclopaedic Universe with Transmedia Storytelling." *Adaptation* 6, no. 2 (2013): 202–14.

Bowman, Sarah. *The Functions of Role-Playing Games*. Jefferson City, NC: McFarland, 2010.

Brabham, Daren C. "Crowdsourcing: A Model for Leveraging Online Communities." In *The Participatory Cultures Handbook*, edited by Aaron Delwiche and Jennifer Jacobs Henderson, 120–29. New York: Routledge, 2013.

Branigan, Edward. *Narrative Comprehension and Film*. New York: Routledge, 1992.

Britt, Ryan. "Why the 1978 *Battlestar Galactica* Doesn't Suck." *Tor*. March 20, 2013. Accessed June 01, 2014. http://www.tor.com/blogs/2013/03/why-the-1978-battlestar-galactica-doesnt-suck.

Brookey, Robert A. *Hollywood Gamers: Digital Convergence in the Film and Video Game Industries*. Bloomington, IN: Indiana University Press, 2010.

Brown, Adam, and Deb Waterhouse-Watson. "Reconfiguring Narrative in Contemporary Board Games: Story-Making Across the Competitive-Cooperative Spectrum." *Intensities: The Journal of Cult Media* 7 (2014). https://intensitiescultmedia.files.wordpress.com/2014/08/2-brown-and-waterhouse-watson-reconfiguring-narrative-pp-5-19.pdf.

Bruns, Axel. *Blogs, Wikipedia, Second Life, and Beyond.* New York: Peter Lang, 2008.

Burleson, Donald R. "Lovecraft's The Color Out of Space." *Explicator* 52, no. 1 (1993): 48–50.

—. "On Lovecraft's Themes: Touching the Glass." In *An Epicure in the Terrible: A Centennial Anthology of Essays in Honor of H. P. Lovecraft*, edited by David E. Schultz and S. T. Joshi, 135–47. Cranbury, NJ: Associated University Presses, 1991.

Bury, Rhiannon, Ruth Deller, Adam Greenwood, and Bethan Jones. "From Usenet to Tumblr: The Changing Role of Social Media." *Participations* 10, no. 1 (2013): 229–318. http://www.participations.org/Volume 10/Issue 1/14 Bury et al 10.1.pdf.

Busse, Kristina, and Karen Hellekson. "Introduction: Work in Progress." In *Fan Fiction and Fan Communities in the Age of the Internet*, edited by Karen Hellekson and Kristina Busse, 5–32. Jefferson, NC: McFarland and Co, 2006.

Butler, David. Introduction to *Time and Relative Dissertations in Space*, edited by David Butler, 1–15. Manchester, UK: Manchester University Press, 2007.

Caillois, Roger. *Man, Play, and Games.* Chicago: University of Illinois Press, 1961.

Call, Lewis. "Death, Sex and the Cylon: Living Authentically on *Battlestar Galactica*." *Science Fiction Film and Television* 5, no. 1 (2012): 85–113.

Cameron, Allan. *Modular Narratives in Contemporary Cinema.* New York: Palgrave Macmillan, 2008.

Carr, David. *Time, Narrative, and History.* Bloomington, IN: Indiana University Press, 1986.

Carter, Lin. *Lovecraft: A Look Behind the "Cthulhu Mythos."* USA: Ballantine Books, 1972.

Cartmell, Deborah. *Screen Adaptations: Jane Austen's Pride and Prejudice: The Relationship Between Text and Film.* York, UK: Methuen Drama, 2010.

Castells, Manuel. *The Rise of the Network Society: The Information Age.* Malden, MA: Wiley-Blackwell, 2009.

Chance, Jane. *The Lord of the Rings: The Mythology of Power*, rev. ed. Lexington, KY: The University Press of Kentucky, 2001.

Clarke, Arthur C. *Profiles of the Future.* London: Gollancz, 1962.

Clarke, M. J. *Transmedia Television: New Trends in Network Serial Production.* New York: Bloomsbury, 2013.

Condis, Megan. "Adaptation and Space: Thematic and Atmospheric Considerations for Board Game Environment Construction." *Intensities: The Journal of Cult Media* 7 (2014): 84–90. https://intensitiescultmedia.files.wordpress.com/2014/08/8-condis-adaptation-and-space-pp-84-90.pdf.

Conners, Sean P., and Iris Shepard. "Who's Betting on *The Hunger Games*? A Case for Young-Adult Literature." In *Critical Insights: Contemporary Speculative Fiction*, edited by M. Keith Booker, 115–36. Amenia, NY: Grey House Publishing, 2013.

Consalvo, Mia. *Cheating*. Cambridge, MA: MIT Press, 2007.

Coppa, Francesca. "Women, *Star Trek*, and the Early Development of Fannish Vidding." *Transformative Works and Cultures* 1 (2007), http://journal.transformativeworks.org/index.php/twc/article/view/44/64.

Costikyan, Greg. "Boardgame Aesthetics." In *Tabletop: Analog Game Design*, edited by Greg Costikyan and Drew Davidson, 179–86. US: ETC Press, 2011.

—. "Games, Storytelling, and Breaking the String." In *Second Person: Role-Playing and Story in Games and Playable Media*, edited by Pat Harrigan and Noah Wardrip-Fruin, 5–14. Cambridge, MA: MIT Press, 2007.

—. "I Have No Words & I Must Design." In *The Game Design Reader*, edited by Katie Salen and Eric Zimmerman, 192–211. Cambridge, MA: MIT Press, 2006.

—. *Uncertainty in Games*. Cambridge, MA: MIT Press. 2013.

Couldry, Nick. *Media Rituals: A Critical Approach*. London: Routledge, 2003.

Cover, Jennifer G. *The Creation of Narrative in Tabletop Role-Playing Games*. Jefferson, NC: McFarland, 2010.

Creeber, Glen. *Serial Television: Big Drama on the Small Screen*. London: BFI Publishing, 2004.

Curwood, Jen Scott. "*The Hunger Games*: Literature, Literacy, and Online Affinity Spaces." *Language Arts* 90, no. 6 (2013): 417–27.

d'Astous, Alain, and Karine Gagnon. "An Inquiry into the Factors That Impact on Consumer Appreciation of a Board Game." *Journal of Consumer Marketing* 24, no. 2 (2007): 80–89.

Davisson, Amber, and Paul Booth. "Reconceptualizing Communication and Agency in Fan Activity: A Proposal for a Projected Interactivity Model for Fan Studies." *Texas Speech Communication Journal* 32, no. 1 (2007): 33–43.

Dena, Christy. "Current State of Cross Media Storytelling: Preliminary Observations for Future Design." *European Information Systems Technologies Event*. 2004. Accessed June 06, 2013. http://www.christydena.com/Docs/DENA_CrossMediaObservations.pdf.

Derrida, Jacques. *On Grammatology*. Translated by Gayatri Chakravorty Spivak. Baltimore, MD: Johns Hopkins University Press, 1967.

Desmond, John, and Peter Hawkes. *Adaptation: Studying Film and Literature*. New York: McGaw, 2005.

Deuze, Mark. "Convergence Culture in the Creative Industries." *International Journal of Cultural Studies* 10, no. 2 (2007): 243–63.

—. *Media Life*. Cambridge, MA: Polity Press, 2012.

—. "Participation, Remediation, Bricolage: Considering Principal Components of a Digital Culture." *The Information Society* 22, no. 2 (2006): 63–75.

Diamond Book Distributors. 2011. Accessed July 08, 2014. http://www.
diamondbookdistributors.com/downloads/DBDProse2011.pdf.

Dietsch, T. J. "Exclusive: Adlard Covers 'The Walking Dead: The Board Game.'" *Comic Book Resources.* 2011. Accessed June 01, 2014. http://www.comicbookresources.
com/?page=article&id=33349.

Dixon, Shanley, and Sandra Weber. "Playspaces, Childhood, and Video Games." In *Growing Up Online: Young People and Digital Technologies,* edited by Sandra Weber and Shanley Dixon, 15–35. New York: Palgrave, 2007.

"*Doctor Who*: The Interactive Electronic Board Game." 2014. Accessed July 10, 2014. http://www.boardgamegeek.com/collection/items/
boardgame/19378?rated=1.

Dovey, Jon, and Helen W. Kennedy. *Game Cultures: Computer Games as New Media.* Maidenhead, UK: McGraw-Hill, 2006.

Dowd, Tom, Michael Niederman, Michael Fry, and Joe Steiff. *Storytelling Across Worlds: Transmedia for Creatives and Producers.* New York: Focal Press, 2013.

Duffett, Mark. *Understanding Fandom: An Introduction to the Study of Media Fan Culture.* London: Bloomsbury, 2013.

Eco, Umberto. "*Casablanca*: Cult Movies and Intertextual Collage." In *Travels in Hyper Reality: Essays,* 197–212. New York: Harcourt Brace, 1986.

"Effect of 'Keep in Play' on 'Thirty-Three' Crisis Card?" *Board & Card Games.* November 24, 2010. Accessed July 10, 2014. http://boardgames.stackexchange.com/
questions/1509/effect-of-keep-in-play-on-thirty-three-crisis-card.

Elias, George, Richard Garfield, and K. Robert Gutschera. *Characteristics of Games.* Cambridge, MA: MIT Press, 2012.

Evans, Elizabeth. *Transmedia Television: Audiences, New Media, and Daily Life.* New York: Routledge, 2011.

Fay, Ira. "Filtering Feedback." In *Tabletop: Analog Game Design,* edited by Greg Costikyan and Drew Davidson, 61–68. US: ETC Press, 2011.

Fernández, Juan José. "Board Game Sales Stats (Now with Sources)." September 12, 2009. Accessed July 09, 2014. http://www.boardgamegeek.com/geeklist/22976/
board-game-sales-stats-now-with-sources/page/6?

Fernández-Vara, Clara. *Introduction to Game Analysis.* New York: Routledge, 2015.

Fine, Gary Alan. *Shared Fantasy: Role Playing Games as Social Worlds.* Chicago, IL: University of Chicago Press, 2002.

Fischer, Craig. "Meaninglessness." In *Triumph of The Walking Dead,* edited by James Lowder, 67–80. Dallas, TX: Benbella Books, 2011.

Fisher, Mark. "Precarious Dystopias: *The Hunger Games, In Time*, and *Never Let Me Go*." *Film Quarterly* 65, no. 4 (2012): 27–33.

Fiske, John. "The Cultural Economy of Fandom." In *The Adoring Audience,* edited by Lisa A. Lewis, 30–49. London: Routledge, 1992.

Flanagan, Mary. *Critical Play: Radical Game Design.* Cambridge, MA: MIT Press, 2009.

Ford, James E. "*Battlestar Galactica* and Mormon Theology." *Journal of Popular Culture* 17, no. 2 (1983): 83–87.

Forde, Teresa. "'You Anorak': The *Doctor Who* Experience and Experiencing *Doctor Who.*" In *Fan Phenomena: Doctor Who,* edited by Paul Booth, 72–82. Bristol, UK: Intellect Press, 2013.

Foucault, Michel. "What Is an Author?" In *Language, Counter-memory, Practice: Selected Essays and Interviews,* edited by Michel Foucault and Donald F. Bouchard, 113–38. Ithica, NY: Cornell University Press, 1980.

Frasca, Gonzolo. "Ludology Meets Narratology: Similitude and Differences Between (Video) Games and Narrative." *Parnasso* 3 (1999): 365–71. http://www.ludology.org/articles/ludology.htm.

Galloway, Alexander. *Gaming: Essays on Algorithmic Culture.* Minneapolis, MN: University of Minnesota Press, 2006.

Garassini, Stefania. "Internet of Things." *Domus* 917 (2008): 113–23.

Garite, Matt. "The Ideology of Interactivity or, Video Games and the Taylorization of Leisure." *Level Up, Digital Games Research Association Conference DiGRA.* 2003. Accessed May 14, 2013. http://www.digra.org/wp-content/uploads/digital-library/05150.15436.pdf.

"The Game of *Alice in Wonderland.*" Boardgamegeek. 2014. Accessed Jul 08, 2014. http://www.boardgamegeek.com/boardgame/130692/the-game-of-alice-in-wonderland.

Gee, James Paul. *Situated Language and Learning: A Critique of Traditional Schooling.* New York: Routledge, 2004.

—. *What Video Games Have to Teach Us about Learning and Literacy,* rev. ed. New York: Palgrave Macmillan, 2007.

Genette, Gérard. *Paratexts: Thresholds of Interpretation.* Translated by Jane Lewin. Cambridge: Cambridge University Press, 1997.

Geraghty, Lincoln. "Aging Toys and Players: Fan Identity and Cultural Capital." In *Finding the Force of the Star Wars Franchise: Fans, Merchandise, and Critics,* edited by Matthew Wilhelm Kapell and John Shelton Lawrence, 209–23. New York: Peter Lang, 2006.

—. *American Science Fiction Film and Television.* Oxford: Berg, 2009.

—. *Cult Collectors.* London: Routledge, 2014.

—. *Living with Star Trek: American Culture and the Star Trek Universe.* London: IB Tauris, 2007.

Gibson, J. J. *The Ecological Approach to Visual Perception.* Boston: Houghton Mifflin, 1979.

—. "The Theory of Affordances." In *Perceiving, Acting, and Knowing,* edited by Robert Shaw and John Bransford, 127–43. Hillsdale, NJ: Lawrence Erlbaum Associates, 1977.

Goffman, Erving. *Encounters: Two Studies in the Sociology of Interaction.* New York: Penguin, 1972.

Gray, Jonathan. *Show Sold Separately: Promos, Spoilers, and Other Media Paratexts.* New York: New York University Press, 2010.

Gumpert, Matthew. "Hybridity's End." In *Cylons in America,* edited by Tiffany Porter and C. W. Marshall, 143–55. New York: Continuum, 2008.

Gunkel, David J. "Do Machines Have Rights? Ethics in the Age of Artificial Intelligence." Interview with Paul Kellogg. *Aurora Online.* 2014. Accessed June 01, 2014. http://aurora.icaap.org/index.php/aurora/article/view/92/114.

—. *Hacking Cyberspace.* Boulder, CO: Westview Press, 2001.

—. *The Machine Question.* Cambridge, MA: MIT Press, 2012.

Gwenllian-Jones, Sara. "Starring Lucy Lawless?" *Continuum: Journal of Media & Cultural Studies* 14, no. 1 (2000): 9–22.

—. "Virtual Reality and Cult Television." In *Cult Television,* edited by Sara Gwenllian-Jones and Roberta Pearson, 83–98. Minneapolis, MN: University of Minnesota Press, 2004.

Hadas, Leora. "The Web Planet: How the Changing Internet Divided *Doctor Who* Fan Fiction Writers." *Transformative Works and Cultures* 3 (2009). http://dx.doi.org/10.3983/twc.2009.0129.

Harrigan, Pat, and Noah Wardrip-Fruin. Introduction to *Third Person: Authoring and Exploring Vast Narratives,* edited by Pat Harrigan and Noah Wardrip-Fruin, 1–9. Cambridge, MA: MIT Press, 2009.

Harvey, David. *A Brief History of Neoliberalism.* Oxford: Oxford University Press, 2005.

Hills, Matt. "As Seen on Screen? Mimetic SF Fandom & the Crafting of Replica(nt)s." *In Media Res.* September 10, 2010. Accessed June 01, 2013. http://mediacommons.futureofthebook.org/imr/2010/09/10/seen-screen-mimetic-sf-fandom-crafting-replicants.

—. "The Cultural Lives of *Doctor Who*: What's Special About Multiple Multi-Doctor Specials?" *Antenna.* 2013. Accessed October 15, 2013. http://blog.commarts.wisc.edu/2013/10/15/the-cultural-lives-of-doctor-who-whats-special-about-multiple-multi-doctor-specials/.

—. *Fan Cultures.* London: Routledge, 2002.

—. "Fiske's 'Textual Productivity' and Digital Fandom: Web 2.0 Democratization Versus Fan Distinction?" *Participations: The Journal of Audience and Reception Studies* 10, no. 1 (2013): 130–53. http://www.participations.org/Volume%2010/Issue%201/9%20Hills%2010.1.pdf.

—. "From Dalek Half Balls to Daft Punk Helmets: Mimetic Fandom and the Crafting of Replicas." *Transformative Works and Cultures* 16 (2014). http://dx.doi.org/10.3983/twc.2014.0531

—. "Mainstream Cult." In *The Cult TV Book,* edited by Stacey Abbott, 67–73. London: IB Tauris, 2010.

—. "Media Fandom, Neoreligiosity, and Cult(ural) Studies." *Velvet Light Trap* 46 (2000): 73–84.

—. "Torchwood's Trans-Transmedia: Media Tie-Ins and Brand 'Fanagement.'" *Participations: The Journal of Audience and Reception Studies* 9, no. 2 (2012): 409–28. http://www.participations.org/Volume%209/Issue%202/23%20Hills.pdf.

—. *Triumph of a Time Lord: Regenerating Doctor Who in the Twenty-First Century.* London: IB Tauris, 2010.

—. "'Twilight' Fans Represented in Commercial Paratexts and Inter-Fandoms: Resisting and Repurposing Negative Fan Stereotypes." In *Genre, Reception, and Adaptation in the Twilight Series,* edited by Anne More, 113–31. Farnham, UK: Ashgate, 2012.

Hite, Kenneth. "Another Form of Story Telling." Presentation at *Capricon 34*, Wheeling, IL, 2014.

—. "Narrative Structure and Creative Tension in *Call of Cthulhu.*" In *Second Person: Role-Playing and Story in Games and Playable Media,* edited by Pat Harrigan and Noah Wardrip-Fruin, 31–40. Cambridge, MA: MIT Press, 2007.

Hocking, Clint. "Ludonarrative Dissonance in *BioShock.*" *Clicknothing: Design from a Long Time Ago.* 07 October 2007. Accessed May 13, 2013. http://clicknothing. typepad.com/click_nothing/2007/10/ludonarrative-d.html.

"How Big Is It?" 2004. Accessed July 09, 2014. https://web.archive.org/ web/20071013162924/http://spielboy.com/printrun.php.

Howells, Sacha A. "Watching a Game, Playing a Movie: When Media Collide." In *Screenplay: Cinema/Videogames/Interfaces,* edited by Geoff King and Tanya Krzywinska, 110–21. London: Wallflower Press, 2002.

Huizinga, Johan. *Homo Ludens: A Study of the Play Element in Culture.* Boston: Beacon Press, 1950.

Hutcheon, Linda. *A Theory of Adaptation,* 2nd ed. London: Routledge, 2012.

Ito, Mimi. *Hanging Out, Messing Around, and Geeking Out: Kids Living and Learning with New Media.* Cambridge, MA: MIT Press, 2010.

Jacklin, Kevin. "Simply Knizia." In *Tabletop: Analog Game Design,* edited by Greg Costikyan and Drew Davidson, 55–60. US: ETC Press, 2011.

Jacoby, Henry, ed. *Game of Thrones and Philosophy.* Hoboken, NJ: John Wiley and Sons, 2012.

Jenkins, Henry. *Convergence Culture: Where Old and New Media Collide.* New York: New York University Press, 2006.

—. "The Cultural Logic of Media Convergence." *International Journal of Cultural Studies* 7, no. 1 (2004): 33–43.

—. "Game Design as Narrative Architecture." In *First Person: New Media as Story, Performance and Game,* edited by Noah Wardrip-Fruin and Pat Harrigan, 118–30. Cambridge, MA: MIT Press, 2004.

—. *Textual Poachers: Television Fans and Participatory Culture,* 2nd ed. New York: Routledge, 2012.

—. "Transmedia Storytelling." January 15, 2003. Accessed June 12, 2013. http://www. technologyreview.com/news/401760/transmedia-storytelling/.

—. "*The Walking Dead*: Adapting Comics." In *How to Watch Television*, edited by Ethan Thompson and Jason Mittell, 373–81. New York: New York University Press, 2013.

Jenkins, Henry, Sam Ford, and Joshua Green. *Spreadable Media: Creating Value and Meaning in a Networked Culture*. New York: New York University Press, 2013.

Jenkins, Henry, with Ravi Purushotma, Margaret Weigel, Katie Clinton, and Alice J. Robison. *Confronting the Challenges of Participatory Culture: Media Education for the 21st Century*. Cambridge, MA: MIT Press, 2009. http://mitpress.mit.edu/sites/default/files/titles/free_download/9780262513623_Confronting_the_Challenges.pdf.

Johnson, Derek. *Media Franchising*. New York: New York University Press, 2013.

Jones, Bethan. "Unusual Geography: Discworld Board Games and Paratextual L-Space." *Intensities: The Journal of Cult Media* 7 (2014). https://intensitiescultmedia.files.wordpress.com/2014/08/6-jones-unusual-geography-pp-55-73.pdf.

Jones, Sara Gwenllian. "The Sex Lives of Cult Television Characters." *Screen* 43, no. 1 (2002): 79–90.

Jones, Steven E. "Dickens on *Lost*: Text, Paratext, Fan-Based Media." *The Wordsworth Circle* 38, no. 2 (2007): 71–77.

Juul, Jesper. *Half-Real: Video Games Between Real Rules and Fictional Worlds*. Cambridge, MA: MIT Press, 2005.

Kaplan, Deborah. "Construction of Character through Narrative." In *Fan Fiction and Fan Communities in the Age of the Internet*, edited by Karen Hellekson and Kristina Busse, 134–52. Jefferson, NC: McFarland, 2006.

Kaufeld, John. "Randomness, Player Choice, and Player Experience." In *Tabletop: Analog Game Design*, edited by Greg Costikyan and Drew Davidson, 33–38. US: ETC Press, 2011.

Klug, Chris. "Dice as Dramaturge." In *Tabletop: Analog Game Design*, edited by Greg Costikyan and Drew Davidson, 39–48. US: ETC Press, 2011.

Knizia, Reiner. "The Design and Testing of the Board Game—*Lord of the Rings*." In *Rules of Play: Game Design Fundamentals*, edited by Katie Salen and Eric Zimmerman, 22–27. Cambridge, MA: MIT Press, 2004.

Koster, Raph. *A Theory of Fun for Game Design*, 2nd ed. Sebastopol, CA: O'Reilly Media, 2014.

Lammers, Jayne C., Jen Scott Curwood, and Alecia Marie Magnifico. "Toward an Affinity Space Methodology: Considerations for Literacy Research." *English Teaching: Practice and Critique* 11, no. 2 (2012): 44–58.

Lancaster, Kurt. *Interacting with Babylon 5*. Austin, TX: University of Texas Press, 2001.

Lang, Eric, with Pat Harrigan. "Design Decisions and Concepts in Licensed Collectible Card Games." In *Second Person: Role-Playing and Story in Games and Playable Media*, edited by Pat Harrigan and Noah Wardrip-Fruin, 85–90. Cambridge, MA: MIT Press, 2007.

Lawson, Cherri. "No Batteries Required: Board Game Sales Soar." *NPR*. December 24, 2009. Accessed June 01, 2014. http://www.npr.org/templates/story/story.php?storyId=121841016.

Librande, Stone. "15 Games in 15 Years." In *Tabletop: Analog Game Design*, edited by Greg Costikyan and Drew Davidson, 69–90. US: ETC Press, 2011.

Linderoth, Jonas. "Exploring Anonymity in Cooperative Board Games." *Proceedings of DiGRA 2011 Conference: Think Design Play*. 2011. Accessed June 01, 2014. http://www.digra.org/wp-content/uploads/digital-library/11312.15167.pdf.

"*Lord of the Rings* (board game)." 2014. Accessed July 09, 2014. http://en.wikipedia.org/wiki/Lord_of_the_Rings_(board_game).

Lovecraft, H. P. "The Dream-Quest of Unknown Kadath." In *H.P. Lovecraft: The Complete Fiction*, 286–364 New York: Barnes and Noble, 2011.

—. "Nyarlathotep." In *H.P. Lovecraft: The Complete Fiction*, 121–23. New York: Barnes and Noble, 2011.

Lowder, James, ed. *Beyond the Wall: Exploring George R.R. Martin's A Song of Ice and Fire, from A Game of Thrones to A Dance with Dragons*. Dallas, TX: Benbella Books, 2012.

Lunenfeld, Peter. "Unfinished Business." In *The Digital Dialectic*, edited by Peter Lunenfeld, 6–23. Cambridge, MA: MIT Press, 1999.

Manovich, Lev. *The Language of New Media*. Cambridge, MA: MIT Press, 2001.

Mariconda, Steven J. "Lovecraft's Cosmic Imagery." In *An Epicure in the Terrible: A Centennial Anthology of Essays in Honor of H. P. Lovecraft*, edited by David E. Schultz and S. T. Joshi, 188–98. Cranbury, NJ: Associated University Presses, 1991.

Marshall, C. W., and Tiffany Porter. "'I See the Patterns': *Battlestar Galactica* and the Things That Matter." In *Cylons in America*, edited by Tiffany Porter and C. W. Marshall, 1–10. New York: Continuum, 2008.

Martens, Todd. "Board Games Return to Popularity." *Los Angeles Times*. November 12, 2012. Accessed June 01, 2014. http://www.jsonline.com/business/boardgamesreturn-topopularitysd7lkjk180549421.html.

Mascheroni, Giovanna. "Citizenship Online: Identity, Subactivism and Participation." *Observatorio Journal* 7, no. 3 (2013): 93–119.

Mathijs, Ernest, ed. *The Lord of the Rings: Popular Culture in Global Context*. London: Wallflower Press, 2006.

—. "Popular Culture in Global Context: *The Lord of the Rings* Phenomenon." In *The Lord of the Rings: Popular Culture in Global Context*, edited by Ernest Mathijs, 1–19. London: Wallflower Press, 2006.

Mazza, Ray. "The Greatest Gift." In *Tabletop: Analog Game Design*, edited by Greg Costikyan and Drew Davidson, 111–28. US: ETC Press, 2011.

McClellan, Ann. "A Case of Identity: Role Playing, Social Media, and BBC *Sherlock*." *The Journal of Fandom Studies* 1, no. 2 (2013): 139–57.

McCloud, Scott. *Understanding Comics: The Invisible Art*. New York: Kitchen Sink Press, 1993.

McCracken, Ellen. "Expanding Genette's Epitext/Peritext Model for Transitional Electronic Literature: Centrifugal and Centripetal Vectors on Kindles and iPads." *Narrative* 21, no. 1 (2013): 105–24.

McFedries, P. "The Age of Spimes." *IEEE Spectrum* 25 (2010): n.p.

McGonigal, Jane. *Reality Is Broken: Why Games Make Us Better and How They Can Change the World.* New York: Penguin, 2011.

McKee, Alan. *Textual Analysis: A Beginner's Guide.* London: Sage, 2003.

Meikle, Graham, and Sherman Young. *Media Convergence: Networked Digital Media in Everyday Life.* Houndsmill, UK: Palgrave Macmillan, 2012.

Mittell, Jason. "Narrative Complexity in Contemporary American Television." *The Velvet Light Trap* 58 (2006): 29–40.

—. "Sites of Participation: Wiki Fandom and the Case of Lostpedia." *Transformative Works and Cultures* 3 (2009), http://dx.doi.org/10.3983/twc.2009.0118.

—. "Transmedia Storytelling." In *Complex TV: The Poetics of Contemporary Television Storytelling*, pre-publication ed., MediaCommons Press, 2012. Accessed May 13, 2013. http://mediacommons.futureofthebook.org/mcpress/complextelevision/transmedia-storytelling/.

Montola, Markus. "Social Constructionism and Ludology: Implications for the Study of Games." *Simulation and Gaming.* 43, no. 3 (2012): 300–20.

Moore, Robert W. "'To Be a Person': Sharon Agathon and the Social Expression of Individuality." In *Cylons in America*, edited by Tiffany Porter and C. W. Marshall, 105–18. New York: Continuum, 2008.

Morgan, Matt. "Cryptozoic's Cory Jones Unearths *The Walking Dead* Board Game." *MTV Geek.* June 15, 2011. Accessed June 01, 2014. http://geek-news.mtv.com/2011/06/15/interview-cryptozoics-cory-jones-unearths-the-walking-dead-board-game.

—. "ZMan Games Set to Debut *The Walking Dead* at SDCC." *MTV Geek.* July 07, 2011. Accessed June 01, 2014. http://geek-news.mtv.com/2011/07/07/z-man-games-set-to-debut-the-walking-dead-at-sdcc.

Norman, Donald. "Affordance, Conventions, and Design." *Interactions* 6, no. 3 (1999): 38–43.

—. *The Design of Everyday Things.* New York NY: Doubleday, 1990.

obsession_inc. "Affirmational Fandom vs. Transformational Fandom." 01 June 2009. Accessed August 21, 2013. http://obsession-inc.dreamwidth.org/82589.html.

Papacharissi, Zizi. "A Networked Self Identity Performance and Sociability on Social Network Sites." In *Frontiers in New Media Research*, edited by Francis L. F. Lee, Louis Leung, Jack Linchuan Qiu, and Donna S. C. Chu, 207–21. New York: Routledge, 2013.

Parlett, David. "Conquest." In *Tabletop: Analog Game Design*, edited by Greg Costikyan and Drew Davidson, 101–4. US: ETC Press, 2011.

—. *Oxford History of Board Games.* Oxford: Oxford University Press, 1999.

Patel, K. "Need to Know: Spime." *Creativity* 17, no. 4 (2009): 74.

Pearce, Celia. *Communities of Play: Emergent Cultures in Multiplayer Games and Virtual Worlds.* Cambridge, MA: MIT Press, 2009.

—. "Theory Wars: An Argument Against Arguments in the So-Called Ludology/ Narratology Debate." *DiGRA Conference: Changing Views—Worlds in Play.* 2005. Accessed June 07, 2013. http://lmc.gatech.edu/~cpearce3/PearcePubs/ PearceDiGRA05.pdf.

Pearson, Roberta. "Anatomising Gilbert Grissom: The Structure and Function of the Televisual Character." In *Reading CSI: Television under the Microscope*, edited by Michael Allen, 39–56. London: IB Tauris, 2007.

—. "Fandom in the Digital Era." *Journal of Popular Communication* 8 (2010): 1–12.

Peters, Ian. "Peril-Sensitive Sunglasses, Superheroes in Miniature, and Pink Polka-Dot Boxers: Artifact and Collectible Video Game Feelies, Play, and the Paratextual Gaming Experience." *Transformative Works and Cultures* 16 (2014), http://dx.doi.org/10.3983/twc.2014.0509.

Peterson, Jon. *Playing at the World*. US: Unreason Press, 2012.

Phelan, James. *Reading People, Reading Plots: Character, Progression, and the Interpretation of Narrative*. Chicago, IL: University of Chicago Press, 1989.

Phillips, Andrea. *A Creator's Guide to Transmedia Storytelling: How to Captivate and Engage Audiences Across Multiple Platforms*. Columbus, OH: McGraw-Hills, 2012.

Price, Robert M. "Lovecraft's 'Artificial Mythology." In *An Epicure in the Terrible: A Centennial Anthology of Essays in Honor of H. P. Lovecraft*, edited by David E. Schultz and S. T. Joshi, 247–56. Cranbury, NJ: Associated University Presses, 1991.

—. "With Strange Aeons: H. P. Lovecraft's Cthulhu Mythos as One Vast Narrative." In *Third Person: Authoring and Exploring Vast Narratives*, edited by Pat Harrigan and Noah Wardrip-Fruin, 225–42. Cambridge, MA: MIT Press, 2009.

Pulsipher, Lewis. "The Three Player Problem." In *Tabletop: Analog Game Design*, edited by Greg Costikyan and Drew Davidson, 17–26. US: ETC Press, 2011.

Rainie, Lee, and Barry Wellman. *Networked: The New Social Operating System*. Cambridge, MA: MIT Press, 2012.

Riley, Brendan. "Zombie People." In *Triumph of The Walking Dead*, edited by James Lowder, 81–98. Dallas, TX: Benbella Books, 2011.

Robertson, Adi. "How Amazon's Commercial Fan Fiction Misses the Point." *The Verge* June 04, 2013. Accessed June 01, 2014. http://www.theverge.com/2013/6/4/4392572/ does-amazon-kindle-worlds-miss-the-point-of-fanfiction.

Robinson, Michael G. "I Outwit Your Outwit: HeroClix, Superhero Fans, and Collectible Miniature Games." In *Super/Heroes: From Hercules to Superman*, edited by Wendy Haslem, Angela Ndalianis, and Chris Mackie, 335–46. Washington, DC: New Academia Publishing, 2007.

Roth, Lane. "'Vraisemblance' and the Western Setting in Contemporary Science Fiction Film." *Literature/Film Quarterly* 13, no. 3 (1985): 180–86.

Ryan, Marie-Laure. *Narrative as Virtual Reality: Immersion and Interactivity in Literature and Electronic Media*. Baltimore, MD: John Hopkins University Press, 2001.

—. "Transmedial Storytelling and Transfictionality." *Poetics Today* 34, no. 3 (2013): 362–88. http://users.frii.com/mlryan/transmedia.html.

Salen, Katie, and Eric Zimmerman. *Rules of Play: Game Design Fundamentals.* Cambridge, MA: MIT Press, 2004.

Schneider, Dean. "Katniss, Harry, and Percy: *The Hunger Games* by Suzanne Collins and the Lure of Fantasy Series." *Book Links* (2011): 29–32. http://www.booklistonline. com/Books-and-Authors-Katniss-Harry-and-Percy-The-Hunger-Games-by-Suzanne-Collins-and-the-Lure-of-Fantasy-Series-Dean-Schneider/pid=4770980.

Schultz, David E. "From Microcosm to Macrocosm: The Growth of Lovecraft's Cosmic Vision." In *An Epicure in the Terrible: A Centennial Anthology of Essays in Honor of H. P. Lovecraft,* edited by David E. Schultz and S. T. Joshi, 199–219. Cranbury, NJ: Associated University Presses, 1991.

Scolari, Carlos Alberto. "Transmedia Storytelling: Implicit Consumers, Narrative Worlds, and Branding in Contemporary Media Production." *International Journal of Communication* 3 (2009): 586–606.

Scott, Suzanne. "Authorized Resistance: Is Fan Production Frakked?" In *Cylons in America,* edited by Tiffany Potter and C. W. Marshall, 210–24. New York: Continuum, 2008.

—. "*Battlestar Galactica:* Fans and Ancillary Content." In *How to Watch Television,* edited by Ethan Thompson and Jason Mittell, 320–29. New York: New York University Press, 2013.

—. "Repackaging Fan Culture: The Regifting Economy of Ancillary Content Models." *Transformative Works and Cultures* 3 (2009). http://dx.doi:10.3983/twc.2009.0150.

—. "Who's Steering the Mothership? The Role of the Fanboy Auteur in Transmedia Storytelling." In *The Participatory Cultures Handbook,* edited by Aaron Delwiche and Jennifer Jacobs Henderson, 43–52. New York: Routledge, 2013.

Seiter, Ellen. *Sold Separately: Children and Parents in Consumer Culture.* New Brunswick, NJ: Rutgers University Press, 1995.

Sharp, John. "Pandemic." In *Tabletop: Analog Game Design,* edited by Greg Costikyan and Drew Davidson, 129–36. US: ETC Press, 2011.

Shefrin, Elana. "*Lord of the Rings, Star Wars,* and Participatory Fandom: Mapping New Congruencies between the Internet and Media Entertainment Culture." *Critical Studies in Media Communication* 21, no. 3 (2004): 261–81.

Silverstone, Roger. *Why Study the Media?* London: Sage, 1999.

Smith, Jim, and J. Clive Matthews. *The Lord of the Rings: The Films, the Books, the Radio Series.* London: Virgin Books, 2004.

Sobchack, Vivian. *Screening Space: The American Science Fiction Film,* 2nd ed. New Brunswick, NJ: Rutgers University Press, 1997.

St. Armand, Barton Levi. "Synchronistic Worlds: Lovecraft and Borges." In *An Epicure in the Terrible: A Centennial Anthology of Essays in Honor of H. P. Lovecraft,* edited by David E. Schultz and S. T. Joshi, 298–323. Cranbury, NJ: Associated University Presses, 1991.

Staiger, Janet. *Media Reception Studies*. New York: New York University Press, 2005.

Stanitzek, Georg. "Texts and Paratexts in Media." Translated by Ellen Klein. *Critical Inquiry* 32 (2005): 27–42.

Steiger, Kay. "No Clean Slate." In *Triumph of The Walking Dead*, edited by James Lowder, 99–114. Dallas, TX: Benbella Books, 2011.

Stein, Louisa E., and Kristina Busse. "Introduction: The Literary, Televisual and Digital Adventures of the Beloved Detective." In *Sherlock and Transmedia Fandom*, edited by Louisa Ellen Stein and Kristina Busse, 9–24. Jefferson, NC: McFarland, 2012.

Sterling, Bruce. *Shaping Things*. Cambridge, MA: MIT Press, 2005.

Stöckmann, Britta, and Jens Jahnke. "Playing by the Book: Literature and Board Games at the Beginning of 21st Century." *Homo Communcativus* 5 (2008): 128–44. http://www.hc.amu.edu.pl/numery/5/stockjahnke.pdf.

Stoy, Jennifer. "Of Great Zeitgeist and Bad Faith: An Introduction to *Battlestar Galactica*." In *Battlestar Galactica: Investigating Flesh, Spirit and Steel*, edited by Roz Kaverney and Jennifer Stoy, 1–36. London: IB Tauris, 2010.

Sutton-Smith, Brian. *The Ambiguity of Play*. Boston: Harvard University Press, 1997.

Thomas, Angela. "Fan Fiction Online." *Australian Journal of Language And Literacy* 29, no. 3 (2006): 226–39.

Thomas, Sue. "The End of Cyberspace and Other Surprises." *Convergence: The International Journal of Research into New Media Technologies* 12, no. 4 (2006): 383–91.

Thompson, Hamish. "'She's Not Your Mother Anymore, She's a Zombie!' Zombies, Value, and Personal Identity." In *The Undead and Philosophy*, edited by Richard Green and K. Silem Mohammad, 27–37. La Salle, IL: Open Court Publishing Company, 2006.

Tolkien, J. R. R. *The Lord of the Rings: The Fellowship of the Ring*, 2nd ed. London: HarperCollins, 1966.

Van Dijck, José. "'You Have One Identity': Performing the Self on Facebook and LinkedIn." *Media, Culture and Society* 35, no. 2 (2013): 199–215.

Veale, Kevin. "Capital, Dialogue, and Community Engagement—*My Little Pony: Friendship Is Magic* Understood as an Alternate Reality Game." *Transformative Works and Cultures* 14 (2013). http://dx.doi.org/10.3983/twc.2013.0510.

Vossen, Emma. "Where's the Sex?" *First Person Scholar*. June 05, 2013. Accessed June 05, 2013. http://www.firstpersonscholar.com/wheres-the-sex/.

Wagner, Rachel. *Godwired: Religion, Ritual and Virtual Reality*. New York: Routledge, 2012.

Wardrip-Fruin, Noah, and Pat Harrigan, eds. *First Person: New Media as Story, Performance, and Game*. Cambridge, MA: MIT Press, 2004.

Wilson, Kevin. "One Story, Many Media." In *Second Person: Role-Playing and Story in Games and Playable Media*, edited by Pat Harrigan and Noah Wardrip-Fruin, 91–93. Cambridge, MA: MIT Press, 2007.

Wingfield, Nick. "High-Tech Push Has Board Games Rolling Again." *New York Times.* May 05, 2014. Accessed May 05, 2014. http://www.nytimes.com/2014/05/06/ technology/high-tech-push-has-board-games-rolling-again.html.

Woerner, Meredith. "First Full Cast Picture from AMC's *The Walking Dead*." *io9*. July 15, 2010. Accessed June 01, 2014. http://io9.com/5587483/first-full-castpicture-from-amcs-the-walking-dead.

Wood, Megan M., and Linda Baughman. "*Glee* Fandom and Twitter: Something New, or More of the Same Old Thing?" *Communication Studies* 63, no. 3 (2012): 328–44.

Woods, Stewart. *Eurogames: The Design, Culture, and Play of Modern European Board Games*. Jefferson City, NC: McFarland, 2012.

—. "Last Man Standing: Risk and Elimination in Social Game Play." *Leonardo Electronic Almanac* 16, no. 2–3 (2008). http://leoalmanac.org/journal/vol_16/lea_v16_n2-3/ JChatelain.asp.

Yore, Kevin. "Dice and Digital—Rehabilitating the Board Game Geek." *BBC News.* March 01, 2013. Accessed June 01, 2014. http://www.bbc.com/news/business-21615083.

Zagal, José P., Jochen Rick, and Idris Hsi. "Collaborative Games: Lessons Learned from Board Games." *Simulation and Gaming* 37, no. 1 (2006): 24–40.

Zakowski, Samuel. "Time and Temporality in the *Mass Effect* Series: A Narratological Approach." *Games and Culture* 9, no. 1 (2014): 58–79.

Zimmerman, Eric. "Narrative, Interactivity, Play, and Games: Four Naughty Concepts in Need of Discipline." In *First Person: New Media as Story, Performance and Game*, edited by Noah Wardrip-Fruin and Pat Harrigan, 154–64. Cambridge, MA: MIT Press, 2004.

Zipes, Jack. "The Age of Commodified Fantasticism: Reflections of Children's Literature and the Fantastic." *Children's Literature Association Quarterly* 9, no. 4 (1984–85): 187–90.

Zubernis, Lynn, and Katherine Larsen. *Fandom at the Crossroads: Celebration, Shame and Fan/Producer Relationships*. Newcastle, UK: Cambridge Scholars Press, 2012.

List of media

Abrams, J. J. Director. *Star Trek*. Los Angeles, CA: Paramount. 2009.

Battlestar Galactica: A Parker Brothers Game. Pawtucket, RI: Parker Brothers, 1978.

Benioff, David, and D. B. Weiss. Producers. *Game of Thrones*. New York: HBO, 2011–present.

Berman, Rick and Brannon Braga. Producers. *Star Trek: Enterprise.* Los Angeles, CA: Paramount, 2001–05.

Berman, Rick, Brannon Braga, and Michael Piller. Producers. *Star Trek: Deep Space Nine.* Los Angeles, CA: Paramount, 1993–99.

Berman, Rick, Brannon Braga, Michael Piller, and Jeri Taylor. Producers. *Star Trek: Voyager.* Los Angeles, CA: Paramount, 1995–2001.

Collins, Suzanne. *The Hunger Games.* New York: Scholastic, 2008.

Costikyan, Greg, and Doug Kaufman. *Star Trek: The Adventure Game.* New York: West End Games, 1985.

Darabont, Frank. Executive Producer. 2010. *The Walking Dead.* New York: AMC Studios, 2010–present.

David-Marshall, Brian, Keith Tralins, and Matthew Wang. *The Walking Dead Board Game.* Mahopac, NY: Z-Man Games, 2011.

Davies, Russell T. Producer. *Doctor Who.* Cardiff, Wales: BBC-Worldwide, 2005–2010.

Doctor Who Interactive Electronic Board Game. Huntingdon, Cambs, UK: Toy Brokers Ltd., 2005.

Doctor Who: The Time Travelling Action Game. Huntingdon, Cambs, UK: Toy Brokers Ltd., 2007.

E.T. The Extra-Terrestrial. Pawtucket, RI: Parker Brothers, 1982.

Elliott, Mike, Bryan Kinsella, and Ethan Pasternack. *Star Trek: Fleet Captains.* Hillside, NY: WizKids Games, 2011.

French, Nate, Eric M. Lang, and Christian Petersen. *A Game of Thrones: The Card Game.* Roseville, MN: Fantasy Flight Games, 2008.

Guild, Christopher, Bryan Kinsella, and Andrew Parks. *The Hunger Games: District 12 Strategy Game.* Hillside: WizKids Games, 2012.

Hyra, Matt. *Walking Dead: The Best Defense Board Game.* Lake Forest, CA: Cryptozoic Entertainment, 2013.

Johnson, Mike, and Tim Jones. *Star Trek: Countdown.* San Diego, CA: IDW, 2009.

Jones, Cory. *The Walking Dead: The Board Game.* Lake Forest, CA: Cryptozoic Entertainment, 2011.

Kinsella, Bryan, and Wilson Price. *The Hunger Games: Training Day.* Hillside, NY: WizKids Games, 2010.

Kirkman, Robert. *The Walking Dead.* Berkeley, CA: Image Comics, 2003.

Knizia, Reiner. *Lord of the Rings.* Roseville, MN: Fantasy Flight Games, 2000.

—. *Star Trek: Expeditions.* Hillside, NY: WizKids Games, 2011.

Konieczka, Corey. *Battlestar Galactica: The Board Game.* Roseville, MN: Fantasy Flight Games, 2008.

—. *Eldritch Horror.* Roseville, MN: Fantasy Flight Games, 2013.

Lang, Eric M., and Christian Petersen. *Game of Thrones: The Card Game.* Roseville, MN: Fantasy Flight Games, 2012.

Launius, Richard. *Elder Sign.* Roseville, MN: Fantasy Flight Games, 2011.

Larson, Glen A. Producer. *Battlestar Galactica*. Los Angeles, CA: Glen A. Larson Productions, 1978.

The Lord of the Rings: The Complete Trilogy—Adventure Board Game. New York: Pressman Toy Corp., 2012.

Lovecraft, H. P. *The Complete Fiction*. New York: Barnes and Noble, 2011.

Martin, George R. R. *A Song of Ice and Fire Series*. New York: Bantam Books, 1996–present.

Moore, Ron D. Producer. *Battlestar Galactica*. New York: NBC Universal, 2003–10.

Petersen, Christian. *A Game of Thrones: The Board Game*, 2nd ed. Roseville, MN: Fantasy Flight Games, 2011.

Roddenberry, Gene. Producer (1987–91). *Star Trek: The Next Generation*. Los Angeles, CA: Paramount, 1987–94.

—. Producer. *Star Trek*. Los Angeles, CA: Paramount, 1966–69.

Ross, Gary. Director. *The Hunger Games*. Los Angeles, CA: Lionsgate, 2012.

Star Trek: The Final Frontier. UK: Toys and Games, 1992.

Star Trek: The Next Generation: Interactive VCR Board Game: A Klingon Challenge. Milton Bradley, 1993.

Tolkien, J. R. R. *The Lord of the Rings*. London: George Allen & Unwin, 1954–55.

Walking Dead: Season One. San Ragael, CA: Telltale Games, 2012.

Wilson, Kevin, and Richard Lanham. *Arkham Horror*. Roseville, MN: Fantasy Flight Games, 2005.

Index